ASIAN AMERICAN PLAYERS

ASIAN AMERICAN PLAYERS

MASCULINITY, LITERATURE, AND THE ANXIETIES OF WAR

Audrey Wu Clark

THE OHIO STATE UNIVERSITY PRESS
COLUMBUS

Copyright © 2023 by The Ohio State University.
All rights reserved.

Library of Congress Cataloging-in-Publication Data
Names: Clark, Audrey Wu, 1980– author.
Title: Asian American players : masculinity, literature, and the anxieties of war / Audrey Wu Clark.
Description: Columbus : The Ohio State University Press, [2023] | Includes bibliographical references and index. | Summary: "Examines gendered and racialized US militarism through works written during major postmodern American wars, investigating how books by John Okada, David Henry Hwang, Chang-rae Lee, Frances Khirallah Noble, and Viet Thanh Nguyen (re)fashion Asian American masculinity in ways that ultimately mimic masculinist American foreign policy and military strategies"—Provided by publisher.
Identifiers: LCCN 2023007208 | ISBN 9780814215449 (cloth) | ISBN 0814215440 (cloth) | ISBN 9780814283011 (ebook) | ISBN 0814283012 (ebook)
Subjects: LCSH: American literature—Asian American authors—History and criticism. | Okada, John—Criticism and interpretation. | Hwang, David Henry, 1957—Criticism and interpretation. | Lee, Chang-rae—Criticism and interpretation. | Noble, Frances Khirallah—Criticism and interpretation. | Nguyen, Viet Thanh, 1971—Criticism and interpretation. | Masculinity in literature. | Militarism in literature.
Classification: LCC PS153.A84 C57 2023 | DDC 810.9/895073—dc23/eng/20230519
LC record available at https://lccn.loc.gov/2023007208

Other identifiers: ISBN 9780814258811 (paperback) | ISBN 0814258816 (paperback)

Cover design by Brad Norr
Text composition by Stuart Rodriguez
Type set in Adobe Minion Pro

This time, for Dash.

player, *n.*

3a. A gambler; a person who plays cards, dice, etc., for money. *Obsolete.*

▸ *a*1387   J. Trevisa tr. R. Higden *Polychron.* (St. John's Cambr.) (1872) IV. 297 (MED)   He was..coveytous of lordschippe and pleyere at þe dees [L. *aleæ lusor*].

*c*1390 (▸ ? *c*1350)   *St. Bernard* 725 in C. Horstmann *Sammlung Altengl. Legenden* (1878) 53 (MED)   A monk ones he hedde wiþ him..A ribaut and a pleyer grete.

*a*1425   *Medulla Gram.* (Stonyhurst) f. 3   *Aleator*, a tabyl pleyer.

1483   W. Caxton tr. *Caton* B iv b   A player [at dice] demaunded of hym [*sc.* St Bernard] yf he wolde playe his hors ageynst his sowle.

1511   *Churche of Yuell Men* (Pynson) B vj   Oft my players shall say, by the deth such one was a nimble player, for when he came to the play he had but .v.s. & wan .x.s.

?1518   *Cocke Lorelles Bote* sig. B.vi^v Gardeners, and rake fetters; Players, purse cutters money baterers.

1620   *Hist. Frier Rush* sig. C4   I haue beene among players at the Dice and Cardes, and I haue caused them to sweare many great oathes.

1755   S. Johnson *Dict. Eng. Lang.*   Player..a gamester.

3e. *slang* (orig. and chiefly *U.S.*, esp. in African-American usage). Also in form **playa**. A sexually successful person, usually a man; a playboy; (hence more generally) a successful, respected, or influential person, (sometimes) *esp.* a pimp; a criminal.

1968   *Current Slang* (Univ. S. Dakota) **3** II. 37   *Player*, a man or woman who goes out with many members of the opposite sex. [. . .]

2004   *Daily Star* (Nexis) 29 July 11   Sven Goran Eriksson is not an honourable man. He's a chancer, a player, a dodgy dealer.

4. A person who acts a character on the stage; a dramatic performer, an actor.

*a*1400   in T. Wright & J.O. Halliwell *Reliquiæ Antiquæ* (1845) II. 45 (MED)   Riȝt as Pharao..dispiside God, so these myraclis pleyeris..scornen God. [. . .]

*a*1616   W. Shakespeare *As you like It* (1623) II. vii. 140   All the world's a stage, And all the men and women, meerely Players.

—*Oxford English Dictionary*

CONTENTS

Acknowledgments ix

INTRODUCTION	Asian American Players	1
CHAPTER 1	Playing the Korean War: Domestic Containment and the Bluff of Melancholic Asian American Masculinity	37
CHAPTER 2	Playing the Vietnam War: Remasculinization and the Rhetoric of Polarity	66
CHAPTER 3	Playing the Odds of the Virtual Gulf War: World Police and Family Man	95
CHAPTER 4	Playing the Endless War: The Simulacra of Illegitimacy after 9/11	126
CONCLUSION	The Anxieties of Postmodern Wars	163

Bibliography 175

Index 187

ACKNOWLEDGMENTS

Every book has a far-reaching village of people to which it owes itself. A wealth of gratitude goes to my editor Ana Maria Jimenez-Moreno, my two anonymous readers, and The Ohio State University Press's Editorial Board for their enthusiastic support and keen edits. I also greatly appreciate the feedback I received from Sara Jo Cohen, Cathy Hannabach, Jean Lee Cole, and Michelle Velasquez-Potts as this book developed. Words cannot express my gratitude to my forever teachers and advisors: Colleen Lye and Richard Cándida Smith. Many thanks to my steadfast and brilliant writing group members: Mimi Khúc, Mai-Linh K. Hong, Caroline Hong, Leah Milne, Megan Geigner, Calina Ciobanu, Joan Shifflett, Shirley Wong, Alyssa Quintanilla, Jane Wessel, Michael Wagoner, Gabriel Bloomfield, and Mike Flynn. I also thank Allyson Booth, Noah Comet, Jill Fitzgerald, Thomas Ward, and Michelle Allen-Emerson for reading early drafts of this manuscript. I thank Michelle, too, along with Shirley Lin, Sharika Crawford, Eileen Tess Johnston, and Mike Parker, for mentoring me at USNA. Much gratitude goes to Kurtis Swope for aiding my understanding of game theory. I am so grateful for my students at USNA, who are a constant stream of inspiration and joy. I also thank the Naval Academy Research Council and the Volgenau Fellowship for the great support I received as I developed and finished this project. I thank dear friends both in and out of the field for getting me through all my moments of surrender: Christine Hong, Lawrence-Minh Bùi Davis, Sarah Townsend, Jesse Costantino, Brendan Prawdzik, Marlon Moore, Mike Major, Naida García Crespo, Derek Handley, Monica D. Hanna, Emily Alianello, Melody Wukitch, Theresa Rosenthal, Sarah Slye, Kristi Petree, Mindy Lo, and Dara Kao. I thank my local friends, in place and heart, for their tangible support: Kelly Sweeny, Raima Carpenter, Liz Cash, Stephanie Martin, Brenda Salsman, Chelsea Barzal, Abby Meckes, Dawn Morgan, Susan Bausum, Maria Koshute, Jack Ryan, Jhena Sword, Michelle Cable, Evelyn Lunasin, Loretta Lamar, Denise Boucher, Cindy Winnick, Leslie Davis, Brenda Novak, Genny Jorgensen, Jess Samaras, Gloria Cramer, and Aparna Srinivasan. My paternal aunts and their lives will always be a source of awe and creativity for me. I continue to owe a debt of gratitude to all my siblings: Connie Cheng, Alan Cheng, Michael Wu, Nancy Wu, Karen Karyshyn, Bobby Karyshyn, Tony Clark, and Gina Clark. I thank my parents, Dick and Candy Clark, and Hen-Vai and Serena Wu, for their endless, boundless support and for being on this journey of life with me. And for being my haven and rest, I thank Quentin, Dashiell, and especially Charles—the most ethical man I know.

INTRODUCTION

Asian American Players

ON ASIAN AMERICAN MASCULINITY

Throughout the twentieth and twenty-first centuries, both high literary and low popular US culture have persistently depicted Asian American men as ineffectual and effeminate. These effeminate and disempowered representations have corresponded to the ways in which Asian American men have been legally excluded and racialized. During the nineteenth and early twentieth centuries, even when Chinese American men were exploited for their labor, they were still viewed by Americans as being less manly than their white working-class counterparts.[1] The perception of Asian American men as docile, cheap, and industrious labor that threatened white, specifically minoritized Italian and Irish, labor contributed to the conflicting Asian American stereotypes of the model minority and the yellow peril.

In *Racial Castration* (2001), critic David L. Eng insightfully points out that the fetishized feminization of laboring Asian American male bodies suggests the inextricability of race, gender, and sexuality in Asian American subjectivity. Following Eng, Michael Park argues that nineteenth- and early twentieth-century immigration laws against Asian Americans "eclipsed" Asian American

---

1. Lew-Williams, *Chinese Must Go*, 129, 131.

masculinity.² Fictional representations of Asian American throughout this time period bear out these observations. Starting in 1913 and 1925, respectively, early twentieth-century novels (many of which were later turned into films) by Sax Rohmer and Earl Derr Biggers reinforced this gendered, racialized stereotype—as both feminized and Other—by featuring memorable Chinese American male characters, namely the devious, hypersexual criminal mastermind Fu Manchu and the effeminate, docile police detective Charlie Chan. Though Fu Manchu was depicted as hypersexual and threatening, he was never perceived as manly in a normative, white, hegemonic American sense. In twenty-first-century Hollywood blockbusters like *The Hangover* (2009), Asian American men, like the character Leslie Chow played by Ken Jeong, continue to be portrayed as effeminate and flamboyant. On the other hand, playing with the stereotype of the abused, submissive Asian American male, critic Nguyen Tan Hoang theorizes Asian American gay male "bottomhood" as a state of social abjection that "entails the gleeful surrendering of power."³ While Leslie Chow and Hoang thus reproduce and play with the stereotype of the effeminate, abject Asian American man, the Asian American players of this study performatively reject this stereotype in favor of a victimizing masculinity.

As this study shows, Asian American "player" masculinity is the poached mimicry of normalized white hegemonic masculinity. Critic Martin Summers argues that white "hegemonic masculinity—or the dominant cultural ideals of what it means to be a man—becomes the terrain on which all marginalized, or subordinated, masculinities are constructed and performed."⁴ That is to say, masculinity often—but not always—implies domination, and since 1945, a specific kind of masculinity has dominated: that of the player imperialist. In the ideology of player imperialist masculinity, in order to play others, a player must believe himself, at least at some point, to be the best.

US imperialism began to operate as a form of playerism after 1945, when the US emerged from World War II victorious and as the geographically unaffected world leader; this timeframe was also when neoliberalism, described by such political figures as Ludwig von Mises and Friedrich Hayek starting in 1938, coincidentally emerged with what has become Keynesian economics in its defense of free-market capitalism. Distinguishing neoliberalism from classical liberalism, in which the government "is hands-off and/or aims to offset market effects such as unemployment, resource depletion, or pollution," political scientist Wendy Brown has famously argued that "neoliberal ratio-

---

2. See Park, "Asian American Masculinity Eclipsed," 5–17.
3. Hoang, *View from the Bottom*, 20.
4. Summers, *Manliness and Its Discontents*, 14.

nality disseminates the *model of the market* to all domain and activities—even when money is not at issue—and configures human beings exhaustively as market actors, always, only and everywhere as homo oeconomicus."[5] Historian Suzanne Kahn adds that neoliberalism was synonymous with the market-driven, "breadwinner liberalism"—which favored "a breadwinner father and homemaker mother" in the "idealized nuclear family"—that dominated the mid-twentieth century.[6] Historically championed by white, hegemonic (that is, straight and cisgender) men, the neoliberal player, which both challenged and reaffirmed the patriarchal nuclear family, has characterized US war-making since 1945; this discursive figure has followed the model of the free market in terms of playing others, that is women and gendered (Asian and Middle Eastern) nations of color—for his own profit and to win, or defeat others. Brown goes on to argue that "liberal democracy has also carried—or monopolized, depending on your view—the language and promise of inclusive and shared political equality, freedom, and popular sovereignty."[7] In this way, the US, as a neoliberal player, has seduced certain Asian and Middle Eastern nations since 1945 precisely through the promise of democratic inclusion. In US fiction, the feminized Asian American player performs this gendered citizenship and ultimately reveals the promise of inclusion to be a bluff, an offer that continues to be held beyond his reach.

Player imperialism, although racialized and politicized by whiteness and hegemony, is a simulacrum mimicked by Asian American players. The Asian American male player in the context of post-1945 US war-making in and against Asia and the Middle East, regions toward which he might defensively feel akin, demonstrates how player imperialism has pervaded the global ethos during this historical period, particularly since it is predicated on perpetuating the cycle of the victim and victimizer. This idea of the player is simultaneously sexual and scheming, interpersonal and geopolitical; the Asian American mimicry of what I am calling *player imperialism* poses a threat to its authority by mimicking or performing it.

As the epigraph of this book suggests, the player has been a historically high (dramatic performer, actor) and low (gambler) cultural figure whose meaning was conflated with that of a "womanizer" after World War II. The *Oxford English Dictionary* records the first usage of *player* in this sense in 1968 and traces it to the turn of the twenty-first century. Even though the *OED* designates *player* as an especially prevalent slang term among African Americans, this study indicates that the idea of the player has informed the ideology of

---

5. Brown, *Undoing the Demos*, 63, 31.
6. Kahn, *Divorce, American Style*, 15.
7. Brown, *Undoing the Demos*, 44.

white American imperialism since 1945, which, in turn, has influenced all US citizens. The term *player* is now a common concept and term that the larger American, including Asian American, popular low and high cultures have absorbed.[8] In this way, the player, which lies at the confluence of popular low and high cultures—a trademark of postmodernism—represents postmodernism and its multiple significations. The *OED* generally defines the "player" in slang as a man who embarks on serial sexual conquests for empowerment.

Critic Tara Fickle has argued that even though Asian Americans have long been viewed as intensely hardworking and thus, "unplayful," they have nevertheless been implicated in the "game" or gamble of life in the very dicey game of their representation and the social hierarchies that gaming reinforces: "Exclusionists depicted Chinese Americans as 'inveterate gamblers' and dissolute cheaters whose 'cheap labor' constituted not only unfair competition for other immigrant laborers but an affront to the 'fair play' on which U.S. democracy was ostensibly founded."[9] In other words, historically, Asian Americans have been discursively marked as gaming and dishonest whereas other male laborers have been either unmarked or portrayed as honest and fair. In Asian American literature since 1945, the simultaneously high and low cultural figure of the Asian American player seems to enter monogamous relationships with the promise of reciprocal love and equity only to abuse their partners through deception, betrayal, or objectification to empower themselves. At the same time, such protagonists are also victims of racism and are ultimately emasculated. Many post–World War II Asian American novels and plays featured masculinist, cisgender, usually heterosexual Asian American men who "play" or womanize others—often Asian American women—to reclaim a masculinity that has long been denied Asian Americans.

As mentioned earlier, the blending of high and low culture and the multiplicity of significations that the term *player* connotes are the hallmarks of postmodernism; indeed, as I will explain, postmodernism itself has diverse and often conflicting theoretical definitions and intersects with the performance theories and game-playing theories of capitalism that are foundational to the figure of the player. Moreover, postmodernism is usually said to have emerged at the conclusion of World War II and is often demarcated by a theoretical fragmentation that never resolves itself; likewise, the player, which came to mean "womanizer" after 1945, is a psychically fragmented victim who never resolves his victimhood and, instead, becomes a victimizer as a way of coping with his pain.

---

8. *Oxford English Dictionary*, s.v. "player," accessed April 7, 2020, http://www.oed.com.
9. Fickle, *Race Card*, 3–4, 15, 13, 5, 22.

The slang term *player* has become the cultural signifier of the simultaneously lauded and despised behavior of male promiscuity in popular culture. For example, most of the country-turned-pop-singer Taylor Swift's catchy break-up songs that have ranked at the top of the Billboard Music pop charts since 2014 have featured the "player" whom she can't resist but who ultimately betrays, abandons, and devastates her. The popularity of her music indicates that American culture is indeed obsessed, however ambivalently, with these rebellious, sexually objectifying male figures. The player, or its earlier incarnation, the womanizer, is of course not unique to the postmodern era—nor is the cultural love-hate obsession with players a recent phenomenon: In high literary culture, Nicholas Rowe's *The Fair Penitent* (1793) and Lord Byron's *Don Juan* (1819) are famous examples of sympathetic lotharios that predate this period. The 2020 Netflix series *Bridgerton*, which is set in early nineteenth-century London, also revolves around "rakes" or players. This historical, literary, and popular fascination with the stock character of the player suggests that this ambivalent fantasy is a distraction, much in the way that Raymond Williams understands the perpetual, ahistorical myth of the countryside—marked by its "quiet [. . .] innocence [and] simple plenty," its status as both a "metaphorical" and "actual retreat"—to be an effective distraction from the exploitation of workers and industry in the city.[10] Broadly, since 1945, forms of both high and low culture—literature, literary theory, film, television, and the media—have promoted the trope of the masculine player or womanizer, distracting us from the victims he leaves in the wake of his actions.

THE PLAYER MASCULINITY OF AMERICAN IMPERIALISM

The player is an imperialist figure. He believes himself to be the best sexual partner to women—a vague "God's gift to women"—but struggles to maintain the illusion of his dominance. In its achievement and maintenance of global dominance after World War II, the US has taken on a player persona to hold firm to its masculine, military, and economic might. Although this study focuses on American imperialism after 1945, many critics like Amy Kaplan trace the dawn of American imperialism to the US victory of the Spanish-American War in 1898. In his 1901 speech, "Manhood and State-hood," just three years after the Spanish-American War in which the US began to assert itself as a global leader, President Theodore Roosevelt argued that masculine

---

10. Williams, *Country and the City*, 23.

strength was synonymous with American nationhood.[11] After World War II, however, the world watched as the US remained in a permanent state of war through major conflicts such as the Cold War, the Gulf War, and the War on Terror to maintain America's unstable masculine dominance. This study proceeds from critic Mark Breitenberg's argument that

> masculinity is inherently anxious. [...] Anxiety and masculinity: the terms must be wed if only for the obvious reason that any social system whose premise is the unequal distribution of power and authority always and only sustains itself in constant defense of the privileges of some of its members and by the constraint of others; even though historically and culturally specific patriarchal models function with considerable variety, they are by definition forms of social organization that produce distress and disequilibrium.[12]

After 1945, masculinity was premised not only on physical strength but also on playing others; since then, player imperialist masculinity has often been exclusionary, presented as the only legitimate form of masculinity, and usually tied to cisgender male bodies. More importantly, it has always aimed to win and exploit others, particularly in recent less bodily, more technological wars. As an imperialist player, the US had to be aggressive but cunning to respond to the ever-moving target of history and still maintain its masculine dominance.[13]

The US white hegemonic player's attitudes followed the imperialist politics of his home country. As postcolonial critic Anne McClintock has famously argued in *Double Crossings* (2001), gendered Western imperialism has been masculine and sexually exploitative. The US began to temporarily occupy nations through war and military bases to dominate ideologies or exploit resources such as oil after 1945 rather than following an earlier nineteenth-century, explicitly expansionist model of colonialism of seizing land and sending back resources from colonies. Historian David Lake has argued that over the course of 1887 to World War II, the United States was slowly surpassing Great Britain as the global imperial power; even after US power took over the world, it continued to be what Lake calls an "opportunistic" global economic player.[14] Historian John Bodnar points out that, at the same time, after World War I, the US consolidated itself as a nation-state: During World War II, Americans felt the need to fight totalitarianism and fascism, but they also

---

11. Cheung, "Early Chinese American Autobiography," 32.
12. Breitenberg, *Anxious Masculinity,* 2, 3.
13. In *Postmodern War,* Chris Hables Gray argues that since 1945, wars have become "devastating[ly] technologi[cal]" (23).
14. Lake, *Power, Protection, and Free Trade,* 30.

"lusted for" imperialist "dominance over others both within and outside the nation and justified acts of excessive cruelty" to further the myth of American exceptionalism.[15] US temporary occupations of other nations since 1945 for exploitation and sovereignty have been attempts to stabilize US masculine sovereignty through a "player's," or womanizing logic. In this way, American imperialism has "played" or seduced other nations with its promise of democratizing them without fulfilling that promise domestically or abroad; these attempts, in turn, bolster white hegemonic masculinity.[16] In her analysis of totalitarianism during World War II and the Cold War, philosopher Hannah Arendt argues that totalitarianism is the result of the postmodern secularization of time, which involves the separation of religion and politics but also "knows no beginning and no end and which thus does not permit us to entertain eschatological expectations": With no religious endpoint like death and judgment, totalitarianism keeps itself afloat by continually basing its action on hypothesis and oppressing its subjects from the postmodern "empty space" at its center through its player "persuasion."[17] It is worth noting that Arendt, who became an American citizen after immigrating to the US, did not view the US as totalitarian, imperialist, or as a consolidated nation-state.[18] However, as Lake and Bodnar have argued, the US was certainly imperialist. Reliant on persuasion and inherently unstable for fear of being outdone by another imperialist power, white hegemonic masculinity has had a reciprocal relationship with postmodern wars.

In literature and in popular discourse since 1945, white hegemonic masculinity and the player imperialism that has often driven it remain unmarked and are commonly seen as benevolent military interventions in fascist, communist, and terrorist countries. On the other hand, the anxious Asian American male subjects portrayed in contemporary literature reflect the anxieties of hegemonic masculine dominance that have informed postmodern American wars. Thus, the Asian American player is the marked trace of unmarked white hegemonic masculinity and its cultural and historical attendant, player imperialism. Because the US white imperialist player is defined by his contrast to the effeminate Other, the Asian American masculine man, who has historically been feminized by the media and the types of labor offered to him, such as laundry work, gives pause to this assumption that he is indeed feminine.

---

15. Bodnar, *Remaking America*, 21; Bodnar, "Good War," 2.
16. While the same could be said of British ideological imperialism, my focus on US imperialism historicizes the period after 1945 in which the US emerged as the world superpower and explains its impact on Asian American masculinity and those living in the United States.
17. Arendt, *Between Past and Future*, 68, 87, 99, 133.
18. Hill, *Hannah Arendt*, 99.

Focusing on the Asian American sports player, rather than sexual chancer, critic Stanley I. Thangaraj argues specifically that the South Asian American basketball player is a figure that confirms and distorts conventional notions of the masculinity of "manning up" or "being a beast."[19] Thangaraj claims that the easy oscillation in representation between the nerd and the dangerous, perpetually foreign terrorist, particularly during the Gulf War and the War on Terror, suggests the complexity of Asian American masculinity.[20] This complexity, I argue, mimics and exposes player imperialism in exaggerated ways. The Asian American player is postmodern precisely because he deconstructs these power relations through mimicry.

Influenced by America's struggle to maintain its masculine military and industrial imperialism, prominent postmodern theorists Michel Foucault, Jacques Lacan, and Jacques Derrida famously deconstructed power relations of governing authorities. Although they did it from different theoretic vantages, Foucault, Lacan, and Derrida all argued for the postmodern fragmentation of the social subject. By focusing on the anxiety of Asian American masculinity, this book negotiates the historical concurrence of the theoretical destabilization of the social subject that followed the Holocaust and the dropping of the atomic bombs on Hiroshima and Nagasaki that ended World War II, which Foucault, Lacan, and Derrida began to theorize during the Civil Rights era, and the assertion and calcification of masculinist identity politics by scholars and activists during and following the 1960s and 1970s. The performance of Asian American player masculinity reached its apotheosis during the Civil Rights era.

As critic Jachinson Chan argues, in the 1960s and 1970s, Bruce Lee and Marvel's Shang Chi represented Asian American masculinity, with Bruce Lee portrayed as powerful but asexual and Shang Chi as a more "heteromasculine" player figure.[21] Consonant with Bruce Lee's martial arts masculinity in the 1970s, Frank Chin, Jeffery Paul Chan, Lawson Fusao Inada, and Shawn Wong called for Asian American writers to claim America and the "the style of manhood" in *Aiiieeeee!: An Anthology of Asian American Writers* (1974).[22] The groundbreaking publication of *Aiiieeeee!* signified the entry of Civil Rights–era activism into the academy. The editors distinguished between assimilationist texts about Asians and Asians living in the United States and cultural nationalist texts; that is, they pronounced a distinctly cultural national Asian American identity as separate from an Asian identity or one that assimilated

---

19. Thangaraj, *Desi Hoop Dreams*, 5.
20. Thangaraj, 4.
21. J. Chan, *Chinese American Masculinities*, 4.
22. Chin, Chan, Inada, and Wong, *Aiiieeeee!*, 37.

to a white American identity. However, in doing so, the editors problematically limited Asian American identity by defining it according to continental US literature and "the style of manhood," in part to counter decades of discursive xenophobia and feminization of Asian American men in popular culture. African American, Latinx, and Native American literature during and after the Civil Rights era followed the same pattern of calling upon masculinist identity politics in activism and scholarship in the academy: For example, the Black Panthers and Brown Berets were racial, masculinist Civil Rights organizations, as were the masculine labor movement leaders such as César Chávez and Luis Valdez, which coincided with the central theme of masculine action in Gerald Vizenor's theory of Indigenous survivance. However, just as the United States has needed to remain in a constant state of war to maintain its unstable economic power and military imperialism since World War II,[23] the continually reinforced masculinities in the Asian American literary texts of my study already suggest their instability and disintegration. Critic Helen Heran Jun writes that after World War II, the masculinization of Japanese American identity was "haunted" by Asian American and African American racial exclusion and shaped by "black male recalcitrance."[24] Jun also writes that "black Orientalism" signifies the national history of US imperialist intervention in Asia, which the nation must repudiate in the name of "global coprosperity."[25] While Jun focuses on Afro-Asian masculinities, I argue that the ubiquitous white hegemonic masculinity of contemporary US imperialist wars in Asia also fashions the masculinities of Asian American characters in literary cultural artifacts after World War II. This study contributes to and expands studies on Cold War masculinities that emphasize heterosexuality published by Asian American studies scholars such as Daniel Y. Kim and Viet Thanh Nguyen.

TRACKING PLAYER IMPERIALISM: ASIAN AMERICAN PLAYER MASCULINITY IN LITERATURE

The Asian American players of these texts specifically perform masculinity against the Asian American stereotype of femininity and male homosexuality; however, their performances fail when these protagonists face racial discrimination. This failure of performance and impossibility of Asian American masculinity stemmed from stateside culture and politics, which were derived from

---

23. Finlan, *Gulf War*, 7–8, 10; Hastings, *Korean War*, 10.
24. Jun, *Race for Citizenship*, 71.
25. Jun, 9.

the US's engagement in masculine wars in the Middle East and the Far East. Although, as Edward Said has argued, Western domination of the Middle East goes back centuries, the US assumed a new "player" masculinity of temporary occupation to win wars in and exploit the Far and Middle East after 1945. As noted, deconstructive and revelatory postmodernism is usually demarcated as beginning after World War II when American imperialism came to the fore. Then, as now, as critic Cynthia Enloe points out, those in Western governmental and political power have historically been white men.[26] As this study shows, the postwar Asian American player emerges deconstructively as the postmodern, marked trace of this otherwise unmarked or normative form of American imperialism.

As Said first claimed in *Orientalism*, the hegemony of objectification and womanizing after World War II reflects US masculine military interventions into the discursively feminized areas of East Asia and the Middle East. Said argues that Western Orientalism was first applied to the Middle East, then to eastern Asia but was meant to distinguish the Western Self from the Eastern Other. However, as critic Colleen Lye suggests, US Orientalism specifically transformed the Far East into a feminized, US-occupied "proxy" rather than an untouched "antipode" during the Cold War and Vietnam; it did the same to the Middle East during the Gulf War.[27] Critic Amy Kaplan seems to agree more with Said in the American context, arguing that American imperialism has historically conflated domesticity with the nation despite being represented by the white male body.[28] Basing his own theories on the works of Said and historian Ronald Takaki, critic Gary Okihiro points out that Asia has been historically feminized through US military intervention.[29] War brides and hypersexualized Asian villager victims, as exemplified by the 1987 Vietnam War movie *Full Metal Jacket*, mark Asia as a feminized and hypersexual space. Despite the US military having integrated women in 1975, US militarism has always been framed as masculine and gender normative. Intimately close as an invaded "proxy" of the US during major wars but always relegated as Other, Asia is represented by the Asian American "player" characters who don the mask of player imperialism but fail to succeed in this role because they themselves are also feminized and racially disempowered. John Okada's *No-No Boy* (1952), David Henry Hwang's *M. Butterfly* (1988), and Viet Thanh Nguyen's *The Sympathizer* (2015) are all prime literary examples of this phenomenon.

---

26. In *Bananas, Beaches and Bases*, Cynthia Enloe writes, "Most of the time we scarcely notice that governments look like men's clubs" (6).
27. Lye, *America's Asia*, 10.
28. Kaplan, *Anarchy of Empire*, 1, 3; Kaplan, "Black and Blue," 233.
29. Okihiro, *Common Ground*, 18.

I emphasize the historicity of these texts because they are all about war and produced in the US during a period of perpetual war following World War II. Since war and the military often signify masculinity par excellence, the masculinities of the protagonists and antagonists of John Okada's *No-No Boy*, David Henry Hwang's *M. Butterfly*, Chang-rae Lee's *Native Speaker* (1995) and *A Gesture Life* (1999), and Viet Thanh Nguyen's *The Sympathizer* were all influenced by the dominant, player imperialism that characterized each major American war after World War II. As a dominant discourse, player imperialism shapes postmodern American wars, which, in turn, promulgate player imperialism. In this way, the shifting historical player imperialist masculinity of each war influences the Asian American masculinity displayed in each of the texts I examine. While most of these texts explicitly reference earlier wars that are not contemporary to their production, I take a New Historicist approach in arguing that the protagonists' masculinities implicitly reflect and shape the states of American masculinity that emerged from the conflicts that were: namely, the Korean War, the Vietnam War, the Gulf War, and the War on Terror. This method follows what critic Jinqi Ling famously refers to as a "reentanglement" of the "'ideological' with the 'formal'": that is, the influence of historical ideologies on aesthetic form.[30] As the works of my study show, it seems especially incumbent on Asian American men during the American imperialist wars in the feminized Far and Middle East after World War II to prove their analogous Americanness and manhood through their performances.

The remainder of this introduction focuses on the book's theoretical underpinnings by contextualizing the study within postmodernism and American imperialism. Deterrence, bluffing, and preemption, which I will later discuss in detail, are all forms of the racial and gendered privilege, as well as exclusion, that undergirds player imperialism. Thus, *Asian American Players* conceives of the Asian American player as a performer, power-playing womanizer, and game player who indexes the evolving but astonishingly stable playerism or masculine ethos of US foreign policy since 1945.

AN "IN" TO THE SLIPPERINESS OF POSTMODERNISM

Asian American Players: Masculinity, Literature, and the Anxieties of War delineates Asian American postmodernism through the coeval postmodern alienation from and dismantling of identity and masculinity. In this way, post-

30. Ling, *Narrating Nationalisms*, vi.

modernism assumes play. I focus on the trope of the Asian American player and the anxieties that affect his actions in literature as the lens through which to make sense of this contradiction during each major US war since World War II. In the context of this study, I contend that the fantasy of the player—or the consummate lover who is actually bluffing and will, in the end, betray you—transports the self from the reality of perpetual war and misplaces the blame of the abstract damage and doom of the technological wars after 1945 onto the Asian American player. In this way, Asian American players come close to representing the absurd unrepresentability of power in our post–World War II, postmodern condition.

This study is inspired by but departs from Victor Bascara's *Model-Minority Imperialism* (2006), which, like Kaplan's *The Anarchy of Empire*, traces American imperialism back to the US victory from the Spanish-American War of 1898 and argues that, by "self-determination" and "self-naming," the emergence of Asian American literature and culture coincided with the emergence of American imperialism.[31] Contrasting with the timeline of US imperialism cited by Bascara and Kaplan, I find that US imperialism is most clearly refracted through Asian American cultural artifacts in the post-1945 era, partly because of the era's historical coincidence with postmodern theories of dismantling identity. As visible images of masculinity that counter stereotypes of Asian American male effeminacy, Asian American players both challenge the trope of the feminized Asian man and highlight the otherwise unmarked nature of white hegemonic player US imperialism.

As noted, postmodernism is often historically thought of as having begun with the Holocaust but also the masculinist, absurd, and harrowing US acts of dropping the atomic bombs on Hiroshima and Nagasaki that concluded World War II.[32] It has also historically spanned the masculinist Western interventions in the feminized East in major American wars since 1945. However, the content and definitions of postmodernism, specifically the ways in which it can be defined as either conservative or radical, have been more difficult to determine. In *Our Aesthetic Categories*, critic Sianne Ngai writes of the instability of the term *postmodernism*: "My wager in this book is that finding a way to grasp this historically specific configuration, if not exactly 'system' of aesthetic categories, will be similarly salutary for getting a handle on postmodernism (and 'through it, all the other things that are happening to us')."[33] In many ways, postmodernism is itself the inexplicability of the "things that are happening to us": For example, what do we make of the uniquely Ameri-

---

31. Bascara, *Model-Minority Imperialism*, xxvi, xxxvi.
32. Childers and Hentzi, "Postmodernism," 234.
33. Ngai, *Our Aesthetic Categories*, 51–52.

can cultural obsession with the player, or suave lothario? In contrast to Ngai's deconstructive categories of cute, zany, and interesting, the uninteresting but anxious brawn of masculinity, which the postmodern players—that is both the imperialist white hegemonic masculine players and the Asian American players—perform, is both radically deconstructive and conservatively hegemonic and also reflective of the divergent theoretical definitions of postmodernism.

The postmodern Asian American player simultaneously embraces and is alienated by the player masculinity that constitutes American imperialism. In *Framing the Margins,* critic Phillip Brian Harper argues that alienation and decenteredness are hallmarks of the slippery concept of postmodernism.[34] He goes on to assert that leading postmodern theorists Jürgen Habermas, Jean-François Lyotard, and Fredric Jameson perceived postmodern fragmentation differently: For Habermas, it is a conservative force in contemporary life; for Lyotard, it is a progressive method of revelation; and for Jameson, it is a conservative articulation of late capitalism.[35] Jameson famously begins *Postmodernism, or, The Cultural Logic of Late Capitalism* (1991) by making historicization a logical imperative but also critiquing the narcissistic conservatism of postmodernism as the cultural logic of late capitalism: "It is safest to grasp the concept of the postmodern as an attempt to think the present historically in an age that has forgotten how to think historically in the first place. [. . .] Postmodernism, postmodern consciousness, may then amount to not much more than theorizing its own condition of possibility, which consists primarily in the sheer enumeration of changes and modifications."[36] Habermas's[37] and Jameson's definitions of postmodernism as conservative differ from the conception offered by Lyotard, who argues that postmodernism exposes and "de-reifies" ossified relations between individuals and institutions.[38] Lyotard refuses to accept this partition between individuals and institutions and argues that oppositional thinking "is out of step with the most vital modes of postmodern knowledge."[39] The visible performances of the postmodern Asian American player progressively demystify the player imperialism of white hegemonic masculinity and in this way illustrate Lyotard's position. In *The Postmodern Condition,* Lyotard further writes that the postmodern indi-

---

34. Harper, *Framing the Margins,* 4, 5.
35. Harper, 9.
36. Jameson, *Postmodernism,* ix.
37. In his foreword to Lyotard's *Postmodern Condition,* Jameson writes, "For Habermas, indeed, postmodernism involves the explicit repudiation of the modernist tradition—the return of the middle-class philistine of *Spiessbuerger* rejection of modernist forms and values—and as such the expression of a new social conservatism" (xvii).
38. Lyotard, *Postmodern Condition,* 17.
39. Lyotard, 14.

vidual is shaped by the "complex and mobile" conditions of his contemporary moment.[40] Influenced by their contemporary wars, the Asian American player protagonists of my study mimic and divulge the instability of player imperialist masculinity after 1945.

Binaristic thinking defines the actions of the player, specifically the Asian American player. The objectification of another human being requires binaristic thinking. We see these binarisms operating in the masculinities of domestic containment, polarizing remasculinization, world policing/the family man, and illegitimate orphanhood, concepts the four chapters of this book explore in turn. However, through mimicry, the Asian American player also exposes and dismantles the binaristic thinking of player imperialist masculinity. And thus, in keeping with Lyotard, postmodernism, or what Appiah would call the politicized, "misleadingly postmodern" "postmodernization," is revelatory and deconstructive of binary power structures.[41] Reflecting the notions of both Jameson and Lyotard, the Asian American player is simultaneously conservative *and* radical insofar as he mimics but ultimately fails to attain the historicized player imperialism championed by each major US war since World War II. His marked failures expose the domestic failures of democracy and reveal the unmarked, unchecked hegemony of the racialized masculinity undergirding the Keynesian US military-industrial complex that has driven each of the presidential administrations during the major postmodern US wars.

Rather than a criticism of free love or consensual polyamory, my study of the Asian American player is a critique of his power-seeking dishonesty, victimization of others, and perpetuation of player imperialist masculinity. Many of us are guilty of such things. And yet, as Wendy Brown points out, white, heterosexual, cisgender men are inevitably given power in our postmodern society through "'postmodern' techniques of power" even when their power is deconstructed.[42] We continually see the Asian American players insisting on their masculinity even through failures in this study. Although Brown traces the masculinism of freedom and the perpetual empowerment of white, heterosexual, cisgender men to the Enlightenment, she recognizes that the posthumanist critique of freedom, which has become synonymous with white hegemonic masculine American imperialism, issues from our postmodern, post–World War II era.

There are of course stark differences among the major US wars after World War II on which I focus in this book: the Korean War, the Vietnam War, the Gulf War, and the War on Terror. But, as Kaplan argues, "What Virginia Woolf

---

40. Lyotard, 15.
41. Appiah, "Is the Post- in Postmodernism," 352–53.
42. Brown, *States of Injury*, 18, 19–20.

wrote of books, they 'continue each other,' can also be said of wars: Wars continue each other. Wars generate and accumulate symbolic value by reenacting, reinterpreting, and transposing the cultural meaning of prior wars."[43] What was specifically "continued" through these wars were similar game theoretic strategies of deterrence that exemplified American imperialism. Another reason why I focus on post-1945 American imperialism is because of its incorporated culture of play. Critic Alan Trachtenberg has used "incorporation" to discuss the corporatization of the US during the Gilded Age; a century later, the US military-industrial complex corporatized masculinity and playing in an effort to promulgate American imperialism.[44] That is to say, in its military-industrial tactics, the US government incorporated the post-1945 counterculture of play, or what historian Daniel Belgrad calls the postwar "culture of spontaneity" that continued past the Cold War.[45] This culture of playful spontaneity responded first to the postwar fear of totalitarianism, which persisted through all four major US wars I examine.[46] The playful spontaneity specific to Cold War counterculture responded to and was shaped by the serious fear of nuclear holocaust and the communist enemy and those who supported Third World revolution as well as the emergence of the military-industrial complex.[47] As historian Thomas Doherty has indicated, even playful, enjoyable pastimes like watching television featured the serious, threatening images of Senator Joseph McCarthy during the communist witch hunts of the House Un-American Activities Committee years.[48] Likewise, the 1960s countercultural phenomenon of rock and roll, as historian Michael Kramer argues, was absorbed and disseminated by the American military during the Vietnam War.[49] The US counterculture of musical and artistic play and spontaneity, historian Richard Cándida Smith claims, was part of postwar "mythopoetic thinking" that aspired to utopia.[50] And yet, he goes on to point out that "the very theory that allowed the avant-garde to criticize the dominant structures of American society applied to their hopes as well, but, with few exceptions, they did not apply their critique to their own lives, so they did not see, except intuitively, how radical utopia was dependent upon and derivative from the society they hoped to overthrow."[51] The US government had absorbed and

---

43. Kaplan, "Black and Blue," 219.
44. Trachtenberg, *Incorporation of America*, 3–7.
45. Belgrad, *Culture of Spontaneity*, 1–2.
46. Menand, *Free World*, 6.
47. Kuznick and Gilbert, *Rethinking Cold War Culture*, 2.
48. Doherty, *Cold War, Cool Medium*, 16.
49. Kramer, *Republic of Rock*, 17.
50. Cándida Smith, *Utopia and Dissent*, xix, 398.
51. Cándida Smith, 398–99.

incorporated the utopia of counterculture so that its playful "player" military interventions into the East in major post-1945 wars were ironically as much a reflection of American counterculture as they were a pursuit of the utopian imperialism that the counterculture critiqued.

Cándida Smith adds that lust and obscenity were part of American counterculture's utopian aspirations: Referencing US imperial interventions into the feminized East, he goes on to point out that male obsession with the military stemmed from it being a US institution "where sexual fantasies were openly indulged."[52] Historians Peter J. Kuznick and James Gilbert also point to the ways in which the incorporated US counterculture of spontaneity and playfulness extended to the increasing liberalism of sexuality after World War II: The "playboy" counterculture of the 1950s increased the openness of all sexuality, including homosexuality, and led to the discovery of the birth control pill in the 1960s.[53] On the other hand, the US government's incorporation of American sexualized counterculture fueled the masculinist and sexualized interventions into the feminized Far and Middle East.

To maintain its masculine, imperial dominance after it emerged unscathed and victorious from World War II, the US played Eastern nations through its foreign policy of enticing democratization and military and economic imperialism.[54] Claiming their own masculinity, the Asian American protagonists of the texts I examine reflect this US foreign policy by disseminating the uninteresting yet enticing brawn and anxiety of US masculinity; on the other hand, they decenter or delegitimate US imperialism through their performances by virtue of the way they are feminized through their race. While other immigrant populations such as the Irish, the Italians, and the Germans have often been feminized, their assimilation as white over the course of the twentieth century allowed them to take on masculine personas without question. On the other hand, other immigrant and minority populations such as Latinxs, African Americans, and Native Americans, respectively, alternate between feminization and hypermasculinization. Asian Americans remain a unique, unassimilated racial group that is continually feminized despite the dissemination of the masculine Asian American player in the texts I study.

Asian American Players explains why postwar American imperialism has been so enduring and successful by recasting it, including its attendant foreign policy and military incursions, as a seductive masculine player rather than an explicit war machine. This book follows Christine Hong's brilliant book, *A Violent Peace*, in which she defines the postmodern Cold War according to the

---

52. Cándida Smith, 333–34, 366.
53. Kuznick and Gilbert, *Rethinking Cold War Culture*, 5.
54. Freeman, *American Empire*, 50, xii.

twinned multiculturalist, Pax Americana and the US "war machine."[55] *Asian American Players* personifies the US war machine by figuring it as a masculinist player. Masculinity is often conflated with power and strength,[56] and yet the implicit invincibility of masculinity suggests that it is an anxious performance that can be undone or fail at any time.

Asian American playerism is a form of survival within the US's historically heteronormative, patriarchal society; that is to say, in order to succeed within capitalism, retain a job, or achieve progress within the hierarchy of heteropatriarchy, the player must play "others" even as he is othered. The concept of the Asian American player takes as its starting point postmodern theorists Gilles Deleuze and Félix Guattari's landmark claim that sexual desire is constitutive rather than symptomatic of the economic base of society. In *Anti-Oedipus: Capitalism and Schizophrenia*, they argue that schizophrenic subjectivities emerge from the linguistic decoding and rearticulations of capitalist production. That is, capitalism must imperiously colonize others and create seductive conditions in which the others want to be colonized in order to survive. In this way, capitalism produces linear and binary "desiring-machines" out of individuals and systems.[57] These "desiring-machines" perpetuate the endless desire and greed of capitalism. However, they also create schizophrenic bodies or neurotically vacated "bodies without organs" (simply an inside and an outside) that are stuck in the binary of "either, or," which are symptoms of the binary system of capitalism.[58] Whereas capitalism is perpetuated through decoding or deterritorialization and reifying reterritorialization, the unassimilated schizophrenic sticks out like a sore thumb; the schizophrenic thus reflects and exposes the antinomies of capitalism.[59] Deleuze and Guattari lionize the schizophrenic. The schizophrenic's binary state decodes but records the binary limit of capitalism—its seduction and its domination.[60] Likewise, the Asian American player, who is a victim and a victimizer, does not assimilate into player imperialism. In the Asian American player's failure to assimilate, race thus becomes the record, limit, and trace of the masculinist American imperialism of which capitalism is a part; it shows that player imperialism is a performance that is racially specific and thus unsustainable. In other words, Asian American masculinity records the limit of the selective, unsustainable

---

55. Hong, *Violent Peace*, 1.
56. Thangaraj, *Desi Hoop Dreams*, 11.
57. Deleuze and Guattari, *Anti-Oedipus*, 5, 14.
58. Deleuze and Guattari, 9, 11, 12, 16, 224, 225, 12, 75, 160.
59. Deleuze and Guattari, 245–46.
60. Deleuze and Guattari, 246.

capitalist seduction and the failure to fulfill the promises of American democracy, which is part and parcel of American imperialism.

Asian American players are indeed a corollary of American capitalism and military dominance after World War II; however, they are not identical. Asian American players are never fully incorporated as part of the nation; for, even as they mimic white male hegemonic citizenship and copy implicit national behavior by buying into the game of patriarchal masculinity and victimizing (usually women or marginalized) others, they themselves are "played" by the nation when they are the ones who are marked or made visible as the "Fu Manchu" social misfits and degenerate others in high and low American culture. At the same time, the Asian American player, who has either grown up or been socialized or educated in the US, through what critic Karen Shimakawa has called "mimetic abjection," traces unmarked player imperialism: "Asian Americanness is intelligible only as abject," or a "'radical jettisoning' that produces [white American] inside/outside, subject/object, deject/abject [which] can be brought into being differently."[61] In certain cases, the Asian American protagonists who were perceived as dominant subjects in their countries of origins found that they would not continue to hold such a status in the US where they were feminized. Contextualizing Asian American players within the contemporary postmodern wars of their fashioning demonstrates, through an examination of mimicry, the performativity and instability of American imperialism that was demonstrated abroad. As the Double Victory campaign of World War II, in which African Americans fought for integrated troops while the US fought fascism abroad, demonstrated, the US continued to fight dual wars at home and abroad against racial minority groups after World War II. American player imperialism is, in turn, mimicked by Asian American men characters in contemporary cultural artifacts. I argue that, by entering into the international game arena of patriarchal masculinity, Asian American players bear the trace of American zero-sum "poker" strategies of imperialism as implemented overseas since World War II. In other words, Asian American players womanize in the masculinist spirit of American imperialist gameplay in masculine military dominance and Keynesian deficit spending, which I discuss in the next section.

This claim prompts the question: What happened after World War II that brought racially minoritized men, such as Asian American men, to the center stage of masculinist American politics? In his magisterial study of the 1930s Popular Front culture, American studies scholar Michael Denning argues that the vast failure of the Congress of Industrial Organization's strike at the end

---

61. Shimakawa, *National Abjection*, 104, 102.

of World War II, which coincided with the beginning of the Cold War, served as the last nails in the coffin of the "Cultural Front" or an American culture of the laboring class. However, this period also invited a "racialization of American politics."[62] According to Denning, this discursive shift away from making labor visible and toward emphasizing race in American politics resulted from interracial conflicts in the consolidated American working class in the North and West.[63] All of the Asian American players I examine in this book are working class or newly transitioned middle class; as anti-establishment "rebels," all of them expose the racism and social injustices they face in their historical moments in the US only to reveal and reinforce the unstable, patriarchal masculinity championed by the US overseas.

THE ASIAN AMERICAN PLAYER'S CAPITALIST GAME: GAME THEORY IN US MILITARY AND ECONOMIC IMPERIALISM

Asian American masculinity, in its performance of and failure to reproduce white hegemonic masculinity, underscores the binary limits of US capitalist imperialism and seductive but unfulfilled democracy. Specifically, Keynesian economics corporately exemplifies a player's method of deception and seeming masculine invincibility; that is, deficit spending offers more money than what the nation has to further American military and economic imperialism, or the military-industrial complex. Since World War II, the US has not just "played" other countries with a performance of military might but also with economic bluffing. This section highlights the ways in which the Asian American player has mirrored American economic imperialism since 1945 by gameplaying through bluffing or pretending. In other words, American capitalism, specifically deficit spending, has been a seductive game of bluffing, which the Asian American player has mimicked. In some low cultural instances, like William Hung's performance on *American Idol*, the Asian American player/performer has even capitalized on his failure to mimic player imperialism, or, in Hung's case, Latinx hypermasculinity or hyperbolic masculinity. While Black and Latinx men have also historically disrupted white hegemonic masculinity, their disruptions have been discursively discounted as hypermasculinity; on the other hand, Asian American player masculinity, which also

---

62. Denning, *Cultural Front,* 24, 466.
63. Denning, 466.

mimics white hegemonic masculinity, is conspicuous because of the historical, enduring stereotype of Asian American male femininity.

The Asian American player's game is conducted on the sexual and financial field and so reflects the larger sociopolitical arena. As Deleuze and Guattari argue, capitalism is binary and linear in its seduction and domination but must appear far-reaching and invincible in its masculinity to maintain its imperialism.[64] The imperial US emerged victorious from World War II, a war not fought on its own soil (with the exception of the attack on Pearl Harbor). Keynesian economics, or deficit spending, was the way in which the US, as a "player" nation, deceived the world about its wealth and appeared invincible even though it was in debt. As most liberal historians will argue, the US immediately delved into the Cold War to shore up its military-industrial complex and guard against a recession.[65] After all, part of the impetus to enter the war was the ideology of Keynesian economics, which had rescued the US from the Great Depression: Historian Lawrence Glickman writes, "A group of Keynesian economists in 1938 described the goal of the New Deal as propping up a free enterprise system that, 'left to its own devices, is no longer capable of achieving anything approaching full employment' by 'restoring the demand for the products of private industry through a vigorous expansion of the public sector.'"[66] In short, Keynesian economics is a mixed economy of private and government-owned public industry in which public spending is used to boost private economy.[67] Keynesian deficit spending is the way in which the US has played other nations since 1945 and thus contributes to the notion of the player as someone who spends what they do not have and seduces others in order to enjoy a life of power.

Keynesian economics played into America's masculine, invincible, imperialist persona. In 1944, in Bretton Woods, New Hampshire, representatives from forty-four nations met to establish the International Monetary Fund (IMF) and the International Bank for Reconstruction and Development (World Bank). In the end, the conference made "the dollar [. . .] the benchmark for currency exchange" and gave the US control over the IMF and World Bank through its contributions.[68] Although the Bretton Woods agreement has become known as the greatest success of the American Keynesian policy, Bretton Woods adopted hegemony under the guise of cooperation; the mon-

---

64. Deleuze and Guattari, *Anti-Oedipus*, 14.
65. Zunz, *Why the American Century?*, 90; Tindall and Shi, *America*, 1327.
66. Glickman, *Free Enterprise*, 108.
67. Glickman, 108.
68. Freeman, *American Empire*, 56.

etary system perpetuated US imperialism during the Cold War.[69] Moreover, as economist Zachary D. Carter writes, Keynes had hoped that the Bretton Wood conference would eliminate global conflict and create a new international order of "balanced, fair trade, regulated by international authorities"; rather the conference produced a Cold War monetary system that the neoliberal United States could use to further its imperialism.[70] Woods goes on to argue that the private and government-led spending of Keynesian economics drove the "military-industrial complex" after World War II, against which President Eisenhower would rail.[71] Throughout each major war after World War II, the US financial policy has been Keynesian in its military spending for imperialist, foreign incursions and domestic bailouts. Freeman writes that defense spending was one way in which the US government spurred on the postwar economy and corporations.[72] Carter likewise states that nearly every presidential administration after the war has deployed Keynesian economics, including Reagan and Obama.[73] Moreover, since there have been liberal and conservative followers of Keynesian economics, it is not a financial model limited to one side of the political spectrum.[74] However, this strategy of Keynesian economics has often backfired: The debt ceiling crises of 1995, 2011, and 2013—two of which led to federal government shutdowns—were, in part, a result of Keynesian economics or widescale, economic bluffing.

The Asian American player mimics Keynesian economics by repeatedly lying about his resources of devotion and love. In terms of game theory, Keynesian economics, or deficit spending, is a form of bluffing other nations about US wealth, even as the US acknowledges to itself that it is lying about its resources. As political scientists Scott Gates and Brian D. Humes indicate, "Any poker player will tell you that bluffing is an essential element of strategy. Bluffing is also important in strategic political interactions. When we bluff we manipulate an adversary's beliefs."[75] Poker, as Gates and Humes and literary critic Gina Bloom point out, is a game of incomplete information, in which "a

---

69. Carter, *Price of Peace*, 441–42.
70. Carter, 441–42.
71. Carter, 309; Freeman, *American Empire*, 107–8.
72. Freeman, 116, 177.
73. Carter, *Price of Peace*, 528–29.
74. In *Price of Peace* Carter writes, "In Washington and academia, the word *Keynesian* no longer carried the subversive connotation it had during the heyday of McCarthyism. There were now liberal Keynesians and conservative Keynesians and reactionary Keynesians who recognized that the tools created by Paul Samuelson, John Hicks, and Alvin Hansen could be deployed for a variety of political ends" (452).
75. Gates and Humes, *Games, Information, and Politics*, 141.

player [is] uncertain of the other player's payoffs."[76] When down to two players, poker becomes a zero-sum game. Likewise, imperialism is a zero-sum game where "one person's gain is another person's loss."[77]

As Gates and Humes claim, game theory has also structured American foreign policy since World War II.[78] Although this study focuses on a substantial time period—1945 until 2013—and covers diverse wars, the United States' approach in all of these wars, in the fashion of a sexual and game player, has been a game theoretic approach; specifically, it has been a zero-sum game where there is only one winner when, really, global foreign affairs are always a mutual "prisoner's dilemma" of keeping peace and ensuring resources for all. The Asian American players in this study evidence the repeated game strategy of the US. Game theorists Avinash K. Dixit and Barry J. Nalebuff define the game theory of the prisoners' dilemma: "The players act at the same time, in ignorance of the others' current actions. However, each must be aware that there are other active players, who in turn are similarly aware, and so on. Therefore each must figuratively put himself in the shoes of all, and try to calculate the outcome. His own best action is an integral part of this overall calculation."[79] In her study of the ways in which interactive gaming structured early modern theater between the "players" or performers and the audience, in which the audience is provided incomplete information, Bloom focuses on games as spaces for trial and error as characters pursue *"patriarchal masculinity"* as a competition of masculine risk over scanty resources.[80] In the postmodern wars following World War II, civilians who did not personally participate in war, specifically Asian American men, were the conscious and unconscious audience members who, witnessing or shaped by these masculinist wars, bought into the poker game of patriarchal masculinity even as they rebelled against white American culture in anti-establishment ways.

In this way, as the imperial "player," the US follows John Nash's game theory of equilibrium in which players use the same strategies and tactics to achieve equilibrium against the anxiety of loss. Nash's dominant game theory "is a set of strategies such that no individual player can become better off by unilaterally changing his or her strategy choice."[81] Although American foreign policy and military strategy were not uniform in all of the major wars after World War II, Gates and Humes focus on the historical repetition in Amer-

---

76. Gates and Humes, 4; Bloom, *Gaming the Stage*, 40.
77. Dixit and Nalebuff, *Thinking Strategically*, 14.
78. Gates and Humes, *Games, Information, and Politics*, ix.
79. Dixit and Nalebuff, *Thinking Strategically*, 33.
80. Bloom, *Gaming the Stage*, 15–16.
81. Gates and Humes, *Games, Information, and Politics*, 26.

ican political science: They argue players often repeat their strategies even if they play the same game with the same opponent again.[82] In each major war, since World War II, the US converted a prisoners' dilemma of keeping world peace and plenty (democratic Pax Americana) to a zero-sum game of imperialism and domination. For example, in his well-known historiography *The Korean War*, Max Hastings writes that the Korean War was "a military rehearsal" for the Vietnam War insofar as the same strategies were used in both.[83] Moreover, historian Rosemary Foot suggests that deterrence, a strategy that predominated in the Gulf War and the War on Terror in the form of preemption, began as nuclear deterrence during the Cold War, specifically as early as the Korean War.[84] The repetitive game strategy that the US used in all of its major wars and forays into the feminized Far and Near East after 1945 was a masculine patriarchal game of poker in which bluffing was deployed in the form of deterrence (of communism or terrorist, antidemocracy) and in which multipolar positions of world powers were ultimately reduced to bipolarities either between capitalists and communists or democratic "freedom fighters" and lawless terrorists. Asian American masculinities trace and reflect the ideology and foreign policy of domestic containment and polarization during the Cold War in that they mirrored the military strategies of surveillance, virtuality, preemption, and ultimately deterrence in the wars fought in the Middle East before and after 9/11. Not necessarily synonymous with imperialism, zero-sum deterrence has nevertheless been a strategy in which the US has repeatedly asserted its dominance over other nations since 1945.

Following World War II, the US fought major wars in Korea, Vietnam, Kuwait, Saudi Arabia, Iraq, and Afghanistan to respectively contain communism and retaliate against terrorism but also to play the odds of its military and economic dominance. The Korean War was a measured victory for the United States, resulting in a national division between North and South Korea, which cost over 2.5 million lives, 33,000 of which were American.[85] By contrast, the Vietnam War, which ended with the surrender of Saigon to the North Vietnamese and the withdrawal of American troops in April 1975, is universally agreed upon as a blight on American history. Although the 1989 fall of the Berlin Wall historically ended the Cold War, some historians argue that the US entered the Gulf War two years later to compensate for the failure of the Vietnam War;[86] abiding by Keynesian economics once again, the

---

82. Gates and Humes, 55–56.
83. Hastings, *Korean War*, 10.
84. Foot, *Wrong War*, 41.
85. Tindall and Shi, *America*, 1320.
86. Finlan, *Gulf War*, 7–8, 10.

war was also an attempt to resolve the leveraged buyout (LBO) bust on Wall Street at the end of the 1980s.[87] Moving away from the "bipolarity" or polarization of the Cold War, the US under the Bush (Sr.) administration, declared war against Iraq after their invasion of Kuwait in August 1990.[88] Nevertheless, McAlister writes, even during the Cold War, the "Middle East has loomed large as a US interest, especially since 1945, when the United States became a global superpower and the Middle East became one of the most contested regions in the world."[89] The technologically based tactics of "shock and awe" of Operations Desert Shield and Desert Storm proved to be a success when the Iraqis fled Kuwait and Bush called for a cease-fire on February 28, 1991. Finally, the US declared a "War on Terror," specifically against the Taliban and al-Qaida following the attacks on the World Trade Center and the Pentagon on September 11, 2001. However, historian Paul Rogers indicates, despite public assumptions, there seemed to be little proof of US military reaction to September 11.[90] Nevertheless, in March 2003, President George W. Bush declared war on Iraq with the intent of overthrowing its president, Saddam Hussein. In December 2006, Hussein was charged by the American-run Iraqi Special Tribune for crimes against humanity and sentenced to death. As theorist Jasbir K. Puar has indicated, US popular culture discursively portrayed both Hussein and the founding leader of al-Qaida, Osama bin Laden, like Asian American and Arab American men—as emasculated, sexually monstrous, heterosexually and homosexually perverse, and Orientally polygamous: "Recall, as an example, a website where weapons are provided to sodomize Osama bin Laden to death."[91] Bin Laden was seized and killed by US armed forces in May 2011. The Cold War, Gulf War, and War on Terror have all been forms of victimizing gameplaying in which the US established military and economic sovereignty.

Despite President Barack Obama's declaration on May 23, 2013, that the Global War on Terror had concluded, the War on Terror has not ended and, therefore, it is difficult to gain a holistic perspective on it. Nevertheless, as critic Annie McClanahan has argued, the American "doctrine of preemptive military action" emerged after 9/11 when the US invaded Iraq, without evidence of their responsibility for the attacks and on the basis of George W. Bush's claim that "we have every reason to assume the worst, and we have an urgent duty to prevent the worst from occurring."[92] As my fourth chapter

87. Tindall and Shi, *America*, 1512–14.
88. Tindall and Shi, 8.
89. McAlister, *Epic Encounters*, 2.
90. Rogers, *Why We're Losing*, 73.
91. Puar, *Terrorist Assemblages*, 38. I thank Leah Milne for making this connection.
92. McClanahan, "Future's Shock," 42, 49.

demonstrates, Asian American players after 9/11 reflected the illegitimate but privileged logic of preemption, a deterrent form of risk and bluffing that is akin to the deterrent strategies of brinkmanship and containment during the Cold War; this preemptive strategy of deterrence manifested itself in legalized domestic and international surveillance such as the Patriot Act (2001), and its renewed iterations have continued to drive the very real but also conceptually abstract War on Terror. In this way, the US deployed a player's strategy of seductive and deceptive deterrence for personal gain. Coupled with the Keynesian approach of economic gain under the guise of militarized justice and the shock-and-awe tactics of military action, deterrence constitutes the corporate, political persona of a narcissistic, player nation, which Asian American players subjectively mimic in the texts I examine.

"DON'T HATE THE PLAYER, HATE THE GAME": THE ASIAN AMERICAN PLAYER AND PERFORMANCE THEORY

Starting where my first book, *The Asian American Avant-Garde*, historically concludes, *Asian American Players* spans the historical period from the end of World War II to the decade after September 11, 2001, in which the US rose to indisputable prominence within the twin international arenas of global capitalism and military imperialism.[93] *The Asian American Avant-Garde* argues that Asian American modernists performed democratic American universalism in a hopeful, dialectical rather than self-cancelling, deconstructive manner. In this way, the hopeful dialectic functions according to Judith Butler's revised theory of performance as outlined in *Contingency, Hegemony, Universality* (2000). On the other hand, *Asian American Players* suggests that, through their performances of white hegemonic masculinity, Asian American postmodern players follow Butler's original theory of performativity, exemplified in *Gender Trouble* (1990) and *Bodies That Matter* (1993), by "denaturalizing" player imperialist masculinity in their performances of it.[94] In *Gender Trouble*, Butler makes the important distinction between the liberating performance and regulatory expression of gender.[95] Although the masculinities of the Asian American players are earnest and conservative "expressions" of player imperialism, their failures to escape their feminizing stereotypes render their expressions performative. Similarly, in "Of Mimicry and Man," from *The*

---

93. I thank Shirley Wong for reminding me of the popular saying quoted in this section's subheading.
94. Butler, *Gender Trouble*, 187.
95. Butler, 192.

Location of Culture, theorist Homi Bhabha writes of mimicry as the "inappropriate" "appropriation" of the colonized who mimics the colonizer and threatens his "normalized" power.[96] The failure of Asian American masculinity in this study underscores its performance and threatens the normalized, white hegemonic masculinity of American imperialism. The Asian American player also coincides with Tina Chen's theory of impersonation—a performance that "resist[s] the binary logics of loyalty/disloyalty, real/fake, and Asian/American" and "by which Asian Americans are constituted and constitute themselves as speaking and acting subjects"—and David Eng's theory of racial melancholia: the "absolute internal exile that exposes a virulent discourse of universalism that contradicts a national project of abstract equivalence and equal representation."[97] However, in keeping with Bhabha's definition of mimicry, the Asian American player is a "perfect" performance that fails due to the race of the performer and, in turn, generates a space for critique of the imperial playerism of white hegemonic masculinity. Thus, in contrast with Chen's and Eng's theories, the temporal lag between failure and critique is crucial in assisting the Asian American player's reformation into an ethical man who realizes the performativity of masculinity. As Butler writes, just as gender performances "parody [. . .] the very notion of an original [. . .] and revea[l] that the original identity after which gender fashions itself is an imitation without an origin," the Asian American player denaturalizes and parodies the masculinist, seemingly invincible originality of American player imperialism and reveals its anxiety to maintain its own performance.[98]

As noted, Asian American masculinity during and after the Civil Rights era corresponded to the contemporary decentering of the subject theorized by influential white European philosophers at the time. Because imperialist masculinity is innately fueled by anxiety and instability,[99] just as player imperialist masculinity requires wars to maintain and legitimate itself, ethnic hypermasculinity, specifically Asian American player masculinity, is always interpreted as a violent threat. Racialized hypermasculinity is likewise fueled by anxiety: Critic Phillip Brian Harper states, "All debates over and claims to 'authentic' African-American identity are largely animated by a profound anxiety about the status specifically of African-American *masculinity*."[100] *Asian American Players* treats race as a social, biological, "external identification" of

---

96. Bhabha, "Of Mimicry and Man," 122–23.
97. Chen, *Double Agency*, xvii; Eng, *Racial Castration*, 199.
98. Butler, *Gender Trouble*, 188.
99. Breitenberg, *Anxious Masculinity*, 2, 3.
100. Harper, *Are We Not Men?*, ix.

ethnicity, which has "larger cultural and historical" implications such as war.[101] Racialization often hyperbolically genders the ethnic subject; that is, race usually hypermasculinizes and hyperfeminizes ethnic men. On the other hand, ethnicity, which is claimed by the subject, acknowledges social disempowerment and seeks re-empowerment and visibility by performing race. Asian Americans have not historically been associated with masculinity and, for this reason, I focus on performances of Asian American (alternating) hypermasculinity and effeminacy.

As a "forever foreigner," the Asian American player is faced with the doubly performative task of acting as a reformed, suave player who has renounced his supposedly innate nerd—that is intellectually robust but physically weak—persona.[102] The Asian American player performatively responds to racially particular model minority / yellow peril stereotypes of social and psychological inscrutability ("poker face") and hypersexualization. The pointed racialization of Asian Americans as perpetual outsiders that vacillate between model minority and yellow peril stereotypes, imaginary fullness and lack, positions them as prime examples of Asian American players. Moreover, their double performance of their racialization as effeminate yet hypersexed complicates their subjectivities.

ASIAN AMERICAN DOUBLE DEALING AND ITS CRITICAL BACKGROUND

In the 1990s, scholars of Asian American studies, African American studies, Native American studies, and Latinx studies were deconstructing the subject in their theorizations of hybridity in ethnic identities. However, Asian American masculinity was already being deconstructed through literary portrayals of unstable masculinity after World War II when the US emerged as a world superpower. In certain ways, these postmodern wars were unofficial, not-declared-by Congress, nebulous things in the same way that nonwhite American citizenship is. The different motivations of the Asian American players and their anxieties about their legitimate citizenship and masculinities characterize and mark the historicity of each war. This book proceeds chronologically: The first two chapters focus on literature produced during and about the Cold War and the ideological bipolarity between capitalism and communism, while the last two chapters center on literature produced during the wars of

---

101. Sollors, *Beyond Ethnicity*, 36.
102. Thangaraj, *Desi Hoop Dreams*, 4.

competing capitalisms that have taken place in the Middle East. As noted earlier, many of the texts I discuss do not specifically reference the wars that are contemporaneous to the texts' publications, but they are all set during or shortly after war and feature anti-establishment protagonists whose masculine interactions with others are complicit with American military strategies and reflect contemporaneous, dominant notions of American masculinity. That is, contemporary wars influence the ways in which masculinity is perceived by the authors: The Asian American players of these texts seduce the objects of their desire with the promise of democratic inclusion but really seek to dominate and use them; in so doing, they sometimes resist but ultimately reflect and expose the player imperialist masculine American military strategies of deterrence—domestic and foreign containment deployed during the Cold War and virtual and preemptive strikes during the Gulf War and the War on Terror. The historicization of all the texts as civilian war literature demonstrates Asian American iterations of imperialist masculinity during each war.

While the marked, racial image of the Asian American player pervaded literature, other high cultural forms of performance theory in literary and cultural studies also took off in the 1990s. Butler's famous theories about the performativity and deconstruction of gender through her study of cross-dressers and hermaphrodites were published in three iterations in the 1990s and early 2000s: In addition to the aforementioned and earlier *Gender Trouble* and *Bodies That Matter*, *Undoing Gender* appeared in 2004. In 1991 theorist Homi Bhabha published his theory on the deconstructive strategies of performance in postcolonial mimicry and hybridity in *The Location of Culture*. The following year, critic Mary Louise Pratt argued for the performative quality of hybridity in colonized cultures in which colonized subjects mimicked and deconstructed the authority of colonizers in the cultural space she dubs the "contact zone" in *Imperial Eyes* (1992). Heavily influenced by Butler and these postcolonial thinkers, major critics in the fields of African American, Asian American, Latinx, and Native American literature such as Paul Gilroy, Lisa Lowe, José David Saldívar, and Elvira Pulitano all published groundbreaking studies about performance and hybridity in their ethnic American subfields from the mid-1990s to early 2000s. Gilroy's *The Black Atlantic* (1993), Lowe's *Immigrant Acts* (1996), Saldívar's *Border Matters* (1997), and Pulitano's *Toward a Native American Critical Theory* (2003) were radical critical texts in their fields and have incited a spate of criticism about the deconstruction of race ever since. These seminal texts explore cultural hybridity—not as blind assimilation to the dominant white, American status quo—but as nuanced performances of ethnic American diaspora that subvert normative American culture and rebel against the establishment.

When conceptualizing performances of power, hybridity theory engages very closely with performance theory. None of the texts I have just named nor any other ethnic American deconstructive criticism that has come after them have explored the subjectivity of the Asian American player, per se. However, all of these texts suggest that performances of stereotypes dismantle the political practice of playerism (that is, if racial subjects can perform player imperialism, then player imperialist masculinity is itself a performance) but also run the risk of reaffirming dominant notions of race and two-dimensional racial stereotypes. The criminalized, or at least denigrated, visibility of Asian American players explains the bifurcation between illegitimate and legitimate violence but also denaturalizes the hegemony of white hegemonic masculinity by underscoring its performativity. Rather than strictly romanticizing or condemning the Asian American player as culturally subversive or complicit to social norms, *Asian American Players* historicizes their subjectivities as part and parcel of, as well as revelatory of, masculinist US military interventions in the Far and Middle East after World War II.

Despite my focus on the Asian American player, I would be remiss to say that he is singular in his proclivities and behavior. As Thangaraj points out, there are multiple masculinities.[103] This range is demonstrated by the players of the texts I discuss in this study, which all come from well-known and canonized Asian American texts—Okada's *No-No Boy,* Hwang's *M. Butterfly,* Lee's *Native Speaker* and *A Gesture Life,* and Nguyen's *The Sympathizer.* These texts all demonstrate the pervasiveness of the player trope, but the various players seduce those around them in diverse ways, according to the historical context of each war. All of the protagonists of these texts succeed at seducing and deceiving their sexual partners through their abilities to "play up" or mimic imperialistic, white hegemonic masculinity through methods both endearing and repulsive to their sexual partners. The Asian American player "plays" on two levels: He interpersonally performs—deconstructs and reasserts—racial and hyperbolically gendered stereotypes for visible self-empowerment, but he also reflexively plays the geopolitical zero-sum game of white hegemonic masculinity trumpeted by American imperialism in wars fought after 1945. On the other hand, player imperialism is hyperbolic but legitimized as "just right" or even invisible by virtue of the global expanse of American imperialism whereas the extremity of or deficiency in the masculinities of Asian American players becomes visible and culturally criminalized in the US.

Although the Asian American player exists in low, popular culture, the case studies in this book mainly focus on Asian American male protagonists

---

103. Thangaraj, 16.

in the high culture of literature. The stereotypes of the Asian outsider or perpetual foreigner and the deceptive, dangerous trickster seem to comprise the "bad boy" underbelly of the Asian American player's charm. The Asian American player/trickster is similar to the African American folk hero "trickster" who is, according to critic John W. Roberts, heteronormative and masculine.[104] However, distinct from other racial stereotypes, the model minority racialization of Asian Americans socially robs them of their countercultural "cool." Whether he performs model minority effeminacy like William Hung did in *American Idol* in 2004 or countercultural African American hypermasculinity as Wei Chen and Eddie Huang do in *American Born Chinese* and *Fresh off the Boat*, respectively, the Asian American player reflects, in different ways, the invisibility of the white hegemonic masculinity championed by American imperialism after World War II. Moreover, like Song's gender performances in *M. Butterfly*, the alternately hypermasculine and effeminate performances of Asian American players I examine are alternatives to what critic Celine Parreñas Shimizu calls Asian American "straitjacket sexualities," or the asexuality, effeminacy, and homosexuality often attributed to Asian American men.[105]

All of the Asian American players examined in this book have the potential to realize what Parreñas Shimizu calls inclusive "ethical manhoods" or inclusive "manhoods that care for others," particularly women and women of color, but their potentials are directly tied to the democratic approaches of US foreign policy during each major war and the result of each war.[106] As I mentioned earlier, not all masculinities are imperialist. Likewise, in "Punks, Bulldaggers, and Welfare Queens," critic Cathy J. Cohen argues for a political alliance between nonnormative heterosexual men and women, who are "demonize[d]" and "oppress[ed]" by "various segments of the population" along with the LGBTQ+ community.[107] At the same time, she makes the proviso that she does not mean to undermine the experiences of gay men, lesbians, or bisexual and transgender people or conflate them with those of marginal heterosexual women and men: "There is no doubt that heterosexuality, even for those heterosexuals who stand outside the norms of heteronormativity, results in some form of privilege and feelings of supremacy."[108] Because I am interested in this middling figure of the Asian American player—one who is racially oppressed but also privileged by his gender and heterosexuality—I focus on performances of toxic or abusive masculinities by cisgender

---

104. Roberts, *From Trickster to Badman*, 2.
105. Shimizu, *Straitjacket Sexualities*, 3.
106. Shimizu, 4.
107. Cohen, "Punks, Bulldaggers, and Welfare Queens," 457.
108. Cohen, 458–59.

gay (masquerading as straight) and straight men of color, specifically Asian American men, rather than subversive masculinities of transgender subjects and queer women and women of color. While theorist Eve Kosofsky Sedgwick famously pointed out that masculinity is distinct from men, I recognize that masculinity is tied to male bodies in this study.[109] Even in rebelling against the norm, Asian American masculinities both challenge and reinforce the status quo of heteronormativity and American imperialism through mimicry. Asian American players are not consensually polyamorous with their partners, as they are understood to be monogamous men who treat women inequitably. Moreover, Asian American players do not, for the most part, espouse an ethical manhood that promotes social equity and inclusion. However, many of the Asian American players examined here start to realize their ethical manhood when they recognize the performativity of player imperialist masculinity and, like their victims, the disempowerment they face, or the organic disempowerment of all men. Their potential for ethical manhood suggests that those who espouse white hegemonic masculinity have the same potential to divorce themselves from player imperialism: White hegemonic masculinity does not have to be toxic and injurious to others, and Asian American players who have turned to ethical manhood exemplify this possibility. As Arendt argues, if player persuasion is the method of totalitarianism and imperialism, it can also be the vehicle of "egalitarian order."[110] The potential of ethical manhood—a practice of democracy—for the Asian American players in these texts reflects the contradictory coincidence of the US twin projects of democracy and capitalist imperialism since World War II.

Asian American masculinities are discursively hyperbolic in their hypersexual fullness or lack; they are historically shaped by but also expose, through mimicry, player imperialism and the instability of American imperialism, foreign policies, and military strategies overseas during the Cold War, Gulf War, and War on Terror. American Studies scholar Melani McAlister writes that "foreign policy is a semiotic activity, not only because it is articulated and transmitted through texts but also because the policies themselves construct meanings."[111] Even when unacknowledged, postmodern American wars and their gendered strategies have broadly affected civilian life. That is, covered by physical and virtual newspapers, postmodern wars are constructed by and contribute to an imagined community of national perceptions of gender. As a result, Asian American men mimic player imperialist masculinity as a form of assimilation, which ultimately fails. While dominant American society

---

109. Sedgwick, "Gosh, Boy George," 11–20.
110. Arendt, *Between Past and Future*, 133, 92–93.
111. McAlister, *Epic Encounters*, 5.

perceives Asian American players as delinquent, their mimicry exposes the unstable playerism of the US nation.

PLAYED OUT: CHAPTER SUMMARIES

My first chapter, "Playing the Korean War: Domestic Containment and the Bluff of Melancholic Asian American Masculinity," examines John Okada's *No-No Boy*, which was written and published during the Korean War (officially, 1950–53). Even though *No-No Boy* (1957) is set before the Korean War, it was heavily influenced by the "Forgotten War." Although the novel does not explicitly allude to the Korean War and is set immediately after World War II, the anxious machismo of the protagonist Ichiro Yamada is a symptom of and participates in the ideologies and political practices of the contemporary war. Seemingly free to assimilate in a racially desegregating US, the figure of the womanizing player in *No-No Boy* mirrors the US intervention and dominance in the Korean War. This chapter demonstrates that Ichiro's and other Japanese American characters' womanizing actions index the US as the masculinist "player" in the Cold War arena that takes advantage of the stereotypically feminized Asian nations South Korea and Japan to rally them against its communist opponents North Korea, China, and Russia. The masculinity of Okada's protagonist is shaped by and reflects the player imperialist masculinity that was promoted during the Korean War. In imitating US Cold War player imperialism, the Asian American male protagonist of Okada's novel subverts the Cold War propaganda of championing the patriarchal, American nuclear family as an avenue of "domestic containment" or a way to shore up the nation's defenses against communism. While US imperialism also took the form of a playboy who forgets or uses his previous alliances whenever convenient, the Asian American players of the novel are forgotten and, in this way, invisible. Although his masculinity appears culturally diverse (Ichiro mimics both African American and white American masculinities), Ichiro vacillates between imitating imperialistic, white American masculinity and experiencing his racialization as invisible and effeminate, just as Korea is discursively depicted during the war. In part, because the US is victorious insofar as it succeeds in establishing the 38th parallel during the Korean War, the characters of this chapter can come to grips with their democratic, ethical manhoods.

My second chapter, titled "Playing the Vietnam War: Remasculinization and the Rhetoric of Polarity," focuses on the ways in which the minoritized Asian / Asian American and French characters of Hwang's *M. Butterfly* reveal the discursive, hegemonic reclamation of violent masculinity in military strategy and American popular culture during the Vietnam War; this ideological reclamation of violent masculinity diverts the Asian American player in this chapter away from ethical manhood during this period. This chapter continues with analyzing Asian American playerism in the later Cold War by relating the intersectional ethnic inferiority of Asian American men. For example, although Song from *M. Butterfly* appears to perform the role of the model minority—the ideal fantasy of an Asian woman—he slips back into the role of the inferior yellow peril when he reveals that he is really a male spy.[112] In *M. Butterfly*, the rhetoric of polarization (between unmarked, privileged capitalism and marked, disenfranchised communism), which predominated in Vietnam War negotiations, pervades the framing of privileged white American heterosexual masculinity as a metaphor for the US and its occupation of Vietnam, Laos, and Cambodia during the war. The nonwhite or non-American male characters in *M. Butterfly* are unable to live up to the paragon of white American hegemonic masculinity despite their womanizing exploits. In this chapter, I argue that the asymmetrical bipolarity between the US and Russia during the Vietnam War contributes to the discourse of metaphorical self-portrayals that constricts Song and Gallimard from *M. Butterfly* to the stereotypes of the white American masculine heterosexual ideal *or* the passive Asian woman. This polarizing rhetoric of either/or, is / is not delineates the binary system of capitalism, according to Deleuze and Guattari, but also Roman Jakobson's linguistic definition of the metaphor, which is, according to Jakobson, defined by trial-and-error substitution. Failing to fully conform to the Vietnam War–era image of player imperialism, despite their player behavior, these characters only have recourse to fashioning themselves according to metaphorized stereotypes as *either* the submissive Asian woman *or* the player imperialist white American man. Because they are unable to name and problematize player imperialism as such, Gallimard and Song are trapped in metaphoric prison houses of asymmetrical binaries: white/nonwhite, man/woman, straight/gay, American/non-American. Song's playerism, which is based on and advances conceptual binaries—man/woman, dominant/submissive—in the play, reflects the polarization of the US and the Soviets, who manipulated other countries to promulgate their opposing ideological agendas. The chapter seeks to historicize *M. Butterfly* by situating its politics as part and parcel of the Manichean Cold War ideologies of the Vietnam War. The aphasic speech of the characters, in which they are stuck speaking in metaphors, thus reflects this "either/or" bipolar mentality of the Cold War.

---

112. Hwang, *M. Butterfly*, 90–91.

Player imperialist masculinity becomes less explicit once it is reframed as the world police masking itself as the caring family man during the virtual Gulf War. In my third chapter, titled "Playing the Odds of the Virtual Gulf War: World Police and Family Man," this subtle masculinity, which the Asian American players expose, is nevertheless an ideology difficult for Asian American players to identify and renounce. This chapter examines Asian American literature following the end of the Cold War and the beginning of the wars in the Middle East in the 1990s. Because Arab American literature had not yet been established in the American popular and social imaginary, the chapter examines contemporary Asian American literature that does not explicitly mention the virtual Gulf War; it investigates post–Cold War Asian American spies in Chang-rae Lee's *Native Speaker* and *A Gesture Life*. Embodying "inferior" yellow peril figures, Henry Park from *Native Speaker* and Doc Hata from *A Gesture Life* are portrayed as insidious menaces to society. These characters are not only seen as fraudulent Americans, they also disidentify with those within their ethnic and work communities, including their espionage colleagues. Moreover, Park and Hata are problematically perceived as foreign, disloyal double agents. An absent presence in both texts, the Gulf War imposes the rhetoric of virtual warfare on the first-person narratives of *Native Speaker* and *A Gesture Life*. Moreover, in reflecting the race riots and the competing capitalisms of the Gulf War era, these two texts exhibit the contemporaneous impulse of devising adversarial difference (a zero-sum game) out of similarity—meaning, similar minoritization or oppression (a prisoners' dilemma)—in trumpeting American imperialism in the Middle East. The unmarked invisibility and racism of American imperialism are figured in the degradation of Lee's Asian American male protagonists by white female lovers and patriarchal figures as they fail to live up to the paragons of white American masculinity. They, in turn, exercise their subjectivities by objectifying, "playing," and victimizing Asian American women in the narratives. As Gulf War–era texts, they mirror the imperialist American military strategies of constructing adversarial difference out of similarity and deterrence, converting prisoners' dilemmas to zero-sum games.

My fourth chapter, "Playing the Endless War: The Simulacra of Illegitimacy after 9/11," focuses on the ways in which Asian American players trace the deterrent ideology of illegitimate preemption and risk which, as McClanahan argues, has expanded finance capital, motivated American intervention in the Middle East since the 1990s, and driven the abstract War on Terror.[113] Whereas the previous chapters unveil the implicit playerism of Asian Ameri-

---

113. McClanahan, "Future's Shock," 51.

can protagonists, this chapter reflects the expansion of bluffing finance capital through the explicitness of Asian American and Arab American players. This logic manifests itself in the orphanhoods and other feelings of illegitimacy of the narrator of Viet Nguyen's *The Sympathizer* and the protagonist of Frances Khirallah Noble's *The New Belly Dancer of the Galaxy* (2007). *The Sympathizer* and *The New Belly Dancer of the Galaxy* respectively feature an unconventional Asian American player—an unnamed Vietnamese communist sympathizer, spy, and refugee after the Fall of Saigon—and an Arab American player named Khalil, who is going through a midlife crisis. To compensate for their discursive effeminacy and illegitimacy, the characters objectify women and turn to the War on Terror era's white hegemonic masculinity of seduction and illegitimate preemption. In the end, the protagonists I study in this chapter are made self-conscious of their playerism, reflective of the consciousness of American imperialism after 9/11, and choose to redeem themselves by embracing ethical manhoods. These novels demonstrate that the deconstruction of the fetishized player more aptly reflects American military intervention into the Middle East since 9/11, where the enemy is nebulous and the threat perpetual. The chapter claims that the cunning codes of preemptive risk and (financial and emotional) debt that structure finance capital also influenced American military strategy after 9/11. In the War on Terror, the US has applied finance capital strategies of change, speculation (investment), and deterrence (preemptive action) to its military interactions with foreign nations such as Iraq and Afghanistan. These strategies are reflected in the womanizing behaviors of Nguyen's sympathizer and Noble's Khalil.

Like these protagonists, the US has lived a fantasy of inexhaustible funds and egalitarian politics to fuel the War on Terror. However, the actions of Asian American players, who reflect the foreign interventions of the US nation, are visible just as the exploitative actions of the US are also exposed to American society after 9/11 and during the War on Terror. Thus, the Asian American players are able to realize the violence of their behavior and consciously embrace ethical manhoods of egalitarian care. In these texts, the Asian American players are both victimizers and victims but can break out of this binary in the realization of inclusive, ethical manhood—a practice and partial fulfillment of democracy. Even though some of their narratives take place well before 9/11, the contemporaneousness of the conceptually wily War on Terror and elusive finance capitalism to these texts' publications contribute to the lack of reality that the sympathizer experiences. Exemplified by the sympathizer, Asian American players are themselves victims of racism and undemocratic, social disempowerment who then victimize others to compensate for their social lack; they subjectively mimic the geopolitical military-industrial complex, or the militarized and corporate nation, by interpersonally objectifying people, usually Asian American women or other women of color, in fiction and drama during periods of war. Broadly, the Asian American player exposes the political practice and anxiety of historical iterations of player imperialism—which has ideologically constituted American imperialism since 1945—and, in turn, proposes an ethical manhood for all who seek it.

CHAPTER 1

Playing the Korean War

Domestic Containment and the Bluff of Melancholic Asian American Masculinity

A KOREAN WARTIME NOVEL

Until recently, critics have not viewed Ichiro Yamada, John Okada's protagonist in *No-No Boy* (1957), as a player. Instead, most critics have perceived him as a Japanese American victim of racism and American nationalism: He is forced to choose between his Japanese heritage, embodied by his overbearing mother, and his American patriotism during World War II as he is imprisoned for refusing the draft. However, Tara Fickle has recently cited Ichiro's sexual relationship with the Japanese American character Emi as a "game theory" attempt to redeem his manhood: "If sexual intercourse with Emi offers Ichiro an opportunity to symbolically change his answer to a 'life-giving yes,' Ichiro, as an extension of Kenji, ostensibly plays an equally heroic role in rescuing her from symbolic death by nominal widowhood."[1] Although Fickle does not focus on the term "player" as womanizer, she does identify that Ichiro games Emi, specifically, in his interactions with her. This chapter focuses on the masculine privilege of deterrence that Ichiro and other Japanese American male characters use in their interactions with women, especially Asian American women; in this way, *No-No Boy* reflects and reveals the gaming deterrence

---

1. Fickle, *Race Card*, 73, 74.

of domestic containment that US player imperialism performed during the Korean War.

Since its publication, *No-No Boy* has been firmly ensconced in the canon of Asian American literature.[2] Critics of Okada's novel, such as Daniel Y. Kim, Viet Thanh Nguyen, Jinqi Ling, as well as Sau-Ling C. Wong and Jeffrey J. Santa Ana, have historically framed it as a Cold War novel. Nguyen writes that the Cold War restricted Americans and perpetuated hierarchical race relations in the US.[3] However, most critics have overlooked the specific historicity of the novel as Korean Wartime literature in its concurrent reflection of the player imperialist masculinity. Daniel Y. Kim has argued that "the Korean War marked a turning point in the US history of race" with Thurgood Marshall's dispatch to Korea to investigate the large population of courts-martialed Black soldiers and Truman's racial integration of troops in his previous Executive Order 9981.[4] In *No-No Boy*, Asian American characters are racialized as alternately hypermasculinized and emasculated during the Korean War. Although *No-No Boy* takes place in 1945, it was written during and influenced by the "forgotten" Korean War (officially, 1950–53). As critic Jinqi Ling points out, Okada started writing *No-No Boy* in the early 1950s, during the Korean War: Under the conditions of the United States' newly formed alliance with Japan, Okada's publisher Charles E. Tuttle sought out Japanese American writers who could write narratives of peaceful cultural encounters and successful assimilation into US society.[5] Given its context of war and the historicity of its publication, *No-No Boy* is a Korean Wartime novel: It features Asian American players whose masculinities reflect the related game theoretic military strategy of deterrence and are shaped by contemporary domestic containment, a form of deterrence. Through Ichiro's and other Japanese American characters' mimicry of player imperialism—perfect in imitation but imperfect in nonwhite racialization—Okada's *No-No Boy* divulges the deterrent political strategies of US foreign policy during the Korean War and the nation's championing of player imperialism in the years after World War II. Specifically, the US espousal of a "domestic containment" policy in Asia was a form of the Cold War strategy of deterrence; domestic containment—a domestic offshoot of international containment—informs the strategies of the US as a Korean War player, as it "played house" with Japan and South Korea for its own imperialist gain; Ichiro futilely, on account of his race, attempts to exemplify this player imperialism through his subjectivity.

---

2. Entin, "'Terribly Incomplete Thing,'" 85–86; Ling, *Narrating Nationalisms*, 36.
3. Nguyen, "Wounded Bodies," 162.
4. D. Kim, *Intimacies of Conflict*, 3.
5. Ling, *Narrating Nationalisms*, 35; Ling, "No-No Boy," 144–45.

Through his subjective, "bluffing," womanizing behavior, Ichiro resists and exposes the Cold War propaganda of the American nuclear family, or "domestic containment." During the early Cold War, domestic containment was a local, interpersonal form of communist deterrence, which the ideology of American player imperialism paradoxically championed even as its subject, the white hegemonic patriarchal player, threatened the American nuclear family through his faithlessness.[6] Patriarchal American policies were also of course exercised in the domestic sphere. In her well-known study of the resurgence of the cult of domesticity following World War II, Elaine Tyler May writes that the US and Soviet Union cemented their hostility during the Cold War as the US focused its containment of communism at home with "visions of carefully planned and secure homes, complete with skilled homemakers and successful breadwinners. The fruits of postwar America could make the family strong; the family, in turn, could protect the nation by containing the frightening potentials of postwar life."[7] Specifically in the decade following World War II, Cold War ideology reinforced security by fighting against communist totalitarianism in the domestic and foreign spheres.[8] In her analysis, May gestures toward but does not explicitly make the link between the United States' role as the "successful breadwinner" in its domesticated relationship with Japan during the Cold War. A form of deterrence or communist containment, domestic containment was a zero-sum US strategic policy against communist totalitarianism. But while performing white paternalism and patriarchy on an international scale, the US was not exclusive in its exploitative alliance with Japan. The US also "played" South Korea as a pawn in its ideological struggle with Russia during the Korean War. This perspective complicates the perception of the US as a domestic family man who is providing "security" for its family of allied nations and also positions it as a double-dealing player that has its international alliances do its wartime bidding. The depiction of masculinity in *No-No Boy* suggests that, as a strategy of communist deterrence, "domestic containment" feigned protecting the integrity of the atomic family and, by extension, the nation; in reality, through the lead of US foreign policy, it privileged the patriarchal player, like Don Draper from *Mad Men* (which spanned the Cold War of the late 1950s to the 1970s), who sought profligate relationships for his own sense of empowerment.

In the international arena, the player imperialism that the Korean War perpetuated was a sexualized discourse of the West invading the East; it privileged a white hegemonic masculine rhetoric internalized by Ichiro and other

---

6. E. May, *Homeward Bound*, 15. See also D. Kim, "Once More, with Feeling," 70.
7. E. May, *Homeward Bound*, 90.
8. E. May, 208.

Japanese American male characters in Okada's *No-No Boy*. Beginning with Said's tidy conceptualization of the West as masculine and the East as feminine, McAlister elucidates that in postwar America, the "universal subject" is not only a male citizen but also premised on the heterosexual couple and its family to legitimize the nation.[9] And yet, American postwar foreign policy and military incursions did not signify a "properly ordered private life" of consent between a heterosexual couple.[10] Instead, American imperialism during the Korean War followed Truman's imperialist principle "that the United States should not be dishonored."[11] Regarding China, the US played the deterrent odds by alternating between the "reduced means" strategy of "Titoism"— passively dealing with China—and a "harsher, more punitive stance toward Peking."[12]

US player imperialism emerged after World War II, in part, because it did not need to recover from war fought on its mainland. Although, as noted earlier, some trace the development of US imperialism from the Spanish-American War, historians generally agree that the US became a global superpower after World War II. With nothing to lose and everything to gain, the US occupied Japan from 1945 to 1952 while it began its military foray into Korea. Historian John Dower writes of the "schizophrenic" US occupation of Japan in which the US simultaneously imposed "democratization" and "authoritarian rule."[13] In their war-torn economic and environmental recovery, particularly from the two American atomic bombs, Japan had neither sovereignty nor diplomatic associations during the occupation period.[14] During this time, the US also "abolished" the Japanese army and navy.[15] The Pax Americana plan for Japan, drawn up by Truman, included (1) the rearmament of Japan, (2) a separate peace for US anticommunist Asian allies, (3) non-neutrality, (4) American military bases in Japan, and (5) the recognition of Taiwan as a separate nation-state from communist China.[16] These imperial injunctions exemplified the paternalistic relationship between the US and Japan up through the Korean War period. Setting the tone for such a relationship, the allies who occupied Japan in 1945 seem to have ignored the grave "suffering, poverty, and destruction" all around them.[17] For obvious reasons, many Japanese resented

9. McAlister, *Epic Encounters*, 12.
10. McAlister, 12.
11. Foot, *Wrong War*, 32.
12. Foot, 41, 47, 54.
13. Dower, *Embracing Defeat*, 26–27.
14. Dower, 23.
15. Allinson, *Japan's Postwar History*, 54.
16. Chapman, *Inventing Japan*, 77–78.
17. Allinson, *Japan's Postwar History*, 52.

the American military and political presence after World War II. The office of the Supreme Commander for Allied Powers (SCAP), which was run by General MacArthur, replaced the Japanese constitution with an Americanized one and purged individuals from the political left (socialists and communists) and right (Japanese capitalists who promoted family-run zaibatsu, or large capital) from positions of political and social power in Japan.[18] Because it excluded the emperor and demilitarized Japan immediately following World War II, SCAP was criticized by the Japanese public for its neocolonial methods of "induced democratization."[19] Moreover, as historian Gary D. Allinson points out, the US exercised "punitive peace" in Japan, rendering it subordinate and effeminate by demilitarizing Japan in the years before it invaded Korea.[20] Player imperialism reciprocally shaped white hegemonic masculinity, which was, in turn, mimicked by Asian American cultural products such as the male characters in *No-No Boy*. Critics have not mentioned Ichiro's role as a Japanese man who operates as a reflection of the Korean War, given the fraught history of Japanese imperialism in Korea.

ICHIRO AS VICTIMIZED PLAYER

It was in this historical context of US international "playing," or the domestic containment and deterrence of communism in Japan and South Korea during the Korean War, that *No-No Boy* was published; it was unfortunately poorly received. Jinqi Ling writes that the American nationalism articulated in the novel "coincides with official cold war celebrations of American nationalism," but the novel's critiques of American racism ran counter to the image of loyal nisei that the Japanese American community desired to project after World War II.[21] Ling also points out that the novel's poor sales suggest that the politically ambiguous protagonist Ichiro declined to offer a clear ideological position for readers who anticipated a white imperialist, assimilationist view of Asian American life.[22]

---

18. Chapman, *Inventing Japan*, 15, 91; Allinson, *Japan's Postwar History*, 52. In *Japan: Enemy or Ally?*, W. Macmahon Ball writes, "General MacArthur believes that, since Japanese democracy can only be overthrown by the 'extreme Right' or the 'extreme Left,' and, since the 'extreme Right' has been destroyed or converted, the only actual danger is the 'extreme Left.' Hence the danger of Soviet influence" (10).

19. Dower, *Embracing Defeat*, 75.

20. Dower, 76.

21. Ling, "*No-No Boy*," 144–45; Ling, *Narrating Nationalisms*, 51.

22. Ling, 50.

The imprisoned and social invisibility of Okada's Ichiro indeed internalizes the inconspicuousness of the "Forgotten War" to the American public. Comparing the social invisibility of the Korean War to the public impact of the Vietnam War in the US, critic William D. Ehrhart states that the Korean War did not touch or have an influence on Americans in the fifties.[23] Military historian Max Hastings writes of the Korean War that it was a "military rehearsal" for the failures in Vietnam and that Americans did not carry the lessons from the Korean War into the Vietnam War.[24] Moreover, to this day, historians and scholars remain split over their perspective on the centrality of Korean nationalism in the Korean War. Korean literary scholars Hong Sŏng-won and Suh Ji-moon have claimed that the war was a devastating, fratricidal civil war, while historians Kathryn Weathersby and Lary May have argued that the war was fought by proxy between the US and Russia.[25] However, critics universally agree that that war was virtually invisible to and quickly "forgotten" by the American populace as historian Clay Blair has described in his well-known 1987 historiography on the Korean War.[26] In addition to its lack of social attention, the Korean War was a political war that was waged not only between the US and Russia but also between President Truman—whose approval ratings were declining at the start of the war on account of his foreign policies—and his disapproving, largely Republican Congress.[27] Historian Harry L. Huey writes that President Truman acted precipitously when North Korea invaded South Korea for fear that it, like China, would fall to the communists and that "Truman did not want the Republicans to have another issue in the upcoming off-year elections."[28] Truman was critiqued by his political adversaries as an "imperial president" who circumvented Congress's customary declaration of war and dismissed General Douglas MacArthur for undermining his order to negotiate the restoration of the 38th parallel between North and South Korea and issuing an unauthorized ultimatum to China instead.[29] The Korean War was vital to the continued economic prosperity of the United States following World War II despite its controversy and public invisibility.[30]

23. Ehrhart, "Ch. 3," 41.
24. Hastings, *Korean War*, 10.
25. Suh, "Ch. 6," 95, 35; Stueck, "Ch. 10," 190; L. May, "Ch. 7," 112.
26. See Blair, *Forgotten War*.
27. Brune and Leach, "Congress during the Korean War," 345; Tindall and Shi, *America*, 1317, 1318.
28. Huey, "Public Opinion," 409.
29. Brune and Leach, "Congress during the Korean War," 345; Tindall and Shi, *America*, 1318.
30. Brune and Leach, "Congress during the Korean War," 360.

Like the invisible Korean War, US player imperialism has historically been undetected because of the invisibility of unmarked white supremacy and the mythology of the US as a colonized victim of Great Britain that only relatively recently supplanted British imperialism after World War II. Like Ichiro, players are often first victims. Reflecting the invisibility of the Korean War contemporary to the novel's publication and his social invisibility after imprisonment, Ichiro holes himself up in his room to escape political persecution for being a no-no boy in post–World War II Seattle.[31] The phrase *no-no boy* referred to the Japanese American men who were imprisoned for refusing to serve in World War II during the period of Japanese American internment. The name specifically came from answering "no" to both questions 27 and 28 of the US War Department's 1943 "Application for Leave Clearance," which were as follows: "Are you willing to serve in the armed forces of the United States on combat duty whenever ordered?" and "Will you swear unqualified allegiance to the United States of America and faithfully defend the United States from any or all attack by foreign or domestic forces, and foreswear any form of allegiance or obedience to the Japanese emperor, to any foreign government, power, or organization?"[32] The infantilization ("boy") and double-negative of the phrase and title of the novel suggest that, because of his decision to refuse the draft, Ichiro's manhood is erased from or made invisible to American society. At the same time, he is criminalized for his lack of legitimate, white hegemonic masculinity, in refusing the draft, and his Asian American masculinity, in standing up for his family's ethnic nation of origin. As critic David Palumbo-Liu points out, although the Japanese internment camps were made visible to the American public,[33] they form an invisible backdrop to the novel as they are hardly mentioned. Ichiro's anxiety over and refusal to fight in World War II demonstrates the impact of war, specifically the contemporary Korean War of the novel's publication, on his masculinity.

Since US nationhood and manhood were conflated in the Cold War period as the Korean War was a proxy, "cover-up" war between masculinist superpowers US and Russia, Ichiro is denied both gendered and national belonging on account of his fraught decision to avoid fighting in war. Helen Heran Jun claims that Ichiro's refusal of the draft incites a simultaneous crisis of national and gender identity since the military embodies masculinity and the nation.[34] Moreover, Apollo O. Amoko argues that Okada makes clear the impossibility of American nationalism for Japanese Americans who were racialized as

---

31. Ling, *Narrating Nationalisms*, 39.
32. Palumbo-Liu, "Discourse and Dislocation," 1.
33. Palumbo-Liu, 5.
34. Jun, *Race for Citizenship*, 62.

such during World War II.³⁵ And yet, the novel opens with Japanese American war veterans anxiously and violently distinguishing themselves as imperial US citizens and superior to the disloyal no-no boys. When Ichiro steps off the bus that transports him from the prison to downtown Seattle, he meets Eto Minato, an old acquaintance of Ichiro's and a Japanese American war veteran. When Eto surmises that Ichiro is a no-no boy, he calls him a "rotten, no-good bastard" and spits on him, threatening to "piss on [him] next time."³⁶ Meanwhile, rejecting the discourse of Asian American effeminacy, Ichiro idolizes military masculinity and disproportionately regards him as "God in a pair of green fatigues, U.S. Army style."³⁷ Although he is Japanese American, Eto embodies a "God-like" imperialist, white hegemonic masculinity to Ichiro. By contrast, war veterans vilify Ichiro and consider him "the emptiness between" the Japanese American soldiers and first-generation Japanese immigrants.³⁸

As he returns home, Ichiro finds himself unable to shirk his identification as a no-no boy, which is given to him. The involuntary mark of a new identification is, as Althusser suggests, part of a hermetically sealed social system that is inevitable and a form of victimization that Ichiro endures throughout the novel.³⁹ Because of this moniker, his brother Taro betrays him and organizes an attack on him outside of a bar.⁴⁰ In addition to Eto, Bull, another Japanese American war veteran, accosts Ichiro as he is sitting with his friend Kenji. Referring to Ichiro and rejecting him on account of his identification, Bull tells Kenji, who is also a war vet, "a friend of yours [. . .] is a friend of yours."⁴¹ Both Japanese American war veterans and prejudiced African Americans victimize Ichiro. At the beginning of the novel, after being spit upon by Eto, he encounters African American men who yell "J**," "Go back to Tokyo, boy," and "To-ki-yo; J**-boy, To-ki-yo." Alienated ("Tokyo") and emasculated ("J**-boy") by these names, Ichiro perpetuates the racism of this confrontation by saying to himself, "Friggin' n*****."⁴² Jun argues, "Ichiro counters the black men's emasculating anti-Japanese remarks with an assertion of antiblack Americanism ('friggin n*****') in an attempt to undermine the nationalist authority that these black men are figured to possess."⁴³ His name calling is a form of deterrent baiting in which he challenges their authority over him by

---

35. Amoko, "Resilient ImagiNations," 40.
36. Okada, *No-No Boy*, 4.
37. Okada, 4.
38. Okada, 19.
39. I thank Michael Wagoner for this insight.
40. Okada, *No-No Boy*, 78–79.
41. Okada, 75.
42. Okada, 6, my elision.
43. Jun, *Race for Citizenship*, 52.

belittling them. As he calls them a racial epithet, Ichiro perceives the African Americans in this scene as hypermasculine and native, yet inferior to himself, despite being emasculated as the yellow peril / model minority. However, the mutually disempowering racial insults between Ichiro and the African Americans suggest that their ethnic masculinities are inherently tenuous, even if in different ways. Nevertheless, Ichiro takes on the hypermasculinity of the African Americans by mimicking their racializing behavior. His hypermasculinity is premised on objectifying women—which I will discuss later—and, like that of the African Americans in this scene, on racism.

In framing Ichiro and other Asian American characters as players whose masculinities are constantly threatened, I argue that the enduring, intersectional stereotypes that diametrically oppose the masculinities of Asian American and African American men that arose in the post–Civil Rights era were collapsed during the Korean War. As critic Chong Chon-Smith writes,

> In the racial architecture of post-civil rights America, Asian and black men are positioned along binary axes that define a system of social meanings in symmetrical contrast to each other—brain/body, hardworking/lazy, nerd/criminal, culture/genetics, acceptability/monstrosity, submissive/aggressive, self-reliant/government dependent, student/convict, feminization/hypermasculinization, technocrat/athlete, and solution/problem—which I term *racial magnetism*.[44]

Ichiro and the African American men whom he meets at the beginning of the novel exhibit all the characteristics of these social binaries that construct the "racial magnetism" between Asian and African American men. And yet, the reputations of these characters are all harmed to various degrees; the African American characters face general social criminalization in the US even as they discriminate against Ichiro, and Ichiro is a womanizing player whose masculinity teeters on the brink of femininity when his sexual exploits fail or he is explicitly racialized. Many critics have emphasized the centrality of vexed masculinity in Okada's *No-No Boy*. Nguyen argues that, in *No-No Boy*, masculinity and heterosexuality define the American public society against the subordinated feminine sphere of private domesticity.[45] By putting women "in their place" of privacy and keeping the secrets of their abuse, Ichiro attempts to mimic but ultimately fails to achieve the white hegemonic American masculinity of player imperialism. Critic Shirley Lim

---

44. Chon-Smith, *East Meets Black*, 3–4.
45. Nguyen, "Wounded Bodies," 162.

specifically claims that *No-No Boy* exemplifies the crisis of Japanese American identity that is premised on masculinity since Americanness is synonymous with manhood and relationships with other men.[46] Simply put, as an Asian American male character, Ichiro fails, of course, to attain the white American heterosexual masculinity that largely constituted the US military. Nevertheless, in a conservative attempt to "man up" and "measure up" to such gender conventions, he does mimic and radically expose the masculinist role that the US politically played in the international arena of the Korean War.

In the novel, white hegemonic masculine discourse is mimicked hyperbolically by Black Americans, who are problematically perceived as hypermasculine, and unsuccessfully by Asian Americans, who are perceived as perpetually feminine. Jun argues that given the gendering racial framework of citizenship in *No-No Boy*, Black masculinity comes up as a frequent but unstable theme in the novel.[47] Mimicking the player imperialism of white hegemonic masculinity, Japanese and African Americans characters direct hypermasculine racism at each other in the novel. For example, when Ichiro and Kenji are at the Club Oriental, the owner Jim Eng says to the Asian patrons, "That crazy J** boy Floyd tried to get in with two n*****s."[48] Another Asian patron replies, "Them ignorant cotton pickers make me sick. You let one in and before you know it, the place will be black as night."[49] Here, there is an interchangeability between Asian Americans and African Americans as African Americans are framed as the "yellow peril": "You let one in and before you know it, the place will be black as night." The interchangeability of the stereotypes, however, does not obviate the mutual racism in the novel. Despite the racist feelings between Asian American and African American men in *No-No Boy*, there are, however, instances in which they work together and fight for one another. Toward the end of the novel, when Ichiro goes to the Christian Rehabilitation Center, he meets Gary, a fellow no-no boy who works there. Gary tells him about his previous job at the foundry which he left because the other men "made it plain that [he] wasn't welcome" on account of his identification as a no-no boy.[50] However, an African American man named Birdie "took a liking to [him . . . and] let everybody know that anyone wanting to give [him] a rough time would have to deal with [Birdie]."[51] Because Birdie begins to get "into a couple of fights [. . .] suffering for [him], really suffering," he decides to

---

46. Lim, "Not Waving but Drowning," 38–39.
47. Jun, *Race for Citizenship*, 62–63.
48. Okada, *No-No Boy*, 133, my elision.
49. Okada, 133–34.
50. Okada, 225.
51. Okada, 225.

leave the job and work at the Christian Rehabilitation Center instead.[52] Birdie's hypermasculinity stands in stark contrast to Gary, who appears unable to fight for himself and reasserts the Asian American stereotype of the emasculated nerd. Recognizing the asymmetrical gendering of Japanese and African Americans in the novel, Jun states that the novel positions Japanese American identity against the diverse meanings given to Black masculinity; thus, the postwar Japanese American narrative is "haunted" by both the racializations and exclusions of Asian Americans and African Americans.[53] Reflecting the racial power structure of the Korean War, the Japanese American characters seem to be feminized in contrast to the masculine white characters and hypermasculinized African American characters, and hence they are arguably more invisible than the latter. As a result, Ichiro attempts to recuperate his (hyper)masculinity. The novel's inclusion of African American characters and their friendships with Asian Americans helps to refute the "forever foreigner stereotype," thus signaling *No-No Boy*'s American nativity.[54]

The Cold War clearly impacted Okada in his writing of *No-No Boy*—a novel about race and masculinity. Set just after World War II, *No-No Boy* alludes to the patriarchal American foreign policy in Korea. As a patriarchal figure, the US ordered and militarily maintains the national split between North and South Korea. Daniel Y. Kim likens Ichiro's split national (Japanese and American) identity to Korea's split by the 38th parallel—a psychic threat that many Koreans faced after the Korean War.[55] In a stream-of-consciousness meditation on his split nationality, Ichiro mentally tells his mother, "I am only half of me and the half that remains is American by law because the government was wise and strong enough to know why it was that I could not fight for America and did not strip me of my birthright. [. . .] I am not your son and I am not Japanese and I am not American. [. . .] I wish with all my heart that I were Japanese or that I were American."[56] For Ichiro, his split consciousness renders him neither Japanese nor American rather than half. This split consciousness is related to the postwar American occupation of Japan, a staging ground for the Korean War. Ichiro's mother fuels his split or lack of identity as she is delusional in her belief that Japan won World War II. She says of Japanese American war veterans and those who believe (know) the US won the war, "They just don't understand that Japan did not lose. I try not to hate them but I have no course but to point them out to the authorities

---

52. Okada, 226.
53. Jun, *Race for Citizenship*, 72.
54. C. Kim, *Bitter Fruit*, 16.
55. D. Kim, "Once More, with Feeling," 79.
56. Okada, *No-No Boy*, 16.

when the ships come."⁵⁷ Despite her psychosis, her conflicted attitude toward other Japanese Americans reveals the contradiction of the Japanese American identity after World War II, particularly after the American atomic bombing of Hiroshima and Nagasaki. Palumbo-Liu underscores this historical identity crisis: "*No-No Boy* calls forth the manners in which ideology shapes the Asian American subject, initiating contradictions within the individual by means of a discourse that elides its own basis in contradiction."⁵⁸ Sato specifies that it is "the loyalty oath" that "reveal[s] how the concept of dual identity limited the terms of Okada's narrative."⁵⁹ Ling argues that, in addition to the oath that names Ichiro a no-no boy, the nationalist Japanese extremism of the Japanese American community and the US nationalism of the war veterans also contribute to Ichiro's sense of homelessness and crisis of identity.⁶⁰ Moreover, the patriarchy of US intervention in the East following World War II, such as the occupation of Japan and the beginnings of the Korean War, perpetuates the alienating split of the Japanese American identity Ichiro experiences in the novel.

In some ways, Ichiro reproduces the patriarchy of imperialistic communist containment by objectifying other women. When he steps off the bus at the beginning of the novel, he sees "half a dozen women who failed to arouse him even after prolonged good behavior" in prison.⁶¹ He continues to sexualize women at first glance when he visits family friends with his mother upon his return home:

> Reiko brought in a tray holding little teacups and a bowl of thin, round cookies. She was around seventeen with little bumps on her chest which the sweater didn't improve and her lips heavily lipsticked a deep red. She said "Hi" to him and did not have to say look at me, I was a kid when you saw me last but now I'm a woman with a woman's desires and a woman's eye for men like you. She set the tray on the table and gave him a smile before she left.⁶²

Through his perspectival narrative, Ichiro reveals his objectifying (mis)perception that Reiko's "heavily lipsticked [. . .] deep red" lips are meant to entice him when all she does is smile at him "before she le[aves]." When he recalls the first time he has sex with a girl to Kenji, he frames the act in objectifying

---

57. Okada, 24.
58. Palumbo-Liu, "Discourse and Dislocation," 2.
59. Sato, "Momotaro's Exile," 239–40.
60. Ling, *Narrating Nationalisms*, 37.
61. Okada, *No-No Boy*, 1.
62. Okada, 23.

terms: "I remember the first time I laid a girl. She was a redhead in my history class. Knew her way around."[63] He refrains from naming her, further objectifying the girl who "knew her way around." Likewise, Ichiro describes Bull, a successful player who walks into the Club Oriental, by showcasing his white escort: "A swarthy Japanese, dressed in a pale-blue suit that failed to conceal his short legs and awkward body, came in with a good-looking white girl."[64] Bull's player achievement of his white escort, however, is undercut by the revelation of his ethnic morphology—"short legs and awkward body." After Bull insults him, he tells Kenji to "go get fixed up with that blond" who had come in with Bull and "take her away from that monkey."[65] Ichiro discusses the "blond" as currency that can be stolen as retribution. Kenji, who witnesses a Japanese man manhandle his white, female escort at the Club Oriental, also views women as a status symbol when he later sits alone at the bar, thinking to himself, "When a fellow goes away, he likes to take something along to remember and this is what I'm taking. It's not like having a million bucks and sitting in the Waldorf with a long-stemmed beauty, but I'm a small guy with small wants and this is my Waldorf."[66] The "long-stemmed beauty" that is objectified simultaneously subjectifies Kenji. Referring to his emasculating "stump" of a leg—a war injury—that is growing shorter and shorter from gangrene, he accepts himself as "a small guy" with equally "small wants." Despite his status as a war veteran, Kenji fails to assimilate in US society and is furthermore disempowered and emasculated by war. Ichiro, on the other hand, is already figuratively emasculated by his identity as a no-no boy even though he has "big wants" as he objectifies women. Despite their obsession with military masculinity and objectification of women, Kenji's and Ichiro's mutual emasculation exposes, and demonstrates their failure to imitate, masculinist American foreign policy abroad after World War II.

Player imperialism was at the heart of domestic containment, which was practiced at the international scale of US foreign policy. At the start of the Korean War, in 1950, the US played, or used, both Korea and Japan to its own ends. Demonstrating its inconsistent treatment of Japan, the US threw out its policy of punitive peace and remilitarized Japan to fight in the Korean War.[67] The US depended on Japan for its wartime supplies.[68] Moreover, as the imperial occupant of Japan, the US stood to profit from the small economy of Japan

---

63. Okada, 72.
64. Okada, 74.
65. Okada, 76.
66. Okada, 134, 132.
67. Dower, *Embracing Defeat*, 526, 548.
68. Allinson, *Japan's Postwar History*, 77.

in 1950 and the economic stimulants of the Korean War.[69] Japanese Americans also took the opportunity to show their patriotism and fight in the Korean War.[70] In the context of the Cold War, specifically the Korean War, US imperialism politically took the form of a masculinist international player who had conveniently forgotten previous national enmities and alliances when it served his own purposes. For example, Paul Robeson famously denounced the Korean War as American "imperialism."[71] Critic Lary May also writes that the Cold War ideology of forgetting was the core of anticommunist doctrine and permeated Korean War films. In this way, discourse succeeded at encouraging Americans to forget about the failures of the war and perceive it as a victory.[72] Lary May goes on to argue that Korean War films disseminated this popular ideology by centering on "themes of guilt, forgetting, and redemption."[73] Historian John Gaddis writes that although the United States and the Soviet Union had been conceived "in revolution," the two superpowers needed and agreed to "cover up" their animosity since it was dangerous to be at war with each other.[74] In other words, the structure of imperialism rendered all who played vulnerable to loss. The Korean War was, therefore, a "cover-up" war between the US and the Soviet Union. Gaddis goes on to argue that it was during the Cold War that the world seemed to "reach a consensus" "that only democracy confers legitimacy" and empowerment.[75] Likewise, historian Ralph B. Levering claims that the main problem with Stalin's strategy in Korea was that it would obstruct Korean national self-determination with his kind of stagist communism.[76] In addition to being an international practice of US domestic containment, the Korean War was an imperialist "cover-up" war between the US and the Soviet Union and inspired, in Americans and their allies, a "self-determining" masculinist rhetoric in which its own theater of war and victims were quickly forgotten.

Ichiro's playerism reflects this "cover-up" in his emasculation for being an imprisoned "no-no boy." Although the novel provides flagrant examples of Ichiro's objectification of women, it only documents two of Ichiro's sexual exploits—the first time he has sex with the unnamed redheaded girl, which he brings up in a conversation with Kenji, and the night he spends with Emi. In

---

69. Allinson, 78.
70. Tamaki, "Japanese Americans Recall."
71. Jackson, *Ralph Ellison*, 402; Dudziak, *Cold War Civil Rights*, 62.
72. L. May, "Ch. 7," 130.
73. L. May, 133.
74. Gaddis, *Cold War*, 7, 60.
75. Gaddis, 265.
76. Levering, *Cold War*, 7.

this sense, Ichiro does not seem to be a serial player or womanizer. However, his treatment of women, particularly Emi, suggests otherwise. Ichiro describes Emi as "slender, with heavy breasts" and as having "rich, black hair which fell on her shoulders and covered her neck." The description continues, "Her long legs were strong and shapely like a white woman's."[77] Emi's objectified figure—"heavy breasts" and "long legs[, . . .] strong and shapely"—is problematically made ideal when she is likened to a white woman. Emi's positive comparison to white women suggest that white women are currency that masculinize nonwhite men through association. That is, the racial hierarchy of women validates the player's game. Fickle underscores the deterrent strategies of Ichiro's playing: "Ichiro's sexual relations with Emi can be figured not simply as a masculinity-redeeming consummation, but as a choice in the game theory sense."[78] Other critics, such as Daniel Y. Kim, have commented on the contrast between Emi's "shapely" figure and Mrs. Yamada's body, which Ichiro describes as "small, flat-chested, shapeless."[79] Despite Mrs. Yamada's performance of masculinity and Emi's of femininity, for Ichiro, their bodies indicate their essences. Mrs. Yamada's masculinity is evident through her flat-chested shapelessness, whereas Emi's body suggests her "maternal generosity."[80] Picking up on this contrast, Ling and Entin both write that Emi, although a cliché, is a kind-hearted and ethical woman committed to love and its potential to heal.[81] Ichiro's cisgender male heterosexuality is tied to his focus on essentializing masculine and feminine women, which covers up his player imperialism.

His mother's repulsive masculinity, in contrast with Emi's attractive maternalism, unsettles Ichiro's gender essentialism and, likewise, his playerism. Ichiro's mother's seemingly unnatural or denaturalized masculinity, symbolized by her shapelessness, challenges Ichiro's interpersonal identity as a player and his subjective mimicry of geopolitical, player imperialist masculinity. Just as the East had been figured as feminine and objectified through American military intervention during the Cold War, Japanese Americans had been gendered as feminine even as they attempted "to identify with the patriarchal authority of the U.S. state" through player imperialist masculine discourse.[82] The discursive feminization of Japan (and Korea during the writing and publication of the novel), however, incites the masculinist and racist attitudes of the Japanese American characters of the novel, specifically Ichiro. When he returns

---

77. Okada, *No-No Boy*, 83.
78. Fickle, *Race Card*, 73.
79. Okada, *No-No Boy*, 10; D. Kim, "Once More, with Feeling," 74.
80. D. Kim, 74.
81. Ling, *Narrating Nationalisms*, 47; Entin, "'Terribly Incomplete Thing,'" 95.
82. Jun, *Race for Citizenship*, 62–63.

to Seattle and is introduced to his parents' new grocery store and attached apartment, he is dismayed to find that he, his parents, and brother are to share the only bedroom. In this moment, Ichiro documents and performs his own tough manhood through his self-description as a man "who had been big enough for football and tall enough for basketball in high school" and crudely wondering "if his folks still pounded flesh." Sex, for Ichiro, seems to be an endeavor of violence and domination. Moreover, he contrasts his own macho build with his father's "pudgy hand."[83] Throughout the novel he resentfully references his father as effeminate and passive: Ichiro thinks to himself, "Pa's okay, but he's a nobody. He's a goddamned, fat, grinning, spineless nobody."[84] Later, he says, again, "Pa's okay, what there is of him, but he missed out someplace. He should have been a woman. He should have been Ma and Ma should have been Pa."[85] Describing his father as defined by a lack—"he missed out someplace," "he should have been a woman"—and his mother as defined by butch, masculine fullness, Ichiro is ashamed of his father's effeminacy and resentful of his mother's masculinity. His parents' performative denaturalization of gender plays Ichiro: It dismantles his essentializing identity of and reveals his performance of player imperialism.

Nevertheless, Ichiro values what is hard and tough and thus reinforces what he knows to be masculine in his player mentality. In response to this realization about the performativity of gender, he still insists on a naturalized and toxic masculinity: He violently and misogynistically wishes that his father had practiced domestic violence to "straighte[n] [his mother] out long ago."[86] Jun argues that Ichiro's father fails to make a place for himself in the masculine "public domain," whereas his father's private sphere, which Ichiro resents, is "foreign and feminized" as defined by his mother; however, it is clear that Ichiro resents his mother's performance of aggressive masculinity: "Ma is the rock that's always hammering, pounding, pounding, pounding in her unobtrusive, determined, fanatical way until there's nothing left to call one's self."[87] The "self" that he wants to "call" is the player imperialism of white hegemonic masculinity, but his mother's masculine performance reminds him of his own denaturalized mimicry of it. Daniel Y. Kim, likewise, argues that Mrs. Yamada is the active, masculine force who robs Ichiro of his manhood by encouraging him to evade the draft.[88] Kim goes on to historicize Mrs. Yamada as an exam-

---

83. Okada, *No-No Boy*, 7.
84. Okada, 12.
85. Okada, 112.
86. Okada, 112.
87. Jun, *Race for Citizenship*, 68; Okada, *No-No Boy*, 12.
88. D. Kim, "Once More, with Feeling," 69.

ple of the Cold War ideology of momism.⁸⁹ It is precisely the subversiveness of his mother's performative masculinity that unsettles Ichiro's masculine playing. In the space of his futile mimicry of it, Ichiro humanizes white hegemonic masculinity and its potential break from player imperialism.

While Mrs. Yamada is the vehicle to Ichiro's emasculation, Emi is a conduit to his remasculinization but not his ethical manhood of disavowing playerism. In line with the Cold War imperialist ideology of momism, critic Jeanne Sokolowski argues that Ichiro's mother represents the fissured relation between the individual and the nation whereas Emi is a figure of reconciliation through which Ichiro develops his identity as a US citizen.⁹⁰ While it is not his mimicry of white player imperialism that gets Ichiro in trouble, per se, it is his race as a Japanese American who had been forced to choose loyalty to either a foreign nation of origin or a discriminating adopted nation that dooms his playerism. As critics have indicated, Emi's political position is more ambiguous than a reconciliatory nationalism.⁹¹ After she and Ichiro spend the night together, she tells him, "This is a big country with a big heart. There's room here for all kinds of people. Maybe what you've done doesn't make you one of the better ones but you're not among the worst either."⁹² Like his mother, Emi challenges Ichiro's power as a man, making him her social equivalent here when she leads this statement with, "Are you blind? [. . .] Deaf? Dumb? Helpless? You're young, healthy, and supposedly intelligent. Then *be* intelligent. Admit your mistake and do something about it."⁹³ While these statements suggest that she promotes "continuist, progressivist narratives of American nationalism," her earlier comment to Ichiro suggests otherwise: "It's because we're American and because we're Japanese and sometimes the two don't mix. It's all right to be German and American or Italian and American or Russian and American but, as things turned out, it wasn't all right to be Japanese and American. You had to be one or the other."⁹⁴ Ling argues that Emi's contradictory attitudes toward nationalism "problematize[ ] both the textual solution of Ichiro's plight and the assumption that postwar racial divisions in America can be healed by

---

89. Daniel Y. Kim writes, "In his characterization of Mrs. Yamada, Okada follows a well-trodden path: like many U.S. cultural texts of the 1950s, *No-No Boy* makes liberal use of a larger narrative at the heart of containment culture that Elaine Tyler May terms 'momism.' [. . .] Michael Rogin extends May's analysis in his study of Cold War cinema. He notes the prevalence of momism in Hollywood films that identified a certain kind of nuclear family as particularly vulnerable to communist infiltration" ("Once More, with Feeling," 70).

90. Sokolowski, "Internment," 84.
91. Amoko, "Resilient ImagiNations," 42.
92. Okada, *No-No Boy,* 95.
93. Okada, 95.
94. Amoko, "Resilient ImagiNations," 42; Okada, *No-No Boy,* 91.

strategies of forgetting and benevolence."[95] Ling also suggests that Emi's "emotional involvement with Ichiro and mental detachment from his bitterness, her unconventional attitude toward sexual love and political pragmatism, and her sense of America's 'weakness' and belief in its 'strength'" is Okada's attempt at fashioning a complex, three-dimensional female character.[96] Despite Emi's physical embodiment of femininity, she performs aggressive masculinity when she challenges Ichiro's nationalism. Nevertheless, insisting on his player masculinity, Ichiro continues to objectify Emi.

When Emi tells Ichiro that she is divorcing her estranged husband Ralph after Mrs. Yamada's funeral, Ichiro objectifies her by saying, "It'll be nice for the fellows to have you back in circulation."[97] He does not consider a long-term relationship with Emi despite sleeping with her and his professed emotional reliance on her: Earlier he inquires of her, "I've ruined my life and I want to know what it is that made me do it. I'm not sick like them. I'm not crazy like Ma is or your father was. But I must have been."[98] Instead, he sends her, like a prostitute, "back in circulation." Likewise, when Kenji and Ichiro visit, they sexually exploit her. Desiring to be with Emi but unable to sexually perform because of his injury, Kenji tells Ichiro:

> "I'm only half a man, Ichiro, and when my leg starts aching, even that half is no good."
> The hot color rose to his face as he lashed out at Kenji angrily: "So you're sending in a substitute, is that it?"
> Kenji sighed. "The conversation is getting vulgar, but the facts are wrong or loose or dirty or vulgar. You can sleep on the floor or take the car and go back to town." He threw the keys on the sofa beside Ichiro.[99]

Whether vulgarly stated or not, Kenji *does* send Ichiro as a substitute for himself to receive "sexual and physical comfort" from Emi.[100] This substitution in the act of objectifying Emi flags the way in which their womanizing reflects and reveals the performative, player endeavor of the Korean War.

Abandoned by her husband and treated as a sexual object by her male friends, Emi is altogether excluded from Ichiro's vision of a better America at the end of the novel:

---

95. Ling, *Narrating Nationalisms*, 47.
96. Ling, 47.
97. Okada, *No-No Boy*, 207.
98. Okada, 91.
99. Okada, 89.
100. Sokolowski, "Internment," 87.

He wanted to think about Ken and Freddie and Mr. Carrick and the man who had bought the drinks for him and Emi, about the Negro who stood up for Gary, and about Bull, who was an infant crying in the darkness. A glimmer of hope—was that it? It was there, someplace. He couldn't see it to put it into words, but the feeling was pretty strong.

He walked along, thinking, searching, thinking and probing, and, in the darkness of the alley of the community that was a tiny bit of America, he chased that faint and elusive insinuation of promise as it continued to take shape in mind and in heart.[101]

Joining the brotherhood of Ken, Freddie, Mr. Carrick (the white man who had offered him a job in Portland), Gary, Bull, and even strangers such as Birdie and the white man who had bought him and Emi drinks, but not Emi, Ichiro "chase[s] that faint and elusive insinuation of promise" of American democracy at the novel's conclusion. This imagined fraternal nation seems to be in line with Cold War patriarchy and ideologies of the domestic family as a form of communist containment, but as Entin points out, the novel refuses to reproduce the nuclear family of domestic containment as the relationship between Emi and Ichiro is not forged by commitment.[102]

Despite his insistence on his player masculinity, Ichiro faces the cracks in his identity as his mother's and Emi's masculine performances slowly chip away at them. He begins to imagine an alternative lifestyle of domestic containment in which the nuclear family is synonymous with citizenship: "He was still a citizen. He could still vote. He was free to travel and work and study and marry and drink and gamble."[103] However, citizenship is itself a gamble because it can appear in form but not in fact because of racial discrimination; thus, national belonging is a fantasy for Ichiro. Similarly, he only bluffs ("gamble[s]") when he considers the atomic family, as it is only something Ichiro dreams of: "In time, he thought, in time there will again be a place for me. I will buy a home and love my family and I will walk down the street holding my son's hand and people will stop and talk with us about the weather and the ball games and the elections."[104] This image is also a fantasy particularly when one considers his unhappy family life before and imprisonment during World War II. His dream of family, which includes drinking and gambling and "holding [his] son's hand," rather than a daughter's, is contradicted by his womanizing behavior and also perpetuates the patriarchy of this Cold

---

101. Okada, *No-No Boy*, 250–51.
102. Entin, "'Terribly Incomplete Thing,'" 99.
103. Okada, *No-No Boy*, 51.
104. Okada, 52.

War ideology. On the other hand, he thinks the American dream of "that place with the clean, white cottages surrounding the new, red-brick church with the clean, white steeple, where the families all have two children, one boy and one girl, and a shiny new car in the garage and a dog and a cat"[105] either does not exist or is simply "not for me."[106] His renewed version of domestic containment, however, still includes tidbits of playerism such as "gambling" and privileging men.[107] Ichiro avoids marriage or any committed relationship altogether. In this way, he rebels against momism and the anticommunist player imperialist ideology of domestic containment, reinforcing the patriarchal, atomic American family to fight communism domestically and abroad.

"I'M NO GOOD FOR YOU. NO GOOD FOR ANYBODY": ICHIRO AS MELANCHOLY BLUFFER

Resisting one form of patriarchy (the atomic family), however, Ichiro pursues other forms such as womanizing and proving his masculinity, which domestic containment arguably entails. For example, when he first meets Kenji in the novel, they play the game of "Whose is bigger?"—that is, whose wound is bigger?[108] Although it is essentially a contest of muscle-flexing masculinity, their ironic comparisons of emotional and physical lacks or losses indicate their melancholia. In his famous essay, "Mourning and Melancholia," Sigmund Freud distinguishes between mourning as a "reaction to the loss of a loved person, or to the loss of some abstraction which has taken the place of one, such as fatherland, liberty, and ideal and so on."[109] Melancholia, on the other hand, is a condition in which "one cannot see clearly what has been lost" and where the ego cathects or attaches itself to the lost object, which results in "an extraordinary fall in self-esteem" as he belittles the lost object, which has become a part of himself.[110] Melancholia, in essence, is a form of unconscious self-deception. Burdened by his loss of citizenship and self-esteem, Ichiro fetishizes Kenji's masculine "fullness" as a Japanese war veteran:[111]

---

105. Okada, 159.
106. Okada, 159.
107. Although, shortly before his passing, Kenji recommends interracial marriage as a cure for social ills such as racism (Okada, 164).
108. Okada, 64; D. Kim, "Once More, with Feeling," 68.
109. Freud, "Mourning and Melancholia," 164.
110. Okada, *No-No Boy,* 167.
111. D. Kim, "Once More, with Feeling," 22.

I'll change with you, Kenji, he thought. Give me the stump which gives you the right to hold your head high. Give me the eleven inches which are beginning to hurt again and bring ever closer the fear of approaching death, and given me with it the fullness of yourself which is also yours because you were man enough to wish the thing which destroyed your leg and, perhaps, you with it but, at the same time, made it so that you can put your one good foot in the dirt of America and know that the wet coolness of it is yours beyond a single doubt."[112]

Suffering from self-loathing, Ichiro desires to exchange his invisibility, his no-no boy status, for the "full," "eleven inch," phallic "stump" of gangrened leg that claims Kenji's life. As a war wound, nevertheless, the "stump" represents American citizenship and belonging for Ichiro and the other no-no boys like Gary and Freddie. Continuing her work on racial melancholia, in which the racial subject is turned into the object that has been lost, critic Anne Anlin Cheng conceptualizes "ornamentalism" as "a peculiar fusion between 'thingliness' and 'personness.' As such, ornamentalism often describes a condition of subjective coercion, reduction, and discipline, but it can also provoke considerations of alternative modes of being and of action for subjects who have not been considered subjects or subjects who have come to know themselves as object."[113] Identifying as an ornamental object—a no-no boy—despite his performances of white hegemonic masculinity, Ichiro longs for the "thingness" of Kenji's stump that signifies Japanese American citizenship. This reduction begins to allow him to relate to other ornamentalized Asian American women like his mother and Emi. Although his mother's and Emi's gender performances reveal his own performance of player imperialist masculinity, Ichiro continues his melancholic bluff of citizenship—the privilege he has in form but not fact. His imprisonment for refusing the draft and his family's internment during the war call his bluff, but he still insists on playing the melancholic game of qualifying for citizenship.

Ichiro's melancholic bluff of citizenship and deterrent domestic containment reveals the melancholia—specifically the compensatory, psychic loss of masculinity—of US player imperialism. On a geopolitical level, the US bluffed about the mighty funds it had during the Korean War. That is, the Korean War was the example of the Keynesian-driven military-industrial complex that dominated the US economy after the Second World War.[114] Dwight D. Eisenhower took over the US presidency toward the end of the Korean War

---

112. Okada, *No-No Boy*, 64.
113. Cheng, *Ornamentalism*, 18.
114. Carter, *Price of Peace*, 309.

and traveled to Korea as president-elect in hopes of ending the war in 1952. In a 1953 speech in response to the Soviet peace initiative, he warned against Keynesian military spending: "The cost of one modern heavy bomber is this: a modern brick school in more than thirty cities. It is two electric power plants. [. . .] We pay for a single destroyer with new homes that could have housed more than eight thousand people." But, according to Joshua B. Freeman, "Eisenhower succeeded only in modestly checking defense spending and ended up presiding over the elaboration of the very political and social arrangements he warned against."[115] The military-industrial complex during the Korean War was a form of economic playerism in which the US spent more funds than it actually had to appear masculine and invincible and for the purposes of economic and military imperialism.

Unable to achieve American belonging, the no-no boys, Ichiro and Freddie, unconsciously and subjectively mimic the political practice of American imperialism, demonstrated through masculinist foreign policy, and chase women as a substitute for their racial loss of citizenship. When Freddie and Ichiro go to a drive-in restaurant, Freddie "ogle[s] [the female carhop] shamelessly," telling Ichiro, "I'll make it yet. [. . .] Boy, [. . .] she'd be a nice change from the fat pig."[116] Objectifying both the carhop and his Japanese neighbor with whom he is having an affair—"the fat pig" who "can't get enough of it"—Freddie manically womanizes to fill his diasporic void of national homelessness.[117] Freud describes mania as a form of melancholia in which the maniac believes he has surmounted the loss to which he has attached himself and, bluffing, "runs after new object-cathexes like a starving man after bread."[118] Freddie also demonstrates his masculine mania by going to bars and picking fights with Japanese war veterans such as Bull. Freddie's vehicular flight from his final fight with Bull results in a collision in which his body is cut in half, figuratively symbolizing his split, unreconciled identities as a Japanese and American. Freddie's shocking and macabre death unites Ichiro and Bull in a moment of reflective mourning: "Ichiro put a hand on Bull's shoulder, sharing the empty sorrow in the hulking body, feeling the terrible loneliness of the distressed wails, and saying nothing."[119] Despite his "hulking body," Bull cries "like a baby in loud, gasping beseeching howls."[120] Bull cries because, for all of his hulk, he has helped kill a no-no boy who is, in the end, like him. Ichiro

---

115. Freeman, *American Empire*, 107–8.
116. Okada, *No-No Boy*, 199.
117. Okada, 47.
118. Freud, "Mourning and Melancholia," 176.
119. Okada, *No-No Boy*, 250.
120. Okada, 250.

and Bull, no-no boy and war veteran alike, accept their castration as Asian American men in the United States.

And yet, old habits die hard: Their castration becomes a bluffing form of empowering play that objectifies and disempowers women. Earlier in the novel, when Mrs. Yamada tells Ichiro that she is not crazy and that Japan has won the war, Ichiro yells "Balls [. . .] Balls! Balls!" at her, which incites her "surprise, then fear."[121] Here, "balls," or testicles, signify falsehood or the absence of truth, which Ichiro uses to overpower (create "surprise" and "fear" in) his mother and foreclose any further argument with her. Likewise, it is his emotional loss that allows him to womanize or "play" women. When Emi begs Ichiro to "come and see" her, Ichiro melodramatically tells her, "I'm no good for you. No good for anybody."[122] Even though Emi cries, "It isn't [true], it isn't, it isn't!," his statement simultaneously takes himself out of a committed relationship with Emi or "anybody" and back into the "circulation" of womanizing. Ichiro's playerism here suggests that at the compensatory center of player imperialism is melancholic loss.[123]

Like the player imperialist allure of US democracy, Ichiro's player allure is quite literally his baroque literary style—the promise of lasting content and devotion. Existing scholarship on Okada's *No-No Boy* has neglected examination of the novel's long, agrammatical sentences written in stream of consciousness about repetitive family memories and a war-torn region/nation, which are characteristic of William Faulkner's writing.[124] While the stream of consciousness which Okada employs is ubiquitous in Anglo-American modernist texts, Okada articulated Ichiro's stream of consciousness in long, analytical lines that are reminiscent of William Faulkner's works. For example, in the

---

121. Okada, 43.
122. Okada, 207.
123. Okada, 208.
124. Since Okada's biographical information is quite scant, the degree to which he was familiar with Faulkner's works is difficult to precisely assess. However, he did receive his bachelor's degree in English at the University of Washington upon his return from the war and a second Bachelors of Arts from the University of Washington in library science after completing his Masters of Arts in sociology at Columbia University. See Abe, Robinson, and Cheung, *John Okada*, 60, 69. Thereafter, he worked at several libraries including the Seattle Public Library, the Detroit Public Library, and then as the assistant head of the circulation department at the library of the University of California, Los Angeles (Abe, Robinson, Cheung, *John Okada*, 77, 78). Working in several library systems during an era in which Faulkner won the Nobel Prize in Literature (1950) and in which his reputation famously rose in both the United States and Japan, Okada was at least familiar, if not intimately acquainted, with Faulkner's work and style as he completed *No-No Boy*. Since Okada's wife Dorothy burned all of his papers shortly after his death, it is difficult to determine whether he consciously stylized his work after Faulkner's; and yet, the formal overlaps between the two authors seem quite overt. See Chin, Afterword to *No-No Boy*, 257.

novel, Ichiro clearly seems to regret his decision to refuse the draft, for which he blames his mother, whose Japanese patriotism has driven her to insanity:

> There was a time when I was your son. There was a time that I no longer remember when you used to smile a mother's smile and tell me stories about gallant and fierce warriors who protected their lords with blades of shining steel and about the old woman who found a peach in the stream and took it home and, when her husband split it in half, a husky little boy tumbled out to fill their hearts with boundless joy. I was that boy in the peach and you were the old woman and we were Japanese with Japanese feelings and Japanese pride and Japanese thoughts because it was all right then to be Japanese and feel and think all the things that Japanese do even if we lived in America. Then there came a time when I was only half Japanese because one is not born in America and raised in America and taught in America and one does not speak and swear and drink and smoke and play and fight and see and hear in America among Americans in American streets and houses without becoming American and loving it. But I did not love enough, for you were still half my mother and I was thereby still half Japanese and when the war came and they told me to fight for America, I was not strong enough to fight you and I was not strong enough to fight the bitterness which made the half of me which was you bigger than the half of me which was America and really the whole of me that I could not see or feel. [...] And the reason I do not understand it is because I do not understand you who were the half of me that is no more and because I do not understand what it was about that half that made me destroy the half of me which was American and the half which might have become the whole of me if I had said yes I will go and fight in your army because that is what I believe and want and cherish and love.[125]

In this passage, Ichiro holds his mother responsible for inciting his Japanese half to figuratively murder his American half by refusing the draft. And yet he makes her visible by commemorating her and attributing strength to her maddening patriotism to Japan: "I was not strong enough to fight the bitterness which made the half of me which was you bigger than the half of me which was America." Just as Quentin Compson of Faulkner's *The Sound and the Fury* and *Absalom, Absalom!* conflictedly loves and hates the South, Ichiro repudiates his mother—and, by extension, Japan—and her insanity when he states, "And the reason I do not understand it is because I do not understand you who were the half of me that is no more." However, the loss of his mother

---

125. Okada, *No-No Boy*, 15–16.

reveals his love for her, even though he had resented her subversive, performative masculinity. Here he surrenders to their similarity in gender performativity—"the reason I do not understand it is because I do not understand you who were half of me that is no more." He recognizes the social construct of gender division since his mother was "half" of him.

Furthermore, Ichiro is like Quentin, who attempts to document the family history of Rosa Coldfield and the dismantled culture of the postbellum South in *Absalom, Absalom!* through long, formally experimental sentences that articulate stream of consciousness. Exposing the US player imperialist history of the Korean War, Ichiro also attempts to record the history of his mother, who seems to represent the "enemy" and defeated homeland of Japan. Ling writes that Ichiro's mother, who had once been filled with hope in the American dream, has become disillusioned, openly pronouncing her allegiance to Japan and belief in its victory.[126] Despite his mother's monolithic (and delusional) national allegiance to Japan, Ichiro still sees fit to memorialize her in his narrative vision of a democratic America as he mourns her suicide:

> Dead, he thought to himself, all dead. For me, you have been dead a long time, as long as I can remember. You, who gave life to me and Taro and tried to make us conform to a mold which never existed for us because we never knew of it, were never alive to us in the way that other sons and daughters know and feel and see their parents. [. . .] I have had much time to feel sorry for myself. Suddenly I feel sorry for you. Not sorry that you are dead, but sorry for the happiness you have not known. So, now you are free. Go back quickly. Go to the Japan that you so long remembered and loved, and be happy. It is only right. If it is only after you've gone that I am able to feel these things, it is because that is the way things are. Too late I see your unhappiness, which enables me to understand a little and, perhaps, even to love you a little, but it could not be otherwise. Had you lived another ten years or even twenty, it would still have been too late. If anything, my hatred for you would have grown. You are dead and I feel a little peace and I want very much for you to know the happiness that you tried so hard to give me.[127]

His sympathetic exhortation to her to return "quickly" to Japan effectively mirrors his own desire to make counteruniversalist performance into empirical reality. Despite resenting her performative masculinity, Ichiro "love[s] [her] a little" and "want[s] very much for [her] to know the happiness that [she] tried

---

126. Ling, "Race, Power, and Cultural Politics," 364.
127. Okada, *No-No Boy*, 186–87.

so hard to give [him]." After continuously failing in his mimicry of the player imperialism of contemporary white hegemonic masculinity, "U.S. Army style," and witnessing his mother's performative masculinity during his life, Ichiro starts to espouse an ethical manhood of inclusion and care as he wishes for his mother to experience the happiness she had coveted for him.[128] This narrative turn reveals the performativity of masculinity within the player context of American imperialism and US masculinist incursion into Korea. However, the novel ends soon after, so it is difficult to assess whether Ichiro continues to turn from his player ways to espouse a long-lasting ethical manhood of care. Ichiro's long, lyrical, Faulknerian lines peacefully commemorate his burdened mother and, by extension, the lost or destroyed Japanese nation, which she comes to symbolize at the end of her life. In her famous literary criticism of Faulkner, *Class and Character in Faulkner's South*, Myra Jehlen writes of the "apparent" "rich complexity" of Faulkner's seductive narratological style.[129] Although Ichiro's Faulknerian style does not seem to directly seduce his female victims, it lures us as readers to side with Ichiro and meditate solely on his victimization as a no-no boy who is discriminated against and who bears the burdens of his parents' devotion to Japan after World War II.

The deterrent, game-playing performances of masculinity, specifically through the figure of the womanizing player in the novel, reflect the US intervention in the Korean War—what some historians consider a zero-sum proxy war for the ideological conflict between the US and Russia, that is, capitalism and communism.[130] In other words, the US used both Japan and Korea to deter or contain Russian communism in the decade following World War II. This chapter frames the US as the dominant Cold War "player" that uses the stereotypically feminized nations of South Korea and Japan as occupied allies against North Korea and the latter's communist patrons, China and Russia.[131] The Korean War, now popularly known as the "Forgotten War," was largely invisible to the American public.[132] The "paternalistic" and "patriarchal authority of the U.S. state" licensed the US to act, through the international policy and war tactic of deterrence, as a player who courts, uses, and abuses "feminized" Asian nations—specifically Japan and Korea—to gain the

---

128. Okada, 4.
129. Jehlen, *Class and Character*, 16.
130. Suh, "Ch. 6," 95.
131. Jun, *Race for Citizenship*, 62. In "Ch. 10: In Search of Essences: Labeling the Korean War" William Stueck cites historian Kathryn Weathersby as stating, "North Korea was utterly dependent economically on the Soviet Union [and] was simply unable to take any significant action without Soviet approval" (190).
132. Ehrhart, "Ch. 3," 41.

advantage over Russia in the Korean War.[133] The white hegemonic masculinity which informs America's "playerism"—including its refusal to commit to one political partner—is internalized by the protagonist Ichiro Yamada in Okada's *No-No Boy*, which is reflected by his attempt to size up his tenuous—and, at times, stripped-away—masculinity. When his masculinity is finally stripped away by the recognition of performance and his similarity to his mother, Ichiro embraces inclusive, ethical manhood—likewise a possibility for the white hegemonic masculine subject who actively rejects player imperialism.

ANATOMY OF THE COLD WAR PLAYER

Because of his stark victimization in *No-No Boy*, the playerism or womanizing of Okada's Ichiro has long been overlooked or downplayed by critics. Together with his captivating style in speech, his victimization diverts us from perceiving the ways in which he and other Asian American male characters such as Kenji and Freddie in turn victimize white women and women of color in the novels. Their playerism allows them to evade settling into a nuclear family; therein lies their resistance to the linked Cold War ideologies of momism and domestic communist containment. However, as player imperialism has shown, domestic communist containment involves a faithless "playing house" with multiple nations of interest to shore up US global power. Nevertheless, Ichiro's and other characters' philandering is another form of patriarchy next to the atomic family: They are also retrograde in their Manichean objectification of women as whore—Emi—and Madonna—Mrs. Yamada.

Taking a gamble as philanderers, the Asian American players of Okada's novel attempt to situate themselves as Americans during a period of hostility toward Asian Americans by mimicking the player imperialist masculinity demonstrated by American foreign policy and political war strategy. I have argued that Ichiro takes the African Americans who insult him as his model of ethnic (hyper)masculinity. In keeping with player imperialist masculinity at the time, like the players of *No-No Boy*, the US played China through Titoism and Japan—its former enemy turned ally—against Korea in order to emerge from the Korean War a victor over Russia in forming the Korean Demilitarized Zone (DMZ), separating North and South Korea. While in her study of Cold War momism, Elaine May declines to connect this phenomenon to US war tactics specifically, this chapter demonstrates that the US also "played house" with its alliances with the discursively feminized nations of Japan

---

133. Jun, *Race for Citizenship*, 62.

and South Korea, only using them, according to a player's logic, to gain the upper hand over Russia. This dual patriarchal approach complexifies previous notions of the foreign and domestic policies of "domestic containment." As *No-No Boy* demonstrates, Asian American men rebel against the promulgated Cold War ideology of momism and domestic containment by also womanizing and forgoing the nuclear family. Published during the Korean War, *No-No Boy* evinces itself to be a Korean Wartime novel precisely through its practice of deterrence with those of other races and its identifiable depictions of Asian American players. Mimicking player imperialist masculinity, Ichiro's player performance subjectively demonstrates that the US politically positioned itself in this way, as a masculinist player, bluffing in vowing to protect South Korea when their gendered exploits were invisible.

As demonstrated in *No-No Boy*, the discursive image of the Asian American player is a victimized man, whose victimhood elicits sympathy and attraction and also frames him as simultaneously feminine and hypermasculine. This framing is subversive insofar as it exposes US imperialist strategies; at the same time, Ichiro also continues to pursue a naturalized masculinity through playing women. Ichiro's relationship with Emi, specifically, suggests that part of his draw is the Asian American player's ability to vacillate between genders. Playing, by definition, is performative and stylized. Ichiro plays through the pity he solicits through his melancholic low self-esteem and the stream-of-consciousness Faulknerian style of his speech. As a victim of hate crimes and the white gaze, Ichiro is a melancholic subject that alternatively attaches himself to his lost self, manically objectifying women and seeking sexual relationships with them. In Lacanian terms, he is fullness and lack—successful in seducing women yet racially castrated and excluded from the nation whose politics he attempts to emulate. The Asian American players of this Korean Wartime novel are observable monuments of US masculinity and patriarchy in the international arena during this specific historical juncture. Insofar as they fail to completely imitate the domestic patriarchy of the US nation in dealing with its adversarial and allied (domesticized) feminized nations—China, and Japan and Korea, respectively—the Asian American players decline to fully reflect the prevailing ideologies of US nationalism and domestic containment during the Cold War. His failures allow Ichiro to at least briefly espouse a democratic, ethical manhood of recognizing his own ornamental "thingness"—that is, his organic disempowerment—and his personhood in caring for others. Shimizu states,

> In always threatening to soften, [masculinity's] vulnerability to castration becomes even more prominent. Thus, to make a distinction between the

penis and the phallus then allows for us to identify what is undesirable in aspiring to dominate others. Doing so reveals the crucial role of vulnerability in envisioning manhood, especially for those who attempt to lay a claim to power where little is usually accorded.[134]

Likewise, Ichiro's loss of his mother, which occurs before the conclusion of the novel, allows him to relate to her, recover his love for her, and envision a utopian American democracy at the end.

The US gains during the Korean War, such as its victory of demilitarizing the 38th parallel, created an optimistic environment in which Okada's protagonist can embrace a hopeful, democratically inclusive, ethical manhood. Although Ichiro moves toward espousing ethical manhood at the end of his narrative, he fails to enter inclusive, equitable companionate relationships; as a player, his refusal to submit to the ideology of domestic containment reveals the paradox of the deterrent propaganda of domestically containing the nuclear family and the masculinist American player imperialism during the Korean War. That is, through mimicry, Asian American players expose the American doctrine of early Cold War deterrence, domestic containment, as only the masked sexualized rhetoric of the player imperialist, American incursion into the East but also make possible the universal adoption of ethical manhood during a period of historical optimism.

---

134. Shimizu, *Straitjacket Sexualities*, 6.

CHAPTER 2

Playing the Vietnam War

Remasculinization and the Rhetoric of Polarity

"AS REAL AS HAMBURGER": VIETNAM WARTIME LITERATURE

The previous chapter focused on the Asian American player's mimicry of the early Cold War's paradoxical foreign and domestic containment rhetoric of imperialist but democratizing incursion into the East. This chapter centers on the Asian / Asian American player's reflection of the constraints of the increasingly stark, superpower polarization between American capitalism and Russian communism in the later Cold War; this polarization, which became more evident as the Cold War raged on, depended on the player imperialist masculinity that informed the game theoretic approach of nuclear deterrence or brinkmanship (essentially a large-scale aggressive game of chicken) between the US and Russia. The era's player imperialism confines and shapes the playerism of Chinese and French men characters in David Henry Hwang's *M. Butterfly* (1988). Hwang features an international espionage case in which a Chinese man deceives a white French man into thinking that he is the perfect woman for several decades. Nevertheless, these characters alternately perform the masculine player and the conflated Asian and Asian American stereotype of the hyperfeminine and submissive "Butterfly" / Lotus Blossom, which has historically emasculated Asian American men. The play was written after but about the Vietnam War. Hwang's Tony Award–winning play, *M. But-*

terfly, was published and first performed on Broadway in 1988, a year before the fall of the Berlin Wall, which signaled the end of the Cold War. Taking place from the 1960s to around 1988, during the Vietnam War (1955–75) and after, the play reaches its turning point when the Chinese transvestite spy Song Liling finally undresses in front of his/her lover, the white French diplomat Rene Gallimard, to reveal himself as a man after a twenty-year-long seemingly heterosexual love affair while Song spied on the French. Disgusted by the sight of Song's male body, which "pollut[es] the room," Gallimard tells Song at the end of the play, "You're as real as hamburger."[1] Although the play is set partially in flashbacks in Beijing and in the present moment in Paris, and is about Chinese and French characters, Gallimard's metaphorical comparison of Song's unspectacular male body to the quotidian American meat product coincides with other aspects of the play that qualify it as a specifically American play. Although Song is not Asian American, this metaphor conflates Asianness and Asian Americaness in the play's portrayal of the common stereotype of the Lotus Blossom. Moreover, the play is written from the perspective of an American—David Henry Hwang. Song's deception demonstrates Rene's failure in performing player imperialism and thus the ideological distinction between player imperialism and white hegemonic masculinity. In other words, the player got played. However, the US loss of the Vietnam War and the American culture of "conflict and divisiveness" in the 1960s and 1970s create a pessimistic environment in which neither Song nor Gallimard can realize an ethical manhood.[2] Thus, player imperialism and white hegemonic masculinity remain twinned throughout this play.

The risk of Song and Gallimard's decades-long sham relationship reflects the contemporary global brinkmanship between the US and the Soviet Union. Song understands and plays with Gallimard's obsession with the stereotype of the submissive Asian woman, or the Lotus Blossom. Like the players of the previous chapter, both Song and Gallimard objectify Asian and Asian American women, in this case by performing hyperfemininity and pursuing masculinist ownership of it. Song and Gallimard are exemplary players: They seduce and trick each other by performing player imperialism and its antithesis, submissive, Asian femininity, in a play within a play. Despite recognizing these stereotypes of Western masculinity and Eastern femininity, Song appears to play the part of the Lotus Blossom stereotype to spy on Gallimard; and yet this performance is riven by contradictions from the outset of the play. Together, they continually perform the gender binarism of the "perfect,"

---

1. Hwang, *M. Butterfly*, 90.
2. Bodnar, *Remaking America*, 206.

submissive Asian woman and the dominant, powerful white man. In playing the contemporary, player imperialist game of brinkmanship, Song and Gallimard demonstrate that men from both the East and West are imprisoned by an oppressive white hegemonic masculinity during the late Cold War period.

Dixit and Nalebuff write about the theory of brinkmanship during the Cold War:

> The essence of brinkmanship is the deliberate creation of risk. This risk should be sufficiently intolerable to your opponent to induce him to eliminate the risk by following our wishes. [. . .] Like any strategic move, it aims to influence the other's actions by altering his expectations. In fact brinkmanship is a threat, but of a special kind. To use it successfully, you must understand its special features.[3]

Brinkmanship was a feature of the polarities of US capitalism. On the one hand, the US did not want a nuclear war; on the other hand, it was going to pursue a nuclear war if it meant exerting dominance over the Soviet Union. Deleuze and Guattari claim that capitalism creates the condition of "destructive and morbid" schizophrenic behavior of seductive and imperial colonization—of being dominated and wanting to be dominated—such as the sexual deception of players: Players want to win the object of desire to prove their dominant masculinity, but in doing so, they risk failure and emasculation; as victimizers and victims of systemic oppression and their own endeavors, they thus must continue playing this "game" of risk to prove their masculinity. This game exemplifies the "crisis of desire" of capitalism that Deleuze and Guattari discuss.[4] Although capitalism and schizophrenia both create a crisis in desire, it is capitalism that *causes* schizophrenic behavior or the neurosis that is needed to maintain capitalism. The flows of capitalism are pervasive but also create hierarchies of domination.[5] The Vietnam War was another imperialist, antidemocratic war of Keynesian military spending that demonstrated America's masculine invincibility: However, Keynes's dream was to eliminate imperialism, which neither the US nor the Soviet Union wanted. Carter adds, "The U.S. military presence existed to prevent Vietnam—North and South together—from holding an election to form a national government. U.S. leaders recognized that the winner of that election would almost certainly be Ho

---

3. Dixit and Nalebuff, *Thinking Strategically*, 207.
4. Deleuze and Guattari, *Anti-Oedipus*, 245.
5. Deleuze and Guattari warn us that, despite the "great" "affinity" between capitalism and schizophrenia, "it would be a serious error to consider *capitalist flows and the schizophrenic flows* as identical, under the general themes of a decoding of the flows of desire" (245).

Chi Minh. The anti-communist rationale for intervention was also an attack on democracy and the promise of postcolonial nationalism."[6] Democracy, during the Vietnam War, was ironically (mis)represented by player imperialist masculinity.

Reflective of the antinomies of American capitalist imperialism and its crisis of desire, Song and Gallimard's player relationship is one of domination, risk, and brinkmanship—that is, when will Gallimard find out that Song is not a woman, let alone the "perfect woman," over the course of twenty years? Having apparently never seen Song naked in the twenty years of their relationship, Gallimard had all along assumed s/he was "the Perfect Woman" and he, the opposing white "cad."[7] The American polarizations that I underscore in this chapter are manifold: Most importantly, the gender polarities that Song and Gallimard perform demonstrate their imprisonment by player imperialist masculinity; this imprisonment reflects and traces the polarities of US capitalism and its corollary, late Cold War brinkmanship. However, Hwang's play about the Vietnam War purposefully features a Chinese antagonist and a French protagonist since the Chinese and French historically rebelled and fought, during this period, against the ideological polarization of the US-Soviet Cold War, which I discuss further in this chapter. Despite this historical backdrop and their culturally diverse backgrounds, Song and Gallimard adopt a particularly American perspective, favoring the ideology of American capitalism: They speak in American English and rehearse Giacomo Puccini's *Madame Butterfly*, which depicts a colonizing affair between an American naval officer B. F. Pinkerton and his stereotypical "butterfly" (meaning, a submissive Asian woman), a Japanese woman named Cio-Cio-san who sacrifices herself when he abandons her. Song and Gallimard constantly recreate *Madame Butterfly* by quoting from it and literally act out the roles in their affair. Song and Gallimard rely on the opera to reproduce American paragons of masculinity during the Vietnam War. The Vietnam War was similar to the Korean War, when the US made aggressive incursions into Asia even if it did not necessarily win. Song and Gallimard perform and capitalize on player imperialist masculinity, but they also perform its antithesis—submissive Eastern or Asian American hyperfemininity: Song appears as the perfect Chinese woman throughout the play but exchanges his kimono for a Western Armani suit when he exerts his domination over and reveals himself as a man to Gallimard. Gallimard practices his American B. F. Pinkerton persona throughout the play but swaps his player imperialist masculinity for the role

---

6. Carter, *Price of Peace*, 442.
7. Hwang, *M. Butterfly*, 4, 7.

of Butterfly when he commits ritual suicide at the end of the play. And yet, his ability to switch his performance from white hegemonic masculinity to the Lotus Blossom suggests his privilege in performing player imperialism. To demonstrate his power, Gallimard remains committed to the notion of the perfect, feminine, and submissive Asian woman. For example, Gallimard says of Song early on, "It is the Oriental in her at war with her Western education."[8] As evident in *M. Butterfly,* the rhetoric of zero-sum polarization between East and West, and between capitalism and communism, which dominated Vietnam War negotiations, rendered the capitalist US unmarked and communist Russia marked as "commies," particularly within the US. What discursively emerged during this period was a linguistic and semantic pattern of asymmetric polarization that privileged white American, heterosexual, cisgender masculinity as a metaphor for the US over the feminized nations of Vietnam, Laos, and Cambodia, which it invaded during the war. Even though Hastings argued that the Korean War was "a military rehearsal for the subsequent disaster in Vietnam," the US gain of the demilitarized 38th parallel that concluded the Korean War allowed for some hope in ethical manhood in literary discourse as demonstrated in *No-No Boy.*[9] Although player imperialism endured in a different form from the Korean War to the Vietnam War, there were no positive military and political outcomes for the US in the Vietnam War, and thus ethical manhood was overtaken by "the crisis of desire"—an aggressive, compulsive, and compensatory masculinity in the popular imagination.

During the Vietnam War, we see again a mapping of gender onto the political players. Elaborating on the white hegemonic masculinity that specifically predominated the Vietnam War, critic Susan Jeffords argues that gender polarities defined the international war: The enemies during the Vietnam War were "depicted as feminine," and, according to Jeffords, "representations of the Vietnam War can be used as an emblem for [. . .] the 'remasculinization' of American culture, the large-scale renegotiation and regeneration of the interests, values, and projects of patriarchy now taking place in U.S. social relations."[10] Meanwhile, the "remasculinization of America" during the Vietnam War followed the women's rights movement of the 1950s and 1960s, which "challenged" "the stability of the ground on which patriarchal power rests."[11] As the masculinist US perpetuated the Cold War in response to the threat of feminism to patriarchy, ethical manhood—individual representations of inclusive, equitable democracy—became conflated with imperial-

---

8. Hwang, 27.
9. Hastings, *Korean War,* 10.
10. Jeffords, *Remasculinization of America,* xi.
11. Jeffords, xii.

ism. Without explicitly referencing the US as the high and low cultural term "player," Jeffords locates the conflated narratives of the US as both masculine imperialist and purveyor of democracy in low cultural Vietnam War films such as *First Blood, Rambo: First Blood, Part 2, Missing in Action, Missing in Action 2,* and *Uncommon Valor*: "The thematics, music, and characteristics of the narratives indicate from the outset [. . .] the successful rescue of POWs and the thwarting of an indifferent government."[12] At the same time, according to Daniel Belgrad, play as an aspect of high American counterculture reached its apotheosis and became more politicized in the 1960s: "The sixties avant-garde turned away from the themes that had defined abstract expressionism and projective verse, embracing irony, neo-dada, and pop art. At the same time, the beat generation gave way to the New Left and the hippie counterculture. These movements embraced important aspects of the spontaneous legacy, but discarded most of its art forms in favor of their own."[13] However, the importation of rock and roll overseas in Vietnam through the military, which established what Kramer calls the playful "republic of rock" between Vietnam and San Francisco, "commodified" hippie culture.[14] The incorporation of countercultural "play" and inclusive, ethical manhood—that is, the folding of democracy—into American imperialism, ultimately seen in the notion of a nontotalitarian world police, is reflected in the imperialist, Eastern and Western performances of white hegemonic masculinity in popular culture and literature. Like its gendering incursions into Korea during the Korean War, US aggressive, masculine dominance during the Vietnam War, despite its discernible losses, is figured in the playing and womanizing escapades of nonwhite and non-American, Eastern and Western male characters of Hwang's *M. Butterfly*; nevertheless, they do not live up to this masculine American ideal. Gallimard pursues the "perfect," hyperfeminine Asian women only to be duped by a Chinese male spy. Even as Song changes from a Butterfly kimono into a masculine Armani suit at the end of the play, he fails to attain player imperialist, white American hegemonic masculinity.[15] During the remasculinizing Vietnam War era, their failed performances reassert the hegemony of player imperialism while dismantling it through performance. The "remasculinization" of America during the Vietnam War depended on the perpetual play of the binaries of player imperialism and submissive, Asian American femininity. These binaries unveil the stark imperialist polarities between the US and

---

12. Jeffords, 6.
13. Belgrad, *Culture of Spontaneity,* 1–2, 12.
14. Kramer, *Republic of Rock,* 5.
15. Hwang, *M. Butterfly,* 90, 83.

Russia in the late Cold War, fueled by nuclear deterrence and game theoretic brinkmanship.

Trained by their superiors to "game" people, Song and Gallimard "play" each other. Song deceives Gallimard through his/her transvestism and capitalizes on his ignorance of the Peking Opera House and its practice of employing male actors in drag. On the other hand, Gallimard instrumentalizes Song to prove his own masculinity and, furthermore, manipulates Song by refusing to recognize him, his fantasized "Butterfly," as a man when he comes out as one; when Song does reveal himself as such, Gallimard actually performs Madame Butterfly instead, conceding to his emasculation. Gallimard's suicide is a reckoning with the notion that the player and the hyperfeminized Lotus Blossom are performative fantasies—fantasies without which he refuses to live. The very medium of the play calls attention to the performativity of Song's and Gallimard's femininities and masculinities. Even as Song and Gallimard alternately perform and potentially deconstruct the metaphor or stereotype of the docile Asian woman—the Lotus Blossom—they nevertheless insist on, call attention to, and reinscribe the dominant discourse of white American, heterosexual, cisgender masculinity as the unmarked metaphor for the US in its "superpower" intervention in the Vietnam War.[16] Though the war is largely seen as an American failure and loss, its costs dramatize its masculine "big guns" incursions into Vietnam; nevertheless, whereas Vietnam, Laos, and Cambodia, combined, lost four million lives, the US lost fifty-eight thousand lives by comparison and further exercised its masculine power by leaving its mark—lasting destruction in Vietnam's ecosystem from Agent Orange.[17]

ATTEMPTS TO EXIT THE POLARIZING GAME

Critics of Hwang's play have commented on how it is set during the Vietnam War but do not explain the significance of the war in the play and its impact on the ways in which the protagonist and antagonist understand themselves and their identities. David Eng writes, "That Hwang chooses to set *M. Butterfly* during the cold war and Vietnam War eras as well as the late 1980s (at the end of Reagan's 'evil empire' discourse) is significant," but does not specify how.[18] The Vietnam War as the war that "remasculinized America," likewise, takes center stage in the development of the plot and characters of *M. Butterfly*.

---

16. Qiang, *China and the Vietnam Wars*, 106.
17. Hwang, 83; Atwood, *War and Empire*, 190.
18. Eng, *Racial Castration*, 147–48.

American masculinity figures itself continually throughout *M. Butterfly*, which is based on a historically true story.[19] When being cross-examined in court by the judge, Song tells him,

> The West thinks of itself as masculine—big guns, big industry, big money—so the East is feminine—weak, delicate, poor . . . but good at art, and full of inscrutable wisdom—the feminine mystique.
>
> Her mouth says no, but her eyes say yes. The West believes the East, deep down, *wants* to be dominated—because a woman can't think for herself.[20]

In addition to self-reflexively reproducing a rape mentality—"Her mouth says no, but her eyes say yes"—Song consciously admits to performing these stereotypes, which suggests his/her transgression of them; however, his/her singular vacillation between the two stereotypes of player imperialism and Asian American hyperfemininity throughout the play suggests that his/her identity has no other alternative. These stereotypes are defined by a spate of polarized metaphors—"big guns, big industry, big money," which signify masculinist, invincible Keynesian military spending and "inscrutable wisdom," or "the feminine mystique." By identifying the racial stereotypes and the rules of American imperialist playing, Song appears to be exiting the game of player imperialist masculinity. But with no other identity to espouse, Song spends the duration of the play performing the metaphor of the "Lotus Blossom" or the ideology it supports—player imperialist masculinity—at the end. Song's strategy of performing the Lotus Blossom stereotype—a woman player—is another mimicry that, in addition to the Asian American male player, punctures further holes in the armor of the imperialist player. On the other hand, a woman player, even more so than the Asian American male player, debases and betrays herself since she is inevitably objectified by US masculine society.

By basing his play on Puccini's opera about an American naval officer and his relationship with a Japanese woman, Hwang critiques Americanized masculinity. The premise of the play centers on China's vested interest in French diplomacy during the Vietnam War. However, like Song's attempt to liberate himself from the gender constraints of player imperialist masculinity, China was very interested in breaking out of the imperialist polarization between the US and the Soviet Union. According to historians, China adopted a "dual-adversary" policy toward the United States and Russia during the Cold War era.[21] While resenting US intervention in the Vietnam War, Chairman Mao

---

19. Hwang, *M. Butterfly*, 94.
20. Hwang, 83.
21. Zhang, "Changing International Scene," 56–57.

Zedong also despised Russia's imperialist "superpower dialogues" over strategies of propagating communism in Vietnam.[22] US involvement in the war also threatened the southern border of China, and yet China carefully avoided escalating the conflict into a separate war with the United States.[23] Zhang goes on to state that between 1868 and 1870, the polarized structure between the US and Soviet Union was moving toward multipolarity in which multiple countries would be global leaders.[24] Despite Chinese and French preferences for multipolarity, the Vietnam War remained largely a policed, zero-sum proxy war of dueling adversaries: the United States and the Soviet Union.[25]

Mao's gambling tactic of evasive confrontation toward the United States evidenced China's lack of a united communist front with the Soviets and its inability to fund a war after the failure of the Great Leap Forward (1958–61).[26] Refusing Russia's intentions to control its military in 1958, China sought to rival Russia in its communist intervention in Vietnam.[27] Moreover, by the late 1960s, Mao neglected foreign affairs to focus on the Cultural Revolution, which was similarly "disastrous for China's domestic and foreign affairs" according to historian Li Jie, and further prevented them from militaristically confronting either the United States or Russia.[28] Contrasting with Hwang's central, pugilistic positioning of China and France through the characters of Song and Gallimard in *M. Butterfly*, China's specific historical conflict with France was ancillary to those with the United States and Russia during the period of the Vietnam War. In fact, according to historian Qiang Zhai, both Mao and French President Charles de Gaulle advocated for anti-American stances.[29] Like the Korean War, the Vietnam War was a "cover-up" of the main conflict between the US and Russia. Likewise, de Gaulle doubted that China was going to be the expansionist threat that the United States had reported

---

22. Qiang, *China and the Vietnam Wars*, 106. For example, Qiang writes, "In the spring of 1965, Moscow asked Beijing to grant an 'air corridor' through which a Soviet airlift could be conducted in defense of the DRV and to cede a base in Yunnan, where hundreds of Soviet military personnel could be stationed to assist Hanoi's war effort. Accusing the Russians of taking advantage of the war in Vietnam to violate Chinese sovereignty, the Chinese turned down the Soviet request" (150).
23. Zhang, "Changing International Scene," 62–63. Zhang notes that the US involvement in Vietnam pushed the hostility between China and the United States; at the same time, China dodged military confrontation with the US (66).
24. Zhang, 66.
25. Blang, *Allies at Odds*, 105.
26. Herring, *America's Longest War*, 113; Qiang, *China and the Vietnam Wars*, 97.
27. Zhang, "Changing International Scene," 58; Qiang, *China and the Vietnam Wars*, 151.
28. Jie, "Changes in China's Domestic Situation," 307.
29. Qiang, *China and the Vietnam Wars*, 146–47.

during the Cold War.³⁰ Although France and China were indeed ideological adversaries during the Vietnam War, their renewed ties in 1964 managed to maintain "cool," temperate relations between the two countries throughout the late 1960s.³¹

In contrast to historical diplomatic relations, Gallimard, as a French diplomat, attempts to sexually dominate Song who, unbeknownst to him, is a Chinese male spy. Gallimard's method of attack is by performing as an American: Benjamin Franklin Pinkerton from Puccini's *Madame Butterfly*. When Gallimard first meets Song at the German ambassador's house in Beijing in 1960, Song performs *Madame Butterfly*. Gallimard is impressed by the concept of the play and meets and compliments Song on his/her "utterly convincing" performance.³² Scoffing at the irony of playing a Japanese woman after the Japanese had colonized China during World War II, Song responds,

> Consider it this way: what would you say if a blonde homecoming queen fell in love with a short Japanese businessman? He treats her cruelly, then goes home for three years, during which time she prays to his picture and turns down marriage from a young Kennedy. Then, when she learns he has remarried, she kills herself. Now, I believe you would consider this girl to be a deranged idiot, correct? But because it's an Oriental who kills herself for a Westerner—ah!—you find it beautiful.³³

Underscoring the gendered stereotypes of the East and West, s/he constructs an inverted analogy of a "blonde homecoming queen" who "turns down marriage from a young Kennedy" over her devotion to a "short Japanese businessman." Like Song—a man who pretends to be a woman in order to play Gallimard and spy on him—President Kennedy also played the Keynesian game of military spending despite the budget deficit to assert American imperialism and to maintain the image of an invincible economy during the Vietnam War.³⁴ In this scene, the reference to a homecoming queen courted by a young Kennedy, as a model of white American, cisgender, heterosexual masculinity, exemplifies the American perspective that the play takes. Gallimard accepts Song's criticism of his gender and racial binarisms but continues to pursue him/her as his Eastern Butterfly. He has the opportunity to exit from the game of player imperialist masculinity, but, without an alternative subjec-

---

30. Blang, *Allies at Odds*, 121.
31. Sullivan, *France's Vietnam Policy*, 23.
32. Hwang, *M. Butterfly*, 17.
33. Hwang, 17.
34. Freeman, *American Empire*, 177.

tivity during the Vietnam War, he clings to the Pinkerton role. After chastising Gallimard for blindly reasserting these stereotypes of the East and West, Song declares, "I will never do Butterfly again, Monsieur Gallimard."[35] The great irony of this statement lies in the moment in which the two consummate their relationship: Gallimard asks, "Are you my Butterfly?" to which Song replies, "Yes I am. I am your Butterfly."[36] They then proceed to cite lines from Puccini's opera as they become intimate.[37] They are trapped in the figurative prison of performing binary metaphors.

Song goes on to embark on a twenty-year-long affair (the approximate length of the Vietnam War) with Gallimard, which implicitly and explicitly replicates the Madame Butterfly–Pinkerton love affair of Puccini's work. When later asked by the judge to explain how he had made it possible to trick Gallimard for several decades, Song states, "One, because when he finally met his fantasy woman, he wanted more than anything to believe that she was, in fact, a woman. And second, I am an Oriental. And being an Oriental, I could never be completely a man."[38] Reinforcing these polarized, gendered stereotypes of the East and West, Gallimard is all too willing to engage in this love affair, fulfilling his fantasy of becoming the player imperialist masculine American naval officer, Benjamin Franklin Pinkerton, whom he calls "the womanizing cad," or player.[39] Pinkerton signifies American imperialism when Gallimard states, "Pinkerton purchased the rights to Butterfly for one hundred yen—in modern currency, equivalent to about . . . sixty-six cents."[40] And yet, Gallimard mentions that Pinkerton is also emasculated by his appearance: "not very good-looking, not too bright, and pretty much a wimp."[41] The individual performativity of Pinkerton's white American hegemonic masculinity is thus underscored. Like Song, Gallimard is stuck in a prison of polarized metaphors of white American hegemonic masculinity and its antipode, Asian American hyperfemininity and hypersexuality; even though the play reproduces the discourse of "the French [as] ladies' men," French masculinity is invisible next to white, cisgender, heterosexual American masculinity.[42] Duped by Song, Gallimard has the potential to encourage the separation between player imperialism and white hegemonic masculinity in his failure. However, his final,

---

35. Hwang, *M. Butterfly*, 17.
36. Hwang, 39, 40.
37. Hwang, 41.
38. Hwang, 83.
39. Hwang, 7.
40. Hwang, 5.
41. Hwang, 5.
42. Hwang, 3.

suicidal performance of Butterfly suggests that he remains married to the Lotus Blossom stereotype that supports the conflation of player imperialism and white hegemonic masculinity.

Despite his ideological insistence on performing player imperialism, Gallimard is a figure of disempowerment. Likewise, the French during the Vietnam War were disempowered by the polarization between the US and the Soviet Union. In fact, France faced a situation similar to China in balancing and staving off both American and Russian superpowers during the Vietnam War. President de Gaulle was deeply suspicious of the American imperialist involvement in what he viewed as Vietnamese civil war but was economically and diplomatically bound to the United States after the 1954 Geneva conference; de Gaulle could only criticize US foreign policies but could not afford to divorce France from its political alliance with the United States.[43] Historian Eugenie Blang writes that de Gaulle wanted to maintain "a policy of cooperation and reaffirmation of historical ties" with the Soviet Union during the Vietnam War.[44] At odds with President Kennedy in 1962 over his desire for neutrality in the war, "De Gaulle preferred a multipolar over the polarized world and hoped that France and Europe as well as the People's Republic of China (PRC) would create a new balanced power system going beyond the nuclear stalemate between the United States and the Soviet Union."[45] In *M. Butterfly,* the French Ambassador Manuel Toulon tells Gallimard of the US: "What a bunch of jerks. Vietnam was *our* colony. Not only didn't the Americans help us fight to keep them, but now, seven years later, they've coming back to grab the territory for themselves. It's very irritating."[46] Turning a prisoners' dilemma of fighting communist totalitarianism and brinkmanship into a zero-sum game of imperialism, the United States, in turn, carefully surveilled what they viewed as the "French paranoic anti-Americanism" that sought to curb American international power after the Geneva conference.[47]

The discourses of surveillance and polarization play out in *M. Butterfly.* Gallimard and Song are socially disempowered representatives of nations that are subordinate to the American and Russian superpowers during the Vietnam War. Like President de Gaulle, Gallimard as a politician has to balance French interest in the face of communist aggression and Western imperialism. It was common practice for the US and the Soviet Union to use other nations as pawns for their own advancement in the war. For example, as his-

---

43. Hwang, xii–xiii, xi, 54–55.
44. Blang, *Allies at Odds,* 104–5.
45. Blang, 108, 105.
46. Hwang, 44.
47. Sullivan, *France's Vietnam Policy,* 63.

torian Qiang Zhai points out, "In a conversation with Wu Lengxi, the Chinese foreign minister criticized the two superpowers for treating Laos as a bargaining chip in their negotiations."[48] Likewise, Song is policed, played, and manipulated by Comrade Chin to seduce and spy on Gallimard while being warned, "Don't forget: there is no homosexuality in China!"[49] Jeffords writes that Vietnam War discourse, as represented in American films, was anxiously homophobic.[50] Likewise, Gallimard expresses his own homophobia when he states, "When a woman calls a man her 'friend,' he's calling him a eunuch or a homosexual."[51] His conflation of eunuchs and gay men articulates his fear of and discrimination against gay men. Gallimard does everything he can to shore up his imperialist, white hegemonic heterosexual manhood by refusing to see a fertility specialist when he and his wife are unable to conceive: He states, "Dr. Bolleart? Of course I didn't go. What man would?"[52] His relationship with his Chinese mistress, Song, is meant to achieve the same end of player imperialist masculinity. In the play, Toulon also plays Gallimard by interrogating him about his new "native mistress" (Song), only to say, "We were worried about you, Gallimard. We thought you were the only one here without a secret. Now you go and find a lotus blossom . . . and top us all."[53] Toulon, who has to "content" himself "with wives of the expatriate community," views extramarital affairs as a game in which one proves one's masculinity by keeping a secret mistress.[54] Moreover, Toulon stereotypes him as the alpha male, colonizing Western man who "top[s] us all" by "find[ing] a lotus blossom."[55]

The increasingly asymmetrical polarization between the US and Russia during the later Cold War, specifically the Vietnam War, constructs a discourse of metaphorical self-fashioning that limits Song and Gallimard to attempt to be or perform *either* the policing white American, masculine, heterosexual male ideal *or* the policed racial stereotype of docile, submissive Asian women. This binary performance itself decenters and reasserts the primacy of player imperialist masculinity. That is, the failed performances of player imperialist masculinity by hyperfeminized others demonstrates the performativity of this hegemony but also its persistence. Thus, these discursive binaries are reflected

---

48. Qiang, *China and the Vietnam Wars*, 106.
49. Hwang, *M. Butterfly*, 48.
50. Jeffords, *Remasculinization*, 71–72.
51. Hwang, *M. Butterfly*, 35.
52. Hwang, 51.
53. Hwang, 45, 46.
54. Hwang, 45.
55. Hwang, 46.

in the Cold War polarization between the United States and the Soviet Union. Even though, as Levering argues, "the leaders of the two chief rivals—the United States and the Soviet Union—deserve credit for repeatedly recognizing the importance of not going to war with each other," the Cold War rhetoric of zero-sum polarization of communism and capitalism, and of superpower police and third world policed, pervaded popular (Vietnam War films) and literary culture.[56] This polarized rhetoric of either/or, is / is not, reflects the binary linearity of capitalism, according to Deleuze and Guattari, but also reflects Roman Jakobson's linguistic theory of the metaphor—one of the two poles (the other being metonymy) that construct language, which operates based on linguistic selection, substitution, and similarity—which was outlined in his famous 1956 essay, "Two Aspects of Language and Two Types of Aphasic Disturbances."[57] As made evident through their language and actions, Song and Gallimard fail to live up to the Vietnam War paragon of imperialist, white American, heterosexual masculinity, despite their "player" lifestyles: Song plays Gallimard by pretending to be the "perfect" cisgender, heterosexual, hyperfeminine Asian woman, and Gallimard attempts to perform player imperialism by capitalizing on Song's performance; ultimately, when he learns that Song is a man, he performs Butterfly himself. In turn, they only have recourse to performing metaphorized stereotypes that are binary in nature: for example, Song and Gallimard can only be *either* a submissive Asian woman *or* an imperialist, fetishizing white hegemonic man. As a professional spy and Asian player, Song undermines the distinction between the model minority and the yellow peril. Gallimard—although white, but not American—both literally and figuratively finds himself in prison at the end of the play as he is also imprisoned by player imperialist masculinity and essentially stuck in performing metaphors of Asian and Asian American stereotypes. Insofar as metaphors are comparisons between or substitutes for different words, the gendered Asian American stereotypes of the model minority and its gendered correlative, the submissive "Butterfly"/Lotus Blossom—which easily flip into the yellow peril and its gendered correlative, the Dragon Lady—are metaphors that Song and Gallimard perform. Discourses surrounding Asian American hyperfemininity criminalized all Asian American women as prostitutes, preventing their immigration to the United States in the Page Act of 1875. In short, such Asian American stereotypes around gender and sexuality that were discursively disseminated during the Vietnam War era become an at times literal prison house for these minoritized characters.[58] The prison house

---

56. Levering, *Cold War*, xiii.
57. Deleuze and Guattari, *Anti-Oedipus*, 14; Bradford, *Roman Jakobson*, 11.
58. C. Kim, *Bitter Fruit*, 20.

of stereotyping metaphors for the yellow peril, racial underclass is a corollary of the conflation of ethical manhood and white American imperialism during this time in which the US started to view itself as world police. Freeman writes, "Only on the political left during the Vietnam War era did imperialism get revived as a way of understanding the United States."[59] During the Vietnam War, the US government largely understood itself within the ideological binary of capitalism/communism, good/evil. *M. Butterfly* exemplifies this Manichean duality of good/evil, Western player/Lotus Blossom while also muddling the binary by suggesting that, like Asian American men, women can be disempowered players.

Song and Gallimard are interpellated and discursively dominated by metaphors of player imperialism and its binary opposite—the hyperfeminized Asian American—during the Vietnam war. Hwang's protagonist and antagonist are imprisoned by these reified terms and definitions and thus suffer from aphasia. In "Two Aspects of Language and Two Types of Aphasic Disturbances" in which he discusses the structure of the linguistic metaphor, Jakobson locates the cause of aphasia, or the "loss of the power to use or apprehend speech," in the interruption of either the linguistic pole of metaphor or that of metonymy (based on combination, contexture, and contiguity).[60] Gallimard and Song therefore suffer aphasia of the first kind: "with a defect in substitution."[61] Never able to completely undermine the unmarked, dominant paragon of player imperialist masculinity as a metaphor for the US during the Vietnam War, the characters can only recognize the criminalizing stereotype of the hypersexual, hyperfeminine Asian American woman they are condemned to reproduce; that is to say, whereas American society accepts white players, it criminalized racialized players who have the same metaphoric "defect in substitution." Jakobson gives a similar example of a patient suffering from an interruption in metaphorical development: "The aphasic with a defect in substitution will not supplement the pointing or handling gesture of the examiner with the name of the object pointed to. Instead of saying, 'This is [called] a pencil,' he will merely add an elliptical note about its use: 'To write.'"[62] Jakobson goes on to argue that "for an aphasic with impaired substitution and intact contexture, operations involving similarity yield to those based on contiguity. It could be predicted that under these conditions any semantic grouping would be guided by spatial or temporal contiguity rather

---

59. Freeman, *American Empire*, ix–x.
60. Jakobson, "Two Aspects of Language," 128; Bradford, 11.
61. Jakobson, "Two Aspects of Language," 122.
62. Jakobson, 122–23.

than by similarity."[63] Tethered to polarized metaphors of player imperialism and "othered" Asian American stereotypes of hyperfemininity and hypersexuality, the characters continue to live in contiguity with these metaphors, repeating them continuously—signaling a crisis of desire. Considering Song and Gallimard as cultural aphasics with an impaired ability to substitute or change their stereotyped identities helps to explain the lengthy drama of Song and Gallimard's twenty-year-long artifice. At the same time, the conscious performances of these stereotypes by Song and Gallimard suggest their cultural transgression. Even though these Americanized characters reaffirm the stereotypes, the performativity of these stereotypes demonstrate that they are hegemonic American cultural constructions. In this way, the political consciousness of these racially and sexually minor characters reflect the coincident rise in political consciousness of the Third World during the Cold War, which historian Robert McMahon argues was reflected by the 1955 Bandung Conference that "echoed with calls for racial solidarity, social justice, and an end to all forms of imperial control."[64] However, even if Hwang's characters aspire to racial solidarity and social justice, they reinscribe imperial control through their homophobia and misogynistic womanizing.

Earlier in the play, Gallimard and his best friend and colleague Marc break the fourth wall, interrupting the Brechtian conventions of realism[65] of the play, to again perform parts of Puccini's opera in which Gallimard plays Pinkerton and Marc plays his friend Sharpless. The sheer repetition of Puccini's opera suggests that the characters are figuratively stuck in the prison house of player imperialist masculinity. And yet, as Gallimard narrates, "In the preceding scene, I played Pinkerton, the womanizing cad, and my friend Marc from school . . . (*Marc bows grandly for our benefit*) played Sharpless, the sensitive soul of reason. In life, however, our positions were usually—no, always—reversed."[66] Gallimard's performance of player imperialism as Pinkerton is quickly undermined when his friend Marc tells him, "You're clumsy and got zits."[67] Gallimard's lack of masculine "game" in school, allows him to reflect on the ironic distance between himself and the character Pinkerton he performs with Marc and, in life, with Song. And yet, this metanarrative of playing and performance with Marc does not aid him in deciphering Song's treachery in their twenty-year relationship. As they once again interrupt the play's Brechtian, epic theatrical conventions and break the fourth wall, Song

---

63. Jakobson, 124.
64. Robert J. McMahon, Introduction to *The Cold War*, 5.
65. I thank Christy Stanlake for giving me these proper terms of notation.
66. Hwang, *M. Butterfly*, 7.
67. Hwang, 9.

later tells him, "You were my greatest . . . acting challenge."[68] The risk of Song's espionage relationship with Gallimard mirrors some of the risks that define brinkmanship; Dixit and Nalebuff write of late Cold War brinkmanship:

> Kennedy cannot credibly threaten an immediate all-out nuclear strike, but he can credibly raise the risks to some degree by taking some confrontational actions. For example, he may be willing to risk one chance in six of nuclear war to ensure the removal of the missiles. Then Kruschchev can no longer conclude that Kennedy's threat is vacuous; it is in Kennedy's interest to expose himself to this risk if it will motivate the Soviets to remove the missiles. If Kruschchev finds this degree of risk intolerable, then the brinkmanship has accomplished its objective: to allow Kennedy to choose a more appropriately sized threat, one big enough to work and yet small enough to be believed.[69]

Through incremental risks, the US turned the prisoners' dilemma of brinkmanship—as neither side ultimately wanted a nuclear war—into an aggressive zero-sum game of imperial power. Within the plot of the play, after Song has revealed his betrayal to Gallimard, which is also a form of risk, he creates "a more appropriately sized threat" and surprises him by saying that he really desires Gallimard and follows his imperious statement with, "Then again, maybe I'm just playing with you."[70] In reversing the roles of power when he reveals himself to Gallimard, Song offensively reproduces the aggressive, "international rape mentality" of the West toward the East.[71] Likewise, earlier, Pinkerton tells Sharpless, "It's true what they say about Oriental girls. They want to be treated bad!"[72] Song discloses his homosexuality and performance of heterosexuality when he makes the admission, "Well maybe, Rene, just maybe—I want you . . . Then again, maybe I'm just playing with you. How can you tell?"[73] Stuck in a prison house of player imperialist masculinity, Song cannot help but play (with) Gallimard. And yet, he reveals his attachment to Gallimard when he tells him, "I'm your Butterfly. Under the robes, beneath everything, it was always me. Now, open your eyes and admit it—you adore me."[74] Admitting that Song's face still feels like his "Butterfly" despite the rev-

---

68. Hwang, 63.
69. Dixit and Nalebuff, *Thinking Strategically,* 210.
70. Hwang, *M. Butterfly,* 86.
71. Hwang, 82, 87.
72. Hwang, 6.
73. Hwang, 85, 86.
74. Hwang, 89.

elation of his manhood, Gallimard nevertheless "plays" him by rejecting his "true self," which is "old and soiled."[75] Trained by their superiors to manipulate others, Song and Gallimard use and deceive each other to compensate for their own deficiencies. Despite his treachery, Song reveals his genuine attachment to Gallimard when he says, "I'm real. Take my hand."[76] He furthermore asks him to "throw away your pride. And come" away with him.[77] As a gay man in China, where "there is no homosexuality," Song clings to his lover of twenty years at the end of the play only to be rejected after he reveals himself to be a man.[78] Instead of Song, Gallimard "choos[es] fantasy" to compensate for his lack of virile, heterosexual, cisgender masculinity.[79] Together, Song and Gallimard reveal the polarities between player imperialism and "played" Southeast Asia, specifically Vietnam, and between the superpowers of the US and Russia.

Clinging to player imperialism, Gallimard states toward the beginning of the play that he is "not handsome, nor brave, nor powerful, yet somehow believe[s], like Pinkerton, that [he] deserve[s] a Butterfly."[80] Unable to live up to an American standard of imperialist, white, heterosexual, cisgender masculinity, he takes a "Butterfly" as a lover, who, unbeknownst to him, is a male transvestite. In other words, like other Asian American players, his failure causes him to play the womanizing game. Earlier in the play, when Marc invites him to go to his father's condo in Marseille where there will be strippers, Gallimard refuses to go because of his own shyness: "Marc, I can't. [. . .] I'm afraid they'll say no—the girls. So I never ask."[81] Gallimard's player performance is underscored by his emasculation. In line with shoring up his masculinity by taking on a "lotus blossom" lover,[82] he objectifies women throughout *M. Butterfly*. In prison for complicit espionage, he tells the audience,

> In real life, women who put their total worth at less than sixty-six cents are quite hard to find. The closest we come is in the pages of these magazines. (*He reaches into his crate, pulls out a stack of girlie magazines, and begins flipping through them*) Quite a necessity in prison. For three or four dollars, you get seven or eight women.

---

75. Hwang, 89.
76. Hwang, 77.
77. Hwang, 90.
78. Hwang, 48.
79. Hwang, 90.
80. Hwang, 10.
81. Hwang, 8, 9.
82. Hwang, 46.

> I first discovered these magazines at my uncle's house. One day, as a boy of twelve. The first time I saw them in his closet . . . all lined up—my body shook. Not with lust—no, with power. Here were women—a shelfful—who would do exactly as I wanted.[83]

As a player, Gallimard objectifies women. His problematic conflation of pornographic images with "women" reveals his desire for power. As a young boy, before he was willing to take risks to trick women into compromising positions as a player, he reveals that playing or objectifying women is a power play that defines imperialism. Likewise, Song calls his player or "cad" performances "imperialist" throughout the play.[84]

In addition to using women for sex and masculine empowerment, Gallimard continually defines himself against the perfect woman that Song embodies. After having developed his confidence as a player with Song, he "embark[s] on [his] first extra-extramarital affair" with Renee, a Danish woman he meets at the Austrian embassy in China. While attracted to Renee, the "picture perfect" woman, whom he objectifies as having "a body like those girls in the magazines," Gallimard's chief complaint with her is that she is "*too* uninhibited, *too* willing, so as to seem almost too . . . masculine."[85] She goes on to emasculate him by calling his penis, or his "little flap of flesh," a "weenie."[86] A reflection of his own name, Renee is Rene's "full" "imago," or what Lacan defined in 1949 as "the total form of his body, by which the subject anticipates the maturation of his power in a mirage."[87] Although she is a picture perfect woman, she also embodies the masculinity that Rene so desires. But instead of confirming his masculinity, she points to its fragmentation by poking fun at his penis.[88] Here, Renee, like Song when Gallimard first meets him, performs the masculine authority as a woman to dismantle Gallimard's own performance of white hegemonic masculinity; although his failure is exposed, he clings to the last vestiges of his identity. After deciding that "this was simply not acceptable," he ends his affair with Renee and resumes his

---

83. Hwang, 10.
84. Hwang, 31, 60, 21, 70.
85. Hwang, 54.
86. Hwang, 55, 54.
87. Lacan, *Écrits*, 76. Lacan published this essay in 1949, a year before the start of the Korean War.
88. In *Écrits* Lacan writes, "The mirror stage is a drama whose internal pressure pushes precipitously from insufficiency to anticipation—and, for the subject caught up in the lure of spatial identification, turns out fantasies that proceed from a fragmented image of the body to what I will call an 'orthopedic' form of its totality—and to the finally donned armor of an alienating identity that will mark his entire mental development with its rigid structure" (78).

first extramarital affair with Song who is able to keep up the appearances of the metaphorized stereotypes of the feminine East and the masculine West as s/he pretends to let him "protec[t] her in [his] big Western arms."[89] Gallimard is simply unable to break out of the binary metaphors of player imperialist masculinity and the Lotus Blossom.

The stage itself is a metaphor for Gallimard's prison. *M. Butterfly* is a frame narrative that begins and ends with Gallimard in prison. Critic Kathryn Remen points out, "Throughout the course of the play, Gallimard never leaves the stage. Thus, we are invited into his prison cell at the beginning of the play and we don't leave until he is dead."[90] Moreover, as I've mentioned earlier, the epic conventions of the play are continually interrupted by Song and Gallimard (impossibly) talking to each other in prison and inserting a metatheatrical moment by addressing the audience. At times, his audience address reinforces the binary stereotypes of the East and West that the play depicts:

> *Gallimard walks downstage. Song exits.*
> GALLIMARD (*To us*): Did you hear the way she talked about Western women? Much differently than the first night. She does—she feels inferior to them—and to me.[91]

While attempting to assert his masculinity to the audience ("she feels inferior . . . to me") by breaking the fourth wall, he also reveals his emasculation and anxiety about his racial and gendered disempowerment at other moments. Thus, he demonstrates, in contemporary Lacanian terms, that masculine fullness is actually feminine lack. Whenever Comrade Chin, Song's superior, enters the prison/stage, Gallimard cowers at her presence:

> *Suddenly Comrade Chin enters. Gallimard backs away.*
> GALLIMARD (*To Song*): No! Why does she have to come in?
> SONG: Rene, be sensible. How can they understand the story without her? Now don't embarrass yourself.
> *Gallimard moves down center.*
> GALLIMARD (*To us*): Now, you will see why my story is so amusing to so many people. Why they snicker at parties in disbelief. Please—try to understand it from my point of view. We are all prisoners of our time and place. (*He exits*)[92]

---

89. Hwang, *M. Butterfly*, 18.
90. Remen, "Theatre of Punishment," 395.
91. Hwang, *M. Butterfly*, 31.
92. Hwang, 47.

His fear of Comrade Chin undermines his self-proclaimed white, albeit non-American masculinity. Presented as an asexual figure throughout the play, Comrade Chin is stripped of her femininity by Song who tells her, "You don't understand the mind of a man."[93] Chin's lack of femininity, like Song's (initially) and Renee's, causes his deep anxiety about the unnaturalness of gender and, still, Gallimard insists on and remains in his prison house of player imperialist masculinity. Moreover, she reminds him of Song's treachery in the Brechtian realism of the play. Furthermore, her intrusions on his private "prison" conversations with Song collapse the only familial space of metaphorical comfort that he has as he states, "We are all prisoners of our time and place"—that is the Vietnam War that is structured by US player imperialism.

The prison house as a metaphor has several layers in *M. Butterfly*: Trapped in the discursive binary metaphors of player imperialism and submissive, Eastern femininity—resulting in his betrayal and imprisonment—Gallimard is imprisoned on stage by Song, Comrade Chin, and an audience who is unsympathetic to his appeals and attempts to assert his masculinity. For example, after Chin memorably tells Song that "there is no homosexuality in China," Song presents another metatheatrical moment through audience address, once again criticizing Chin, who challenges the binary of their metaphorical prison house, for her masculinity:

> SONG (*To us*): What passes for a woman in modern China.
> *Gallimard sticks his head out from the wings.*
> GALLIMARD: Is she gone?
> SONG: Yes, Rene. Please continue in your own fashion.[94]

This time, it is Song, rather than Gallimard, who protects him from Chin in his/her big Eastern arms.[95] In exploring the anxieties surrounding whiteness and race, critic Kalpana Seshadri-Crooks offers some insight into Gallimard's anxious behavior. She writes,

> Anxiety should not be understood as a threat to bodily integrity such as the fear of castration, but rather as "the lack of a lack." Anxiety, *contra* Freud, has an object, but it is no identifiable entity. Rather this object of anxiety is uncanny; it is a phobic object which ultimately sustains the body image. My point is that the racial body is produced in just such a process. [. . .] Whiteness, by attempting to signify that which is excluded in subject constitution,

---

93. Hwang, 72.
94. Hwang, 49.
95. Hwang, 18.

the more-than-symbolic aspect of the subject—the fact that he/she is not entirely determined by the symbolic or the imaginary—produces anxiety.[96]

The excess of race in determining the subject, beyond the symbolic (social and linguistic) or the imaginary (psychically internalized notion of unfragmented fullness) produces Gallimard's anxiety, which is triggered by Comrade Chin, a masculine Chinese woman—a figure who collapses the metaphorical prison of racial stereotypes in which he finds habitual comfort. Chin's masculinity also reflects Gallimard's own in-betweenness as a French, not American, not-quite-heterosexual white man during the Vietnam War. As Cheng argues, Gallimard's real problem is his "lack of *proper* [heterosexual] desire."[97] Likewise, rejected by Comrade Chin and, by extension, communist China as a "homo," Song quells his anxiety of being culturally in-between as a gay transvestite communist by acting out the *Madame Butterfly* fantasy.[98] Cheng poses key questions about the continual reproduction of this fantasy in Hwang's play:

> Gallimard the character seems at times, oddly enough, to "know better." Among derision and awareness, his repeated and conscious re-staging of himself as a "player" within the cultural cliché of *Madame Butterfly*. How do we account for the co-existence of fascination and contempt within Gallimard toward his assigned role? [...] If Song has refused outright to play Butterfly and proceeded to humiliate Gallimard's white assumptions, then why does Gallimard and even Song himself continue to narrativize *and* experience the affair through that myth?[99]

Suffering from the aphasic obstruction of the metaphoric axis of language, specifically imprisoned by the polarized stereotypes of the masculine West and feminine East in their language and actions, Gallimard and Song depend on the contiguity of this repetitive fantasy for their symbolic or social existence. In this way, the binary characterizations that Gallimard and Song perform are Vietnam War–era injunctions. Characters who do not fit these stereotypes such as Comrade Chin threaten the very fabric of this international drama of polarization. The contiguity of the *Madame Butterfly* fantasy, which results in Gallimard's performance of Madame Butterfly and consequent suicide, reflects Chinese and French failed efforts to construct multipolar international powers and divert the polarization between the US and Russia during the Viet-

---

96. Seshadri-Crooks, *Desiring Whiteness*, 37, 38.
97. Cheng, "Race and Fantasy," 181.
98. Hwang, *M. Butterfly*, 72.
99. Cheng, "Race and Fantasy," 177, 178.

nam War. The geopolitical polarization that the play reveals also explains the endurance of player imperialism despite the US failure in the war.

THE BINARY RECEPTION OF *M. BUTTERFLY*

Reflective of the work itself, the criticism of *M. Butterfly* has been polarized in its perception as *either* politically subversive *or* complicitous in its treatment of race and gender. For example, critic Colleen Lye cites Marjorie Garber and Dorinne Kondo as two critics who celebrate the play's deconstruction of gender and Western perceptions of the East. Garber argues, "*M. Butterfly* itself stands at the crossroads of nationalism and sexuality, since the axis along which it plots its dramatic movement is that of West/East and male/female. These principle binarisms are brought immediately into both question and crisis, for one cultural fact of which René and his wife Helga—a diplomatic couple stationed in China—are blissfully ignorant is that the Peking Opera is a transvestite theater: all women's roles are played by men."[100] Likewise, Kondo claims,

> *M. Butterfly* suggests that gender and race are mutually constitutive in the play of identities; neither gender nor race can be accorded some *a priori* primacy over the other. Most important, they are not incidental attributes, accidents ancillary to some primary substance of consciousness of rationality that supposedly characterize a self. In *M. Butterfly*, we find a nuanced portrayal of power and pervasiveness of gender and racial stereotypes. Simultaneously, Hwang de-essentializes the categories, exploding conventional notions of gender and race as universal, ahistorical essences or as incidental features of a more encompassing, abstract concept of self. By linking so-called individual identity to global politics, nationalism, and imperialism, Hwang makes us see the cross-cutting and mutually constitutive interplay of these forces on all levels.[101]

In contrast to Garber's and Kondo's assertions, Lye incisively points out that "*M. Butterfly* enacts a reversal that keeps the binary terms East/West and female/male in place, and that actually renders invisible the structure of power that constitutes them. By reversing the gendering of ethnicity, the play reflects a concern with Orientalism as a problem of cultural stereotyping or myth and

---

100. Garber, *Vested Interests*, 241.
101. Kondo, *About Face*, 48.

therefore as a problem whose rectification involves restituting the masculine as the sign of the 'human truth' of Asian identity."[102] Adding to Lye's claim, I am arguing that the player binarisms of East/West and female/male historicize *M. Butterfly* as a late–Cold War, specifically Vietnam War–era, play insofar as they structurally reflect and index the polarization of the US-Soviet conflict and its proxy in the Vietnam War: China and France, and, of course, North Vietnam and South Vietnam were pitted against each other by Russia and the US. Like these disempowered national pawns, Gallimard and Song—who politically represent their nations of origin as well as feminized Asian American men at large—play, use, and manipulate each other to do the bidding of their superiors. In addition to Garber and Kondo, critics John S. Bak, Karen Shimakawa, Andrew Shin, Robert Skloot, Remen, and Ilka Saal praise the play for its progressive and deconstructive gender and racial politics.[103]

Interpretations of *M. Butterfly* as politically complicitous with and subversive of Cold War American ideologies of white, heterosexual masculinity, which colonizes docile, Asian femininity, precisely qualify it as a Vietnam War play in more than just setting. The critical "playerism"—complicity and subversiveness—of the work emerges from the performers, themselves—Song and Gallimard—who, as players, are both radical and conservative insofar as they engage in the risk of brinkmanship in their sham relationship and thus reinforce patriarchy; their playerism, however, exposes the player imperialist masculinity of Vietnam War strategies of the US of converting a prisoners' dilemma of brinkmanship into a zero-sum game of imperialism. The same cross-dressing, gender, and racial reversal at the end of *M. Butterfly*, when Gallimard dons a wig and a kimono and performs Butterfly, elicits criticism of the play's reinforcement of the stereotypes of dominant, Western masculinity and submissive, Eastern femininity. In addition to Lye, critics Jon D. Rossini, James S. Moy, Sheng-mei Ma, Melanie C. Hawthorne, Joey Lee, and Hsieh-Chen Lin critique the play's seemingly conservative politics: Rossini starkly argues, "Because Song is guilty of 'manipulation,' s/he finally comes across as little more than a disfigured transvestite version of the infamous Chinese 'dragon lady' prostitute stereotype. [. . .] This pattern of subversion establishes not an articulation of Asian desire but rather affirms a nefarious complicity with AngloAmerican desire in its constitution of otherness, both sexual and racial."[104] Likewise, Moy claims, "In David Henry Hwang's *M. Butterfly* [. . .] the genesis of a new representational strategy has emerged, one in which the

---

102. Lye, "M. Butterfly," 276.
103. Bak, "'Vestis Virum Reddit,'" 95; Shimakawa, "'Who's to Say?,'" 353; Shin, "Projected Bodies," 179, 180; Skloot, "Breaking the Butterfly," 62; Remen, "Theatre of Punishment," 397.
104. Rossini, "From *M. Butterfly* to Bondage," 57.

words offer a clear indictment of the cultural hegemony of the West while the characters empowered to represent and speak on behalf of the Chinese or Asians are laughable and grossly disfigured. Thus marginalized, desexed, and made faceless, these Asian characters constitute no threat to Anglo-American sensibilities."[105] Recognizing the in-betweenness of the characters despite their trumpeting of white American heterosexual, cisgender masculinity, Ma nevertheless goes on to make a definitive claim about the play's conservative politics:

> David Henry Hwang is obliged to feature in the bulk of *M. Butterfly* (1986) the dainty Madame Butterfly with all the trappings of Orientalism before he can put in his spin in the last scene. In using pidgin English and in smashing the myth of Oriental woman, these writers try to create their own ethnic identity. But this in-between status involves an excruciating dilemma: their unique Americanness derives in large measure from a resistance to the Orientalist discourse, which in turn presupposes an acknowledgement and even an internalization of the vocabulary of Western constructions of themselves.[106]

Unlike the other critics, Hawthorne comes close to historicizing the play as reflective of the international politics of the Vietnam War by broadly claiming, "So there is a way in which *M. Butterfly* is a colonialist text in a way it does not realize, and that colonialism has as much to do with late-twentieth-century American world dominance as it has to do with nineteenth-century European colonialist attitudes toward Asia."[107] Otherwise, critics have declined to historicize the polarization of the play's politics as reflective of Cold War polarization. Song's and Gallimard's binary prison performances of the submissive, hyperfeminine Asian women and player imperialism dismantle and reaffirm the white hegemonic masculinity of American imperialism during the Vietnam War. In other words, the play, which presents binaristic stereotypes, repetitively reconstructs player imperialist, white American, heterosexual, cisgender masculinity and mirrors and traces the asymmetrical (favoring the US) polarization between the dueling superpowers.

American capitalism is unmarked and thus promoted in the play since the paradoxes of Russian imperialist communism are most noticeable in the communists' mistreatment of Song, a gay spy whose mission is to seduce and spy on a French diplomat even as s/he is criticized for his/her sexual orientation.

105. Moy, "David Henry Hwang's 'M. Butterfly,'" 55.
106. Ma, "Orientalism in Chinese American Discourse," 105.
107. Hawthorne, "'Du That Voodoo,'" 64.

This is to say, because Song's communism is paradoxical, American capitalism is unmarked and endorsed by Song's actions. Song relies on his Armani suit in order to define his manhood at the end of the play: Song declares, "These are Armani slacks [. . .]!" Nevertheless, Gallimard debases him in his masculine apparel by telling him, "You dress like a pimp."[108] His use of the word *pimp* here reduces Song to a man who dominates women without the subtleness of a player. His Armani clothing is a symbol of global capitalism and ethnic (hyper)masculinity.[109] His suit and the cigarettes he smokes at the end of the play when Gallimard dies by suicide, are commodities that reinscribe Song's manhood—an attribute he had denied throughout the course of the play. Even though Song "*stands*" in a dominant position over "*the dead Gallimard*" as he smokes a phallic cigarette and calls Gallimard, "Butterfly? Butterfly?"[110] his manhood is still not secure since it relies on the inherently unstable ideology of capitalism (represented by the commodities of an Armani suit and cigarettes), which exploits him for its definition, and which became increasingly Keynesian in the US during the Vietnam War.

Reflective of the failing game of invincible, masculinist Keynesian economics at the end of the Vietnam War, Song's masculinity is unstable and anxious. Earlier in the play, Gallimard states, "Somehow the American war went wrong too. Four hundred thousand dollars were being spent for every Viet Cong killed."[111] Gallimard's claim here is both economical and ideological insofar as money the US did not have was being spent to exterminate a population of people. Here, he recognizes the principle of playing and objectification of others behind Keynesian economics. Toward the end of the Vietnam War, Keynesian capitalism was still being used but was also failing the United States: Freeman explains that the US was in a difficult position after Nixon left office since stimulating the economy à la Keynesian capitalism would drive inflation even higher.[112] Just as Keynesian capitalism appeared but did not ultimately save the US, the Armani suit cannot fully rehabilitate Song's masculinity. As he tells the judge while on trial earlier: "Being an Oriental, I could never be completely a man."[113] Instead of realizing his long-lost masculinity, which he can perform but not retain, at the end of the play,

---

108. Hwang, *M. Butterfly*, 90.
109. Reich, *Beyond the Latin Lover*, xii. Giorgio Armani is a famous Italian clothing designer and postwar Italian cinema, Reich argues, trumpeted the notion of the hypermasculine, ethnic "Latin lover."
110. Hwang, *M. Butterfly*, 93.
111. Hwang, 68.
112. Freeman, *American Empire*, 322.
113. Hwang, *M. Butterfly*, 83.

he remains entrapped in the enduring, problematic stereotype, the metaphor of the effeminate Asian man. Despite the failures of Song and Gallimard to attain player imperialist masculinity, the complex of power and raced gender remains intact in the play because of a lack of multiple alternatives. This play illuminates the endurance of player imperialist masculinity during the polarized Vietnam War even though the US lost.

The masculinist American politics of the increasingly polarized Cold War are upheld by Song and Gallimard in *M. Butterfly* despite their sexually, gendered, and ethnically (that is, not white American) in-between characterizations. As Vietnam War–era members of a joint ethnic underclass, French and Chinese, which underscores and undermines the model minority myth of the Asian American "Butterfly" / Lotus Blossom, they nevertheless support the standard of the player imperialism of American diplomacy during the Vietnam War by failing to fully imitate it. Their unironic performances of player imperialist masculinity reflect the resurgence of aggressive masculinity in American foreign policy and the incorporation of ethical manhood into American imperialism during the Vietnam War. At the end of the play, neither Song nor Gallimard embrace ethical manhood by acknowledging the humanity and subjectivity rather than the objectivity of the other. Instead of recognizing his twenty-years-long gay relationship with Song, Gallimard chooses an alternative path in performing Butterfly and committing ritual suicide. Whereas Butterfly kills herself in Puccini's opera in her faithfulness to her husband, Gallimard becomes the Butterfly to Song's pimp. Becoming the player imperialist, signified by Benjamin Franklin Pinkerton, is not accessible to Song and Gallimard; they nevertheless succeed in exposing or "playing" the discourse of white American hegemonic, womanizing players. Song, for example, succeeds in turning Gallimard, his/her "greatest . . . acting challenge" into a woman—Butterfly, herself—at the end of the play.[114]

In this way, these characters radically reflect and "out" the dual player imperialist, white hegemonic masculinity of US foreign diplomacy which "played" China and France and, of course, North Vietnam and South Vietnam, by proxy, in its polarized struggle with and battle for dominance over the Soviet Union during the Vietnam War. Nevertheless, Song and Gallimard are constrained in their literal and figurative prison houses of metaphorical stereotype of the criminalized, submissive but hypersexual Lotus Blossom, which is the binary of and further empowers player imperialist, white American, heterosexual, cisgender masculinity. However, the ethnic and sexual "in-betweenness" or "not-quiteness" of the characters delineates the yellow peril,

---

114. Hwang, 63.

underclass myth that racializes Asian Americans during this period. As the polarized Vietnam War discourse speaks its social subjects into existence, these ethnically and sexually "in-between" characters suffer from aphasia with a defect in substitution, which stunts a proliferation of different metaphors and their ethical manhood. For this reason, the characters remain players and rely on the metonymy of metaphorically redundant, player imperialist, white hegemonic masculinity and submissive, Butterfly self-expression through time and space: Gallimard and Song live their obscene fantasy for upward of twenty years in Beijing and Paris.

Despite the contiguity of their travels and the continuous length of their love affair, Gallimard and Song, as the racial and sexual underclass, remain trapped in metaphorical prisons of binary stereotypes. In addition to reflecting but ultimately being imprisoned by their failures to reproduce player imperialist masculinity, their imprisonment by binary stereotypes are traces of the developing role of the US as imperialist world police. Published at the end of the Vietnam War in 1975, Michel Foucault's *Discipline and Punish: The Birth of the Prison* describes the social conditions in which these characters find themselves: "Today, criminal justice functions and justifies itself only by this perpetual reference to something other than itself, by this unceasing reinscription in non-juridical systems."[115] No doubt influenced by the contemporaneous polarization of the Vietnam War and the Cold War more generally, Foucault critiques the way in which the carceral prison system disciplines bodies in binaries, as *either* innocent *or* criminal. Whereas the US military appeared innocent or at least ethical in their gendered incursions into the East during the Cold War, the characters I discuss are castigated as sexually deviant and criminalized for political treachery in their gendered performances. Furthermore, Foucault underscores the prison system's "reinscription in non-juridical systems" as demonstrated in government espionage in *M. Butterfly* (East/West) and the shameless objectification of women by the performances of male characters. As cross-ethnic, "underclass" players that perform and represent the Asian American stereotype of the Butterfly, Gallimard and Song demonstrate that "we are all prisoners of our time and place."[116] As civilian men living during war, they find themselves unable to assert their identities—Song, more so than the others, because of the enduring racial stereotype of Asian effeminacy—in any other way than womanizing or playing others. In the final analysis, they embody the postwar player—imprisoned, with no alternative.

---

115. Foucault, *Discipline and Punish*, 22.
116. Hwang, *M. Butterfly*, 47.

Despite the aggressive, player "remasculinization" of America during the Vietnam War, the war marked the awareness and waning of American imperialism. Nixon's presidency seems to mark a decline in US imperialism.[117] Likewise, when Ford became president at the end of the Vietnam War, the later strategy of easing tensions, or softer polarized "détente[,] had begun to stall" due to the differing situations of US and Soviet imperialisms and resistance to détente within the US.[118] As American imperialism and polarized détente dimmed, player imperialism, which Asian American players continue to mimic in cultural products after the Cold War, went underground; that is, it became less visible. Player imperialist masculinity was reinforced by becoming even more covert and abstract as American war strategies depended on more virtual, rather than physical and on-the-ground, weapons in the Gulf War and the War on Terror.

---

117. Freeman, *American Empire*, 274.
118. Freeman, 324.

CHAPTER 3

Playing the Odds of the Virtual Gulf War

World Police and Family Man

As the Cold War was historically coming to an end, the abstract objectives of the Cold War and the zero-sum approach of American imperialism morphed into the virtually fought Gulf War. This imperialist, virtual warfare, as this chapter argues, was mimicked and traced by contemporary Asian American characters in literature. As opposed to the media coverage of corpses, disfigured flesh, and pervasive civilian carnage of the Vietnam War, televised images of virtual but accurate, GPS-driven strikes on seemingly bodiless military facilities dominated the news on the Gulf War.[1] Historian Alastair Finlan argues that the US, "a nation obsessed with winning," was able to redeem itself during the Gulf War, offsetting its losses in Vietnam with "a decisive military victory which the people had not savoured since the Second World War."[2] Moreover, the divisiveness of the 1960s and 1970s "reinvigorate[d] [American] commemoration of official patriotism and loyalty" in the 1990s.[3] The Gulf War was a welcome opportunity for the US to assert its imperial dominance once again.[4] This time, the US would assert its imperialism by acting as a family man to bring Middle Eastern nations into his fold of democracy through virtual warfare. Critic Susan Jeffords argues that during the Gulf War

---

1. Finlan, *Gulf War*, 71.
2. Finlan, 71–72.
3. Bodnar, *Remaking America*, 250.
4. Freeman, *American Empire*, 414.

of the 1990s, white hegemonic masculinity was refashioning itself as world police under the guise of a family man. As the Asian American players of this chapter demonstrate, the masculine conflation of world police and family man obviated possibilities for the ethical, ideological distinction between white hegemonic masculinity and player imperialism during the Gulf War. To play, during this era of war, was to pose as family man while really inhabiting the position of world police. This emergent, masculine hegemony of world police and family man was a new form of virtual deterrence. Whereas the US was invested in "remasculinizing" itself during the Vietnam War and the late Cold War, by the 1990s, Jeffords argues, white hegemonic masculinity was "a rearticulation of masculine strength and power through internal, personal, and family-oriented values."[5] Although she does not name the American player as such, Jeffords points out that this 1990s white hegemonic masculinity appeared in many popular, low cultural films such as *Kindergarten Cop* (1990), starring Arnold Schwarzenegger as a law enforcer turned family man.[6] And thus, in comparison with the domestic containment of the Korean War and the aggressive masculine imperialism of the Vietnam War era, Gulf War–era American imperialism was refigured in a more subdued but complex masculinity as a personable, ethical family man, an image that masked the accompanying role of invisible world police; in this way, the US as invisible world police surveilled a virtual war. In all its complexities, US player imperialism during the Persian Gulf War threatened to homogenize and replace heterogeneous Middle Eastern cultures with a singular image of white American hegemonic masculinity in the name of democracy.[7] The player imperialist goals to democratize Iraq in the "new world order" was encompassed by this dual figuration of the player imperialist world police under the guise of the ethical, American family man. The protagonists of Chang-rae Lee's debut novel *Native Speaker* (1995) and second novel *A Gesture Life* (1999), Doc Hata and Henry Park, are simulacra of this Gulf War–era dual figuration, but as fathers, they fail to assert their governing authorities and protect their children; instead, they are little more than official and unofficial spies that do the bidding of others. Despite these failures, they, like Song and Gallimard, subjectively cling to their player masculinities and sexually victimize others, namely women of color. As they express their subjectivities, their failures and victimizations mimic, expose, and reassert the American geopolitical, player imperialist masculinity of family man and covert world police.

---

5. Jeffords, *Hard Bodies*, 13.
6. Jeffords, 141.
7. Pease, "New Perspectives on U.S. Culture," 23.

Despite their efforts, the Asian American male protagonists in *Native Speaker* and *A Gesture Life* fail at reasserting their manhoods as interpersonal, ethical, and masculine American family men during the 1990s. In *Native Speaker*, Henry Park is unable to save his son from a premature death. Franklin Hata's daughter Sunny leaves home as a minor in *A Gesture Life*. The earnest, real attempts of these characters to succeed in their respective careers nevertheless flip them into decoys that player imperialist, white American subjects instrumentalize as disposable others. In Lee's *Native Speaker* and *A Gesture Life*, the genuineness of Park's attempt to spy for a private intelligence firm called Glimmer & Company and Hata's effort to feign Japaneseness as an ethnic Korean in the contexts of the Japanese Imperial army during World War II and Americanness in the postwar United States seem paradoxical. And yet, these "player" performances are sincere attempts to assimilate and conform to their societies as citizens; they do so to no avail, as they are constantly rejected as perpetually foreign and, at times, effeminate by Americans of various backgrounds. Although *A Gesture Life* continually loops back to Hata's time in Burma, fighting for the Japanese as a medic during World War II, and *Native Speaker* consistently acknowledges its context of the race riots in Los Angeles and New York between 1990 and 1992, the present contexts of the narratives in each novel take place over the course of the 1991 Gulf War. Moreover, both novels were also published in the same decade as the Gulf War.

A Gesture Life is about war and its emotional aftershocks; thus, Hata's elision of the Gulf War is quizzical since he spends the majority of the narrative revisiting his memories of fighting in World War II. On the other hand, *Native Speaker* consistently acknowledges its context of the race riots in Los Angeles and New York between 1990 and 1992 but fails to mention the 1991 Gulf War, which was bookended by those two events. I would venture to say that the discursive absence of the Gulf War in these two works is symptomatic and constitutive of the ways in which the Gulf War, as a "virtual war"—as many critics have called it—was fought quickly and in a way that was invisible to the public eye.[8] Just as American manhood in the 1990s was framed as the more ambivalent, personal family man, the "world police" re-masculinization of white American men during the 1960s and 1970s went underground, or became less explicitly visible, in the virtual war of 1991. Through this ambivalence, ethical manhood and invisible American imperial masculinity continued to be ideologically fused (as family man and world police) during the Gulf War.

I've chosen Lee's first two novels as cultural artifacts of the Gulf-War and the Asian American and African American race-riots period for several

---

8. Finlan, *Gulf War*, 71.

reasons. First, the transnational scopes of both novels reflect the post–Civil Rights era strides that were made in Asian American studies in the 1990s by critics such as Lisa Lowe who redefined the field as transnational (rather than domestically American) and more flexible in its identity politics than Civil Rights–era critics such as Frank Chin had previously defined it. Second, these first two novels gained Lee (who currently teaches at Stanford University) a professorial position at Princeton University and a reputation as a leading author in the field of Asian American literature and literature, more widely. For example, a *Los Angeles Times* review of his fifth novel, *On Such a Full Sea*, published in 2014, gives him high praise, stating, "I have no choice to ask: Who is a greater novelist than Chang-rae Lee today?" Third, as I mentioned earlier, these novels include the domestic race riots but elide any mention of the contemporary Gulf War despite their preoccupation with war, politics, and racial conflict during the 1990s. Although few historians link the Gulf War and the race riots in the early 1990s, both events were studied and strategically approached through technological developments in surveillance, which showcases the US as invisible world police. During the Gulf War, technological advances in surveillance led to the assessment of Iraq's weakness in naval and air power and the precision of American bombs hitting targets, which was unparalleled by any previous war the US had fought.[9] On the other hand, critic Yoonmee Chang argued that surveillance during the race riots, particularly in the shooting of Latasha Harlins, accomplished the work of "underwriting culturalizations" and placing the blame on ethnic minorities rather than the larger white American public.[10] Moreover, critic Monica Chiu argues that the narrative of a corporate spy in *Native Speaker* deploys the theme of surveillance to understand intricate race relations.[11] Kim takes on a Baudrillardian lens by situating this Gulf War–era novel as a Cold War text, which falls into the genre of a Cold War spy novel through its conventions.[12] Instead, this chapter points to these texts as Gulf War texts through its emphasis on surveillance and virtual conflict.

Instead of acknowledging the contemporary Gulf War and its effects, both *Native Speaker* and *A Gesture Life* explicitly reference only the domestic race riots—the New York boycott of 1990 and the Los Angeles race riots of 1992—that historically flanked the Gulf War of 1991.[13] As he starts to spy on Councilman John Kwang by working for his political campaign for mayor of New

---

9. Finlan, 1, 29, 76.
10. Chiu, *Scrutinized!*, 11–12.
11. Chiu, 12.
12. D. Kim, "Once More, with Feeling," 119.
13. Chang-rae Lee, *Native Speaker*, 150–51; Chang-rae Lee, *Gesture Life*, 3.

York City, Park remarks that Kwang was such an idealist that he "couldn't even speak out against the obvious violence and destruction, after black groups had insisted they were 'demonstrations' against the callousness of Korean merchants and the unjust acquittal of the Korean storeowner who'd shot and killed Saranda Harlans."[14] Here, Park alludes to one real-life event that contributed to the start of the Los Angeles riots: A Korean American female grocer, Soon Ja Du, reflecting white American imperialism, shot and killed an African American young woman named Latasha Harlins after accusing her of stealing orange juice and receiving several blows from Harlins. Reflective of these racial conflicts, in *A Gesture Life,* Hata notes that much like his present moment, thirty years after his arrival in 1963, he found the New York City suburb of Bedley Run (then, Bedleyville) to be much like everywhere else in the United States, a place where "certain groups, such as blacks, or the Chinese in the cities, [. . .] for some reason or another seemed to live apart."[15] This indication of the enduring segregation of African Americans and Asian Americans—two minority groups despite their different racializations—in cities loosely alludes to the Black-Korean conflict in Brooklyn that resulted in the Flatbush Boycott of 1990. According to Claire Jean Kim, the differing racializations of discursively "superior" yet "foreign" Asian Americans and discursively "inferior" yet "insider" African Americans incited the conflict;[16] the differences between the racializations were also undermined by the conflict insofar as both groups were considered inferior and foreign to white American hegemonic masculinity. Moreover, neither novel mentions the occurrence of the contemporary, brief but significant war in the Middle East in 1991. Mirroring the concurrent Gulf War, the power struggle of the race riots depicted in the novels encapsulated an imperialist conflict between two differently minoritized groups who mimicked player imperialist masculinity in the US.

THE PLAYER IMPERIALISM OF GULF WAR-ERA PATERNALISM

The substitution of domestic politics for any mention of the Gulf War in literature that takes place and is published during the 1990s is in itself neither formidable nor necessarily indicative of the absent representations of the Gulf War in the media and American social discourses per se. However, both *Native Speaker* and *A Gesture Life* mirror the paternalistic dynamic between

---

14. Chang-rae Lee, *Native Speaker,* 193.
15. Chang-rae Lee, *Gesture Life,* 3.
16. C. Kim, *Bitter Fruit,* 16.

the US and Iraq during the international Gulf War and, domestically, the privileged invisibility of the Gulf War and the castigated visibility of race riots in the early 1990s through two main representations of American imperialism. The Gulf War redeemed the US as an imperial and policing power through its invisibility as war. Framed as aid to Kuwait and other Middle Eastern countries threatened by Iraq, the war was, of course, not invisible or virtual to those living in the Persian Gulf. The rhetoric of aid but reality of colonization rather than war incited the flight of three million refugees following the 1991 Gulf War.[17] In both novels, the failures of empirical democracy in the covertness and inherent racism of American imperialism—that is, political and capitalistic dominance—are demonstrated through references to the race riots and the subtle subjugation and victimization of the Asian American protagonists by white female lovers and the protagonists' failed attempts to mimic patriarchal figures (family men) as they spy on them. White women and other patriarchal figures and mentors in the protagonists' careers perform player imperialism. Doc Hata, who is later somewhat redeemed by being a caring grandfather to Sunny's son, and Henry Park fail to imitate them with their children. These relationships demonstrate the ways in which they fail to attain player imperialist masculinity even though they abide by its patriarchal logic of deterrence and strategy of preventing apocalyptic moments.

As in the Korean War and the Vietnam War, deterrence was the primary masculinist imperialist strategy of the Gulf War. However, nuclear deterrence in the former morphed into virtual deterrence in the latter. Iraq's invasion of Kuwait in August 1990 triggered a response by the United Nations to place an embargo on Iraq and deploy coalition forces, led by the United States, to enforce a deadline on January 15, 1991, for Iraq's departure from Kuwait—an example of the military strategy of deterrence.[18] Freeman writes that although the United States justified its intervention in Kuwait by criticizing the imperialist sovereignty of Iraq over Kuwait, the Kuwaiti regime was also "wholly undemocratic."[19] Freeman identifies that it was oil, not democracy, that fueled the Bush administration's actions; Iraq's occupation of Kuwait allowed Iraq to control a large portion of global oil production. Fearing Iraq would take over Saudi Arabia, the US intervened for fear that Iraq would become "by far the most important player in the global oil economy."[20] In other words, the Gulf War was driven by oil demands rather than democracy. Militarized engagement with Iraq at the borders of surrounding nations such as Saudi Arabia by

---

17. Galbraith, "Refugees from the War," 1–11.
18. Finlan, *Gulf War*, 29.
19. Freeman, *American Empire*, 412.
20. Freeman, 412.

coalition forces, known as Operation Desert Shield, from August 2, 1990, to January 15, 1991, was complicated, for, up to that point, leaders of the coalition forces—the US, Britain, and France—had participated in a great deal of trade with Iraq.[21] The coalition forces constituted the largest multinational military alliance after World War II. At its helm, the US diverted its attention from guarding Saudi Arabia from Iraqi annexation to offensive attacks on Iraqi forces in Iraq and Kuwait after Iraq failed to withdraw its troops on January 15—a phase known as Operation Desert Storm. Commander-in-chief of the US Central Command General Norman Sckwarzkopf faced the challenge of protecting Saudi Arabia and democratically "liberating" Kuwait; his Operation Desert Storm is known as "one of the most technologically sophisticated military campaigns in human history."[22] With the help of the surveilling global positioning system (GPS), coalition forces were able to efficiently attack their targets.[23] According to Finlan, in the Gulf War, the US was much more efficient in using airpower than previous wars. To put it in perspective, the complete weight of bombs dropped on Iraq was below ninety thousand tons, which was less than the average amount used in just two months of bombing in World War II and the Vietnam War.[24] As I will discuss later, the Asian American player embodied in *A Gesture Life* and *Native Speaker* flips the remasculinization of the US Cold War by reflecting this new virtual, unmarked facet of imperialist warfare.

As I pointed out in the previous two chapters, the Cold War was fought, by proxy, through third-world nations (Korea and Vietnam) and these wars ultimately remasculinized the US. And yet, the measured victory in the Korean War and the loss of the Vietnam War had severely damaged the morale of American imperialism. Moreover, as historian Salim Yaqub argues, the Cold War had little impact on the Middle East; even though the Soviets attempted to gain influence in the Middle East in the 1980s, neither communism nor American capitalism was absorbed by this area.[25] Furthermore, historians such as Finlan view the Gulf War as a welcomed break from the polarization of the Cold War and, specifically, the "nuclear rivalry" between the US and the Soviet Union.[26] However, writing during the contemporary moment

---

21. Finlan, *Gulf War*, 14–15.
22. Finlan, 50, 29.
23. Finlan, 87.
24. Finlan, 30.
25. Yaqub, "Cold War," 22. In *The Cold War* Levering writes, "The fact that crises in the Middle East in 1967 and in Czechoslovakia the next year did not lead to wider conflict underscored the value of the generally positive atmosphere in U.S.-Soviet relations" (114–15).
26. Levering, *Cold War*, 7–8.

of the Gulf War, theorist Jean Baudrillard notes the continuity of the political logic of deterrence from "the cold war (the balance of terror)" to "the dead war—the unfrozen cold war," as he refers to the Gulf War.[27] He states, "We are in neither a logic of war nor a logic of peace but in a logic of deterrence which has wound its way inexorably through forty years of cold war to a denouement in our current events; a logic of weak events, to which belong those in Eastern Europe as well as the Gulf War."[28] Instead of nuclear weapons to effect communist containment—a form of deterrence—the US used technological advancements in military support systems in Operation Desert Storm to deter international policy not favorable to US interests. Baudrillard argues that the "deterrence," accomplished by the virtual warfare of the Gulf War, "inexorabl[y] confus[es]" "the real" and "the virtual," problematically and "spares no-one.[29] No more than the politicians, the military personnel do not know what to make of their real function, their function of death and destruction."[30] The precision and virtuality of the warfare in Iraq and Kuwait made it apocalyptic and "dangerous[ly]" "unreal" for Baudrillard.[31] Finlan refutes Baudrillard's claim about the fakeness of the war in stating, "For postmodernists the Gulf War may have been a 'virtual' war but for the families of the half a million troops in the Middle East, the nature of the conflict was very different."[32] However, Finlan misinterprets Baudrillard's critique of the virtuality of the Gulf War. Rather than arguing that the Gulf War literally "did not take place," he claims that the immediacy and precision of death carried out by drones instead of soldiers are frightening, inhumane, and apocalyptic. Baudrillard argues that it was a virtual war in its technological methods of warfare and in its preemptive or deterrent strategies of preventative combat. Moreover, as he points out, despite the twenty-four-hour coverage of the war and the fact that "the 100,000 Iraqi dead will only have been the final decoy that Saddam will have sacrificed, the blood money paid in forfeit according to a calculated experience, in order to conserve his power," the media did not generate any "real images" of war.[33] However, there was collateral damage, and there were civilian lives lost during the Gulf War. Historian Anthony Tucker-Jones points out that because of the on-point, complete devastation of the technological warfare used during Desert Storm, there was no conclusive

27. Baudrillard, *Gulf War*, 23.
28. Baudrillard, 26.
29. Baudrillard, 67.
30. Baudrillard, 28.
31. Baudrillard, 27, 28.
32. Finlan, *Gulf War*, 71.
33. Finlan, 76; Baudrillard, *Gulf War*, 71–72, 81–82.

body count from the Gulf War; it was only estimated that over 100,000 Iraqis were killed, 300,000 were wounded, and 175,000 were taken prisoner.[34] The US victory in the Gulf War furthered the discourse of white American men as good family men who police their families to avoid danger, albeit in a less visible way.

Like US political practice during the Gulf War, Doc Hata and Henry Park subjectively play, or manipulate, the discourse of deterrence to gain imperialist power but also to survive as Asian American men in a largely, white hegemonic masculine society. The beginning of *Native Speaker* finds Park taking on the role of the good family man and attempting to reconcile with his estranged wife Lelia, a white speech therapist from New England, after the traumatic loss of their seven-year-old son. He continually deters the apocalypse of the end of his marriage by deferring to her every need and desire. He narrates receiving a personal note from Lelia, upon dropping her off to the airport on her way to spend time away from him in Italy, which contains a list of offensive descriptions of him:

> You are surreptitious
> B+ student of life
> first thing hummer of Wagner and Strauss
> illegal alien
> emotional alien
> genre bug
> Yellow peril: neo-American
> great in bed
> overrated
> poppa's boy
> sentimentalist
> anti-romantic
> _____ analyst (you fill in)
> stranger
> follower
> traitor
> spy[35]

Here, Lelia supposedly bares her emotions to Henry by exposing him as a stereotypical model minority / "yellow peril" Asian and a fraudulent "spy."

---

34. Tucker-Jones, *Gulf War*, 115.
35. Chang-rae Lee, *Native Speaker*, 5.

According to various authoritative sources, the model minority myth emerged concurrently with the underclass myth in the 1960s.[36] Claire Jean Kim argues, "Consider the two myths as mirror images: the underclass is lazy, undisciplined, lacking in family values, criminally inclined, unable to deter gratification, deviant, dependent, and prone to dropping out; the model minority is diligent, disciplined, possessed of strong family values, respectful of authority, thrifty, moral, self-sufficient, and committed to education."[37] The Asian American player collapses the binary ethnic distinctions between the model minority and the underclass (or the yellow peril, in the case of the Asian American); as both Henry Park and Doc Hata demonstrate, the model minority, playing the "Good Charlie," quickly devolves into the yellow peril that victimizes women and embodies a life full of ineffectual gestures.[38] As I will later discuss, as both an Asian American victimizer and one who is victimized, Doc Hata melds the binary narratives of the model minority and the underclass.

Henry Park and Doc Hata face how deeply destructive and polarizing the model minority myth is on the Asian American psyche. Historians Sucheng Chan and Ronald Takaki have historically done much to expose the model minority as a myth: Chan writes that, despite the persistence of the model minority myth, discrimination and systemic bias have not disappeared but only morphed into new forms; compared to Black Americans or Latinxs, Asian Americans "live in a state of ambivalence—lauded as a 'successful' or 'model minority' on the one hand, but subject to continuing unfair treatment, including occasional outbursts of racially motivated violence, on the other."[39] This state of racialized ambivalence between the model minority and the yellow peril explains the performative subjectivity of the Asian American player who constantly vacillates between seduction and violence. From a sociological rather than literary or thematic perspective, Takaki debunks the model minority myth and argues that Asian American success is largely exaggerated and Asian American income levels are based on areas of residence that have higher costs of living.[40] The glass or "bamboo" ceiling that proceeds from the model minority myth stems from and perpetuates the racist notion that Asian Americans are "passive" as they are "told they lack the aggressiveness required in administration";[41] the model minority stereotype also treats Asian Ameri-

---

36. C. Kim, *Bitter Fruit*, 19.
37. C. Kim, 20; S. Chan, *Asian Americans*, 167; Takaki, *Strangers from a Different Shore*, 475.
38. Chang-rae Lee, *Gesture Life*, 95.
39. S. Chan, *Asian Americans*, 187–88.
40. Takaki, *Strangers from a Different Shore*, 475.
41. Takaki, 476.

cans as a monolith despite class differences among laborers, refugees, students, and the white-collar professionals.

While Lelia racially denigrates Henry as the model minority, he never assigns her racial epithets or disparages her; he only admits that he has wronged her through donning "[his] mask of serenity and repose" to deter conflicts.[42] Lelia's list above showcases her white supremacy rather than her anger toward or fear of her husband. Lelia declares herself and her speech to be the "standard-bearer" of Americanism early on in her relationship with Henry.[43] The novel concludes with Lelia problematically using racist terms to describe her ESL students ("buck-toothed puppets with big mouths, scary masks") and deploying the white privilege of authoritatively calling on her diversely named students, "speaking a dozen lovely and native languages."[44]

Even as they begin to reconcile their relationship at the end of the novel, when Henry reveals to Lelia the complications of his current mission to inform Glimmer & Co. of Kwang's political activities, Lelia's subjugation and victimizing feminization of Henry do not change:

> Now, I am always coming back inside. We play this game in which I am her long-term guest. Permanently visiting. That she likes me okay and bears my presence, but who can know for how long? I step inside and walk to the bedroom and lie down and close my eyes. She follows me and says that this is her room. I usually sleep on the couch.
>
> Usually? I murmur.
>
> Yes, she says, her voice suddenly closer, hot to the ear, and she's already on me.[45]

Since this "game" or power play is in the context of sex and enacting fantasy, Lelia's actual dominance over Henry is questionable. However, in concert with her actions throughout the novel, she relies on her whiteness and legitimacy as an American to control outcomes and permit him to reenter their shared domestic space. Her power over him demonstrates his failure as an imperialist player.

Like Lelia, Mary Burns, Hata's white, widowed neighbor, dictates the intimacy of her relationship with him in *A Gesture Life*. The first time they attempt to have sex, Hata narrates, "For I am almost sure she wanted me to make love to her, this by the open, willing character of her body, and then by the strength

---

42. Chang-rae Lee, *Native Speaker*, 296.
43. Chang-rae Lee, 12.
44. Chang-rae Lee, 349.
45. Chang-rae Lee, 347.

of her limbs, the way she so tightly wound my legs with hers."[46] And yet, when Hata is unable to sexually perform, she resumes control of their intimacy by assuming that she is responsible for his unresponsiveness: "Mary Burns had the impression that she had done something terribly offending or wrong, and I knew I could not convince her otherwise, at least for the moment."[47] Just as Lelia does, Mary reinforces stereotypes of Asian Americans, specifically that of Asian male effeminacy, in her relationship with Hata when she remarks, "It's just that your face is so unlike my late husband's, I can't tell you. Bradley had such severe features, a long, narrow nose and deep-set eyes and a jutting chin. He was aggressive, in appearance. You have a wonderful gentleness to your face. A softer line to everything."[48] Mary unabashedly genders Franklin's softer, gentler appearance by contrasting it with and subordinating it to her late white husband's jutting chin and aggressive appearance. Young-Oak Lee argues that Hata is subordinate to Mary Burns and their relationship is one of racial, internal colonization.[49] Chang-rae Lee articulates the subtlety and intimacy of American imperialism through racializing relationships between his Asian American protagonists and white American women such as Lelia and Mary. Not only do they seek to dominate the male protagonists, they also reproduce problematic stereotypes: Upon meeting Franklin, Mary assumes his model minority status when she mistakes him for a real physician; when Hata clarifies that he is not a real doctor but is simply called one, she states, "You know, I would have thought you were a doctor anyway."[50] Her dictation of the terms of their relationship showcases his racial and gendered failure as an imperialist player.

Hata and Park are repeatedly victimized or subordinated by their white lovers, who espouse white hegemonic femininity. As Asian American players, their subjectivities are based on their failed performances of the era's player imperialist masculinity of paternalism—world police under the guise of family man; they fail because white women victimize them but also because they are unable to imitate father figures and mentors in their careers. Hata's performance as a doctor, in accepting his Bedley Run appellation, "Doc Hata," and work as a medic (but not a licensed physician) in the Japanese imperial army is nevertheless continually undercut and exposed as fraudulent by his superior, Captain Ono. After demoting Hata from lieutenant to sentry of the

---

46. Chang-rae Lee, *Gesture Life*, 315.
47. Chang-rae Lee, 315.
48. Chang-rae Lee, 70.
49. Y. Lee, "Gender, Race, and the Nation," 154, 155.
50. Chang-rae Lee, *Gesture Life*, 46.

infirmary, Ono reveals to him that he knows of Hata's ethnic Korean heritage and concludes:

> There is the germ of infirmity in you, which infects everything you touch or attempt. Besides all else, how do you think you will ever become a surgeon? A surgeon determines his course and acts. [. . .] You, Lieutenant, too much depend upon generous fate and gesture. There is no internal possession, no embodiment. Thus you fail in some measure always. You perennially disappoint someone like me.[51]

Ono's words become prophetic for Hata's continual sense of fraudulence, inefficacy, and racial difference for the rest of his career in the Japanese imperial army and his "gesture" life in the United States. Ono is an imperial patriarchal figure whom Hata fails to mimic, and whom Hata never critiques for his shortcomings. He admiringly recalls the time he witnesses Ono, the company's surgeon, demonstrating how to hand-massage a heart on a Burmese cobbler who had been sentenced to death for a crime. Without proper anesthesia, he puts the man into "half-sleep with a rag soaked in ether" and stops the cobbler's heart with electrical paddles only to massage it to start beating again.[52] Hata remarks that "Captain Ono himself seemed nonplussed" by the demonstration, which the former describes as "at once God-like and lowly."[53] He wonders if he could perform the same technique on a friend's son who suffers from heart trouble but resigns himself to his subjectification by the patriarchal commanding officer Ono as an ineffectual fraud when he states, "To be truthful, I am sure I'm not a creature who was made to endure."[54] Reflecting the historical moment of his narration, Hata's life appears virtual rather than real and enduring.

Similarly, Henry finds himself unable to truly mirror his father and John Kwang, who becomes a patriarchal figure to him. His father's own Asian American masculinity is dubious as it seems to denigrate yet imitate models of white masculinity: Henry recalls,

> I remember how he would make fun of Joe Namath in those old cologne commercials, remark that he was too ugly a man to have so many beautiful women surrounding him.

---

51. Chang-rae Lee, 266.
52. Chang-rae Lee, 76.
53. Chang-rae Lee, 76.
54. Chang-rae Lee, 77.

> *What a nose!* he'd cry in Korean at the television set. *It looks like a big dried daikon.*
>
> But then there it was, invariably, the little green bottle of musky potion that Joe also used, ready for him on my mother's dresser.[55]

His father gravitates toward Hollywood models of heterosexual, cisgender white American masculinity. Whereas his father makes his masculine presence known by being "forceful with some of his neighbors," and visibly resenting "the town" for "just barely tolerating our presence," he spites his father by becoming invisible to the customers: "I saw that if I just kept speaking the language of our work the customers didn't seem to see me. I wasn't there. They didn't look at me. I was a comely shadow who didn't threaten them."[56] Despite his attempts at invisibility, he nevertheless becomes the one in his family who learns English to document his personal history. Because of his broken relationship with his father, Henry begins to regard Kwang as a surrogate father-figure. Critic Betsy Huang points to the opposing characterizations of Henry's father as "a model of repudiation against the dominant culture's demand for cultural consent" and Kwang, who embraces dominant, white hegemonic masculine culture.[57] And yet, Henry ultimately betrays Kwang and fails to replicate him and fulfill his political aspirations for Henry. Despite his betrayal, he takes it upon himself to shield Kwang from the barrage of race rioters and media personnel that descend upon him, "calling him every ugly Asian name I have ever heard" after the corruption of his campaign is exposed.[58] As Park takes the punches from the crowd that are meant for Kwang, he states that "at the very moment I fall back for good he glimpses who I am, and I see him crouch down, like a broken child, shielding from me his wide immigrant face."[59] In this moment Park, in embodying "the obedient soft-spoken son" to Kwang, takes the visual fall for Kwang, who hides the vulnerability of his "wide immigrant face."[60] The "family-man" paternalistic role of American imperialism during the Gulf War is nevertheless telegraphed through Asian or Asian American patriarchal figures who emasculate the protagonists by pinning their own shortcomings on them through the narrative and their actions.

This type of paternalism, combined with the subtle racism of the protagonists' white lovers, traces the political relation between the US and Iraq

---

55. Chang-rae Lee, *Native Speaker*, 136.
56. Chang-rae Lee, 52, 53.
57. Huang, "Citizen Kwang," 249.
58. Chang-rae Lee, *Native Speaker*, 341.
59. Chang-rae Lee, 343.
60. Chang-rae Lee, 202.

in the international Gulf War and also between the contemporaneous events of the Gulf War and the domestic race riots in the United States. Although the violent tension between racial minorities in the early 1990s mirrored the American paternalistic and imperialistic conflict with Iraq in significant ways, the race riots were sensationalized by the media and public discourse while the Gulf War was virtually ignored by or made unreal to the American public. This historical paradox of unseen national dominance and spectacular racial subjugation is thematic and reenacted in both *Native Speaker* and *A Gesture Life*. In this way, both novels carve out a separate genre of Gulf War literature from a civilian perspective. The related figurations of the Asian American protagonists of the novels as spy and good but fraudulent performer, or player, respectively, problematically collapse the model minority with the yellow peril stereotypes.[61] But, more importantly, their occupations as frauds point to the impossibility of Asian American subjectivity when it is informed by binary, two-dimensional stereotypes of the model minority and the yellow peril. Ultimately, as critics such as Tina Chen have argued, Park and Hata are victimizers, specifically of Asian American women, as much as they are victims.[62]

VICTIMS OF THE VICTIMIZED

Subjugated by white women and patriarchal figures, Hata and Henry fail to attain ethical manhood by stopping the cycle of abuse through selfless care during the Gulf War era in which ethical manhood (family man) was conflated with imperialism (world police). As part of their subjectification, these characters turn to Asian and Asian American women in order to play them as objects for domination, through which they might regain their lost masculinities. Insisting on adopting a daughter for reasons "unknown" to him, Hata feels a sense of "relief" when a "suitable orphan" from Korea, whom he names Sunny, is located for him by an adoption agency.[63] As an ethnically Korean man, he considers himself nationally Japanese and fights in the Japa-

---

61. In *Orientals: Asian Americans in Popular Culture* Robert G. Lee writes, "Six images—the pollutant, the coolie, the deviant, the yellow peril, the model minority, and the g***—portray the Oriental as an alien body and a threat to the American national family" (8). In *Bitter Fruit* Claire Jean Kim states, "The model minority myth, which first emerged during the mid-1960s, was resurrected during the early 1980s just as the underclass myth was gaining ground (Osajima 1988)" (19; my elision).

62. Tina Chen argues, "Ultimately, Henry discovers that he is both victim and perpetrator of the crimes he commits. Before he can own up to the ways in which his many betrayals lead to a self-betrayal, Henry must wrestle with the histories that shape him" (*Double Agency,* 639).

63. Chang-rae Lee, *Gesture Life,* 74.

nese Imperial army. Just as Japan had colonized Korea and enslaved Korean females as comfort women during World War II, Hata adopts a Korean girl to problematically exercise his paternalism over her. Moreover, he is "disappointed" when he first meets Sunny and sees her "dark-hued" skin, assuming she was conceived in "a night's wanton encounter between a GI and a local bar girl."[64] His racism against African Americans here reflects the contemporary race conflicts between Asian and African Americans. Likewise, Young-Oak Lee argues that "he represses Sunny, the object of his racism."[65] Hata racially represses her by incestuously sizing up his daughter, narrating her appearance in a sexual manner: "The dress came just up to her darkly suntanned shoulders, the delicate material clinging to her torso but not so tightly as to be indecent, the handsome drape conveying only the suggestion of the young woman beneath. But the young woman was certainly there, too, the near adultness of her."[66] Playing himself and denying his incestuous gaze, Hata narrates a scene in which he spies on Sunny provocatively dancing for two young men at a party:

> I had never seen her move in such a way. I knew what her body was like, of course, from when she was a young girl, and later, too, when she'd swim or sunbathe at the house in a bikini, which was hardly a covering at all. She was always lithe and strong and sturdy-limbed, never too skinny or too softly feminine. I saw her as I believe any good father would, with pride and wonder and the most innocent (if impossible) measure of longing, an aching hope that she stay forever pristine, unsoiled.[67]

He attempts to justify his incestuous voyeurism: "I saw her as I believe any good father would." And yet his "longing" for his daughter is sexualized ("I knew what her body was like, of course") and contradicts his hopes for the preservation of her virginity ("that she stay forever pristine, unsoiled"). His sexual objectification of his daughter victimizes her.

Moreover, as Mary Burns attempts to mother and mentor Sunny, she critiques Hata's fatherhood by observing, "You adopted her. But you act almost guilty, as if she's someone you hurt once, or betrayed, and now you're obliged to do whatever she wishes, which is never good for anyone, much less a child."[68] Likewise, during her rant in which she calls Hata a "good Char-

---

64. Chang-rae Lee, 204.
65. Y. Lee, "Gender, Race, and the Nation," 153.
66. Chang-rae Lee, *Gesture Life*, 61.
67. Chang-rae Lee, 114.
68. Chang-rae Lee, 60.

lie," Sunny acerbically tells him, "I never needed you. I don't know why, but you needed me. But it was never the other way."[69] As the novel proceeds, it becomes clearer that Sunny is a "needed" unconscious substitute for the woman he "hurt once," the comfort woman K whom Doc Hata meets in Burma where he serves as a medic for the Japanese Imperial army.[70] And yet, he proceeds to victimize Sunny in the same way he victimized K during the war—through sexual objectification.

Ordered and patronized by Captain Ono to guard K from the other soldiers in the infirmary, Doc Hata gets to know K. Like Song and Gallimard, they perform a fantasy and play roles in a context outside of war and imprisonment: Together, they tell each other about their families and fantasize about being "other people, somewhere else, with the most ordinary reasons for keeping such furtive company, just our whispering voices apparent to the night air."[71] Unable to distinguish between fantasy and reality, he believes he has fallen in love with her, despite her sexual enslavement as a comfort woman. Hata plays himself as much as he plays K in their fantasy. He narrates the time he has sex with her, or rather assaults her, as she is enslaved and she appears to be sleeping at the time: "She was sleeping, or pretending to sleep, or somehow forcing herself to, and she did not move or speak or make anything but the shallowest of breaths, even as I was casting myself upon her. [. . .] Then it was all quite swift and natural, as chaste as it could ever be."[72] Here, Hata disguises his rape, "casting [him]self upon her," as paradoxically "chaste." The lack of her consent in the action and circumstances of enslavement is further suggested when he finds her crying afterward.[73] In his analysis of this scene, critic Hamilton Carroll describes Hata's objectification of K: "By the end of the passage, she has turned from an inscrutable, sleeping woman to a piece of art: 'she lay *as if* she were the sculpture of a recumbent girl and not a real girl at all' (emphasis added)."[74] Carroll goes on to argue, "This twinned identification and domination, which culminates in Hata's rape of K and her death at the hands of his fellow soldiers, is evident from their first encounter, in which K recognizes Hata to be Korean."[75] Likewise, critic Christopher Lee concludes *A Gesture Life* expresses its anticolonial nationalism through its criticism of patriarchy and misogyny; the novel frames misogynistic militarism and rape

---

69. Chang-rae Lee, 96.
70. Chang-rae Lee, 60, 96. Y. Lee, "Gender, Race, and the Nation," 153.
71. Chang-rae Lee, *Gesture Life*, 252.
72. Chang-rae Lee, 260.
73. Chang-rae Lee, 261.
74. Carroll, "Traumatic Patriarchy," 602.
75. Carroll, 603.

as forms of imperialism.⁷⁶ In an illuminating moment, K incisively shouts at Hata in a manner that resonates with Sunny's rejection of him earlier in the novel:

> I don't want your help! [. . .] I never wanted your help. Can't you heed me? Can't you leave me be? You think you love me but what you really want you don't yet know because you are young and decent. But I will tell you now, it is my sex. The thing of my sex. If you could cut it from me and keep it with you like a pelt or favorite stone, that would be all. You are a decent man, Lieutenant, but really you are not any different from the rest.⁷⁷

K, who is later gang-raped and murdered by the camp's soldiers, lays bare Hata's perception of her as a sexual object—previously a sculpture, now "a pelt or favorite stone"—and compares him to the other soldiers who rape the comfort women in the camp. Despite K's unveiling of the truth of her victimization, Hata clings to his player masculinity and refuses to leave her alone.

Like Hata, Henry Park also objectifies and plays women of Asian descent. In *Native Speaker*, he recalls

> the single infidelity during my marriage [. . .] with a Chinese woman whose importer husband I was attempting to encounter and track. [. . .] The woman's husband regularly beat her, and I used this to my advantage, terribly, as I was the retailer who would extend her warmth and tenderness on his buying visits. Of course I didn't love her, I hardly liked her, but she was so pitiable and I so fearful and ambitious for my new career that we made love on several occasions in a washroom of their Brooklyn warehouse. But it didn't help any, I was still shut out, and I stopped going to the display store altogether. I eventually reached her husband through his importers' associations, which would later blackball him for undercutting his fellow members.⁷⁸

His playing here imitates player imperialist masculinity and paternalistic figures like Kwang, who also plays women. Eager to please his white boss, Henry is quick to deceive the objects of his espionage, even Kwang, who becomes a father-figure to him. As he works for Kwang, Henry and John "joke[ ] a little more, [. . .] like regular American men, faking, dipping, juking."⁷⁹ Like Hata, who considers himself a "fraud," Henry imitates the duplicitous behavior of

---

76. Christopher Lee, "Form-Giving," 107–8.
77. Chang-rae Lee, *Gesture Life*, 300.
78. Chang-rae Lee, *Native Speaker*, 207–8.
79. Chang-rae Lee, 179.

white "American" manhood.[80] Although they are subordinated by whites and paternalistic figures and fail to perform the masculinity of the white American family man of the era, they victimize Asian women to reclaim their masculinities. In this way, they mimic the player imperialist masculinity of invisible American imperialism and its political incursion into the Middle East in the 1990s.

Likewise, the US and Iraq were victims and perpetrators of the ideology of player imperialist masculinity during the Gulf War. The US had dual aims in Gulf War: to secure political power for itself in the international arena and to stabilize finance capital through reclaiming Kuwait and protecting Saudi Arabia—the two nations that supplied some of the greatest energy sources to the West—from Iraqi invasions. The financial crisis in Iraq initially precipitated the invasion of Kuwait. Virtually unaffected by the Cold War, Iraq nevertheless emerged from the Iran-Iraq War (1980–88) in a severe financial crisis.[81] In the United States, domestic oil produced more energy than the other sources of natural gas and coal, but by the 1970s, domestic production of oil had been exhausted, and the US became dependent on imported oil from countries in the Middle East that belonged to the Organization of Petroleum Exporting Countries (OPEC).[82] Economist Zachary Carter points out that in the United States, the cost of oil rocketed in 1972 and continued to rise when OPEC set an oil embargo to retaliate against the US for siding with Israel during the Yom Kippur War.[83] During the Iran-Iraq War, Saddam Hussein had borrowed large funds from Iraq's wealthier neighboring countries in the Gulf such as Saudi Arabia, Kuwait, the United Arab Emirates, Egypt, Syria, Jordan, and the stateless Palestine Liberation Organization (PLO), but he was unable to repay the debts afterward.[84] Moreover, Iraq was unable to yield enough oil to fill the quotas specified by OPEC.[85] Out of financial desperation, Iraq deployed a hundred thousand soldiers and two thousand tanks to invade Kuwait on August

---

80. Chang-rae Lee, *Gesture Life*, 274.
81. In "The Cold War and the Middle East," historian Salim Yaqub writes, "The Cold War in the Middle East was never a contest between equals" (12). Finlan, *Gulf War*, 15.
82. Freeman, *American Empire*, 296; Finlan, *Gulf War*, 15.
83. Carter, *Price of Peace*, 477.
84. Finlan, *Gulf War*, 15.
85. Finlan explains, "More oil on the international market meant lowering prices per barrel, further reducing Iraq's ability to resolve its financial problems. OPEC had called for a limit of 22 million barrels a day but by 1990 oil production had already exceeded that figure by approximately two million barrels and the price of oil had dipped to $18 a barrel by the spring of 1990. The major culprits in this deliberate overproduction were Kuwait and the UAE whose strategy was to deliberately drive down the price of oil so that more nations became dependent on OPEC oil" (*Gulf War*, 15–16).

2, 1990.⁸⁶ Iraq justified its takeover of Kuwait by claiming that Kuwait had pilfered oil from Iraq's Rumaila oilfield, that Iraq's debts to Kuwait were largely a result of Kuwait's unjust oil overproduction, and, finally, that Kuwait had long been planning to take over Iraqi territory.⁸⁷ Referring to Kuwait as its colonial "19th Province," Iraqi forces engaged in looting at the start of the invasion.⁸⁸ As capitalist competition to the US, Iraq, like the Asian American characters in this chapter, also mimicked the political practice of player imperialist masculinity of the family man and law enforcer in it its invasion of Kuwait.

PLAYING DETERRENCE AND MONUMENTS OF FAILURE

As I mentioned earlier, the protagonists of Lee's novels fail to reproduce the Gulf War masculine paragon of family men and law enforcers; they are consultants acting as spies, ineffective military officers, and disconnected members of society—unable to emotionally provide for others. As Gulf War–period literature, both of Lee's novels, *Native Speaker* and *A Gesture Life* bear the traces of player imperialist masculinity, which is characterized as unmarked and invisible in ways that are analogous to how the Gulf War was fought, through virtual warfare and its attendant surprise, unanticipated tactics of "shock and awe."⁸⁹ As historians have noted, the Gulf War marked the first major war following the end of the Cold War.⁹⁰ But the ideological polarization of imperialism,⁹¹ a relic of the Cold War, nevertheless persisted but in a different form: Instead of a conflict between capitalism and communism in the former era, the Gulf War era evinced a conflict between competing capitalisms, represented by George H. W. Bush and Saddam Hussein. Writing during the Gulf War, Dixit and Nalebuff contrast the strategy of the "zero-sum game" in which "one person's gain is another person's loss" with the strategy of the "prisoner's dilemma" in which "there are possibilities for mutual advantage as well as conflict of interest; both prisoners prefer the no-confession results to its opposite."⁹² In other words, the zero-sum game, in which there can only be one winner, is diametrically opposed to the prisoners' dilemma

---

86. Finlan, 26.
87. Finlan, 25.
88. Finlan, 75.
89. Finlan, 31, 33; Tindall and Shi, *America*, 1531.
90. Finlan, *Gulf War*, 7–8.
91. Finlan, 8.
92. Dixit and Nalebuff, *Thinking Strategically*, 14.

of cooperative survival.[93] The Gulf War conflict could have been a prisoners' dilemma of cooperative survival and gain between formally and similarly capitalist Iraqi and US ideologies—war spending to fix their broken economies and to assert their imperialisms and ideologies (in the US context, the aim of democracy was a red herring)—but was, instead, turned into a zero-sum game between American and Iraqi capitalist imperialisms. McAlister argues that US involvement in the Middle East has often been strategized as "containment and cooptation."[94] What became apparent in the Gulf War was that there was a conversion of a prisoners' dilemma of joint strategies to a zero-sum game between imperialist opponents which was unmarked by the American public. In direct contrast, the domestic conflicts between African Americans and Asian Americans in New York and Los Angeles during this period were marked by the media. Violent conflicts between racial minority groups that were driven by stereotypes adopted from white American discourses came to a head during the race riots in the early 1990s. As Gulf War–period literature, *Native Speaker* and *A Gesture Life* reflect the period's player imperialist masculinity of personable family man and world police, which influenced the war's tactical impulses of constructing adversarial difference out of similarity (victimization) for the purposes of white American imperial gain, surveillance, and (virtual) invisibility. In reflecting the Gulf War period's player imperialist masculinity, the novels also invoke the hegemonic logic of deterrent, virtual warfare and the attendant apocalypse in their depictions of suburban life.

The suburban malaise that both protagonists experience in Lee's *Native Speaker* and *A Gesture Life* during the contemporary periods of their narratives marks the failure of their actions and playing. Suburban despondency depicts the American failure to acknowledge the Gulf War (despite the token "Support Our Troops" yellow ribbons that were tied to cars during this time) and the invisible commodification of people that characterizes finance capitalism, which was concurrently on the rise during this time after the Wall Street bust at the end of the 1980s. Critic Jodi Kim argues that *Native Speaker*, which

---

93. For example, in *Thinking Strategically* Dixit and Nalebuff describe the Iran-Iraq War as a prisoners' dilemma: "Iran and Iraq's situation is analogous to that of the KGB's prisoners. Each of them found it dominant to confess: if the one held out, the other got a better deal by confessing; if one confessed, the other would be foolish not to. Hence whatever one does, the other would be foolish not to. Hence whatever one does, the other wants to confess. But that's true for both. And when both confess, each gets a harsh sentence. Again, the selfish pursuit of one's interests leads to an inferior outcome. When neither confesses, the outcome is better for both. The problem is how to attain such cooperation given the competition to obtain an especially good deal for oneself" (92). Likewise, they assert, when it comes to fixing their economies, "Politicians, too, are prisoners of the same dilemma" (93).

94. McAlister, *Epic Encounters*, 2.

mentions the lucrative job prospects of the "Wall Street" "boom time" during the 1980s, frames the stereotypes of Asian Americans as model minority and yellow peril as intimately related to their ownership of diverse types of capital.[95] Likewise, critic J. Paul Narkunas claims that *Native Speaker* reflects on the state of the human as a kind of capital insofar as Henry Park is stuck between the sphere of international market desires and the political control of ethnic minorities in the US.[96] Symptomatic of the proliferation of finance capital in the late 1980s and 1990s—an offshoot of Keynesian deficit spending—the American, specifically New York City, suburban settings of *Native Speaker* and *A Gesture Life* represent the historical suburban "ideal of the freestanding single family dwelling with lawn, carport, and a bedroom for everyone came, conditioned by ingenious community planning, energetic marketing, new freeways, and the GI Bill within a larger range of families than ever before."[97] At the same time, the suburbs signify a subordinate space to the urban metropole.[98] Moreover, suburbs promoted Keynesian deficit spending to boost the economy: "Between 1990 and 2000 alone, fourteen million housing units were constructed. Home construction and sales became a major economic driving force, with real estate industry employment jumping from less than a million in 1980 to over a million and a half in 2000."[99] According to critic Seongho Yoon, the suburbs, specifically those of New York City in both novels, signify postwar prosperity, and yet capital does not reside with racial minorities who live in the suburbs in *Native Speaker*. In her analysis of the novel, critic Klara Szmańko states that neither Korean Americans nor African Americans have control of significant capital.[100] As failed simulacra of the metropole, the novels' suburban settings are monuments of failure: They represent the protagonists' failed masculinities in imitating player imperialist masculinity and deterring apocalyptic moments in *Native Speaker* and *A Gesture Life*.

In *A Gesture Life*, Doc Hata, who lives a virtual, "gesture" life of inefficacy and preventative measures, attempts to operate according to the logic of

---

95. Chang-rae Lee, *Native Speaker*, 164; J. Kim, "From Mee-Gook to Gook," 135.
96. Narkunas, "Surfing the Long Waves," 328.
97. Yoon, "'Being in a Place,'" 273.
98. In *American Empire* Freeman writes, "People in many circumstances benefited from the economic boom, but the greatest transformation took place in the new suburbs that sprang up across the nation. During the 1950s, a way of life blossomed that came to be seen as the embodiment of what it meant to be American: racially homogeneous, low-density neighborhoods of single-family homes; automobility; tight-knit nuclear families with stay-at-home mothers; and ever-rising levels of consumption. [...] For better or worse, American suburban-style living and its cultural accoutrements came to be a measuring rod for social mores and economic achievement across the globe" (114).
99. Freeman, *American Empire*, 125, 450.
100. Szmańko, "Conflict between African Americans," 82.

deterrence. While *Native Speaker* centers on an actual spy, Henry, *A Gesture Life* focuses on a protagonist who also often finds himself disempowered, on the "outside looking in," and spying on societies in which he lives, specifically on his daughter during her teenage years and on the object of his affection, K, at a Japanese war camp.[101] In his later adult life, Hata does his best to assimilate as a good American, changing his Japanese name Jiro to Franklin (after Benjamin Franklin) and adopting white American customs and acting as a white American family man, such as by always sending thank-you notes to his neighbors.[102] Such actions are preventative measures against rejection, even though these assimilative actions appear racially marked.[103] On the other hand, Hata feels that his Japanese surname "seems both odd and delightful to people, as well as somehow town-affirming."[104] And yet his othering last name actually "affirms" its homogeneous whiteness since he still finds that it "seemed people took an odd interest in telling me that I wasn't *unwelcome*."[105] Despite the vandalism and pranks he experiences in town on account of his race, he goes out of his way to please his neighbors in Bedley Run so much so that his teenage daughter Sunny tells him in a rebellious rant: "You make a whole life out of gestures and politeness. You're always having to be the ideal partner and colleague. [. . .] You know what I overheard down at the card shop? How nice it is to have such a 'good Charlie' to organize the garbage and sidewalk-cleaning schedule."[106] Although he attempts to live according to a logic of deterrence, Hata's "polite" gesture life by which he feels burdened and cursed, since it does not really lead to assimilation to American society, exemplifies the double-bind of the model minority: That is, the mimicry of white hegemonic masculinity only perpetuates the minority and inferior status of Asian Americans. In this way, his playerism is a form of survival in an environment that refuses to accept him. Moreover, Hata's failure to assimilate, despite his model minority performances, demonstrates the harm of the long-standing model minority and yellow peril stereotypes of Asian Americans. His failures in becoming American and an actual surgeon—a career to which he aspires but never attains—lead him to conclude that "nearly every soul I've

---

101. Chang-rae Lee, *Gesture Life*, 356.
102. Y. Lee, "Gender, Race, and the Nation," 153; Chang-rae Lee, *Gesture Life*, 44.
103. In "Transcending Ethnicity," critic Young-Oak Lee points out, "Hata, in choosing Franklin as his first name, reveals his desire to associate himself with a morally upright nation. He has chosen a nation that would provide him with 'the sole legitimate criterion' to which he can return—the land of freedom, liberty and equality" (72).
104. Chang-rae Lee, *Gesture Life*, 2.
105. Chang-rae Lee, 3.
106. Chang-rae Lee, 4, 95.

closely known has come to some dread or grave misfortune."[107] Although he is called the healing "Doc Hata" by the townspeople of Bedley Run on account of his medical supply store, the stereotype of the yellow peril overdetermines his identity, and he causes everyone around him to experience pain.

This tension from his oppositional identities produces tragedy in his life and is reflective of the larger political mechanism breaking down during the Gulf War. From witnessing K's gang rape and dismemberment to assisting in his daughter's abortion, Hata experiences many apocalyptic moments that expose his fundamentally virtual, gesture life, which according to Baudrillard, were the defining features of the Gulf War. Baudrillard writes of the Gulf War: The "media promote the war, the war promotes the media, and the advertising competes with the war. Promotion is the most thick-skinned parasite in our culture."[108] Reducing the tautological relationship between the media and war to the parasitic nature of cultural promotion, Baudrillard decries the technological immediacy of the virtual Gulf War. He states, "Everything is therefore transposed into the virtual, and we are confronted with a virtual apocalypse, a hegemony ultimately much more dangerous than real apocalypse."[109] Gulf War tactics such as "Instant Thunder," which was an offensive air strike that would be quick but precise, fueled Baudrillard's anxiety about an "instant" virtual apocalypse, which he viewed as "much more dangerous than real apocalypse."[110] He names February 22, the start of Operation Desert Storm, as "the day of the Apocalypse: the day of the unleashing of the land offensive behind its curtain of bombs. [. . .] While the tanks advanced to the assault on Kuwait [. . .]"[111] The Gulf War was thus an apocalyptic form of military deterrence.

Despite living according to the masculinist logic of preventative deterrence, Doc Hata fuels and experiences multiple apocalyptic moments. He fails to assist in the comfort woman K's suicide by shooting her when she asks him to; as a result, she is gang raped by the Japanese army and dismembered. Like the players of this study, the Japanese soldiers feel entitled to their power and objectify anyone—in this instance, K, when she cuts one of the soldiers—who threatens their masculinities:

> Then they were all gone. I walked the rest of the way to the clearing. The air was cooler there, the treetops shading the falling sun. Mostly it was like any

---

107. Chang-rae Lee, 346.
108. Baudrillard, *Gulf War*, 31.
109. Baudrillard, 27.
110. Baudrillard, 27. "Instant Thunder" replaced the denigrated prolonged 1960s Vietnam explosive strategy called "Rolling Thunder" (Finlan, *Gulf War*, 31).
111. Baudrillard, *Gulf War*, 78.

other place I had ever been. Yet I could not smell or hear or see as I did my medic's work. I could not feel my hands as they gathered, nor could I feel the weight of such remains. And I could not sense that other, tiny, elfin form I eventually discovered, miraculously whole, I could not see the figured legs and feet, the utter, blessed digitation of the hands. Nor could I see the face, the perfected cheek and brow. Its pristine sleep still unbroken, undisturbed. And I could not know what I was doing, or remember any part.[112]

Hata's disembodiment during this apocalyptic moment documents his trauma. The slow, methodical manner in which he gathers K's remains and the remains of her fetus attempts to reverse the explosive immediacy of her rape and murder. Despite his failure in protecting K, he insists on his player masculinity by paternalistically gathering her remains. Likewise, the detail in which he writes about assisting in Sunny's abortion contrasts with the apocalyptic immediacy of the event that is a severe conflict of interest:

The doctor was right about my presence and participation. For what I saw that evening at the clinic endures, remaining unaltered, preserved. And if in my life I've witnessed the most terrible of things, I've seen what no decent being should ever look upon and have to hold in close remembrance, perhaps it means I should be left to the cold device of history, my likeness festooning the ramparts of every house and town and district of man.[113]

Experiencing apocalyptic moments—"the most terrible of things"—in his life perpetuates Hata's deterrent, gesture life. These seemingly instantaneous apocalyptic moments caricature his inefficacious, effeminate life so that it is his virtual "likeness," not even him, that "festoon[s] the ramparts of every house [. . .] of man." Through his gestures, Doc Hata continually performs and exposes but fails to realize the player imperialist masculinity of his contemporary Gulf War era.

Hata's violent failures to care for K and Sunny are part of his deeper anxiety about his lack of title. Discouraged by Captain Ono from his dream of becoming of physician because he is ethnically Korean and lives a "gesture life," Hata is haunted by a nightmare in which a young pregnant woman shows up at his medical supply store and requires immediate assistance for the spontaneous birth of her child.[114] Failing to care for another woman, when called upon to perform an emergency caesarean section, he "realized then it was a travesty and [he] was not a surgeon, that [he] had never cut into living flesh.

---

112. Chang-rae Lee, *Gesture Life*, 305.
113. Chang-rae Lee, 345.
114. Chang-rae Lee, 266.

That [he] was a fraud and a coward and should not have coveted and accepted as [he] had done the confidence of people, their singular regard and trust."[115] This nightmare reveals his latent and manifest fantasies of being a real doctor only to reveal that he is truly a "fraud" and "coward." Here, Hata is portrayed as an effeminate and passive model minority who will negatively affect others (as the yellow peril) with his "gesture life." His gesturing ultimately reflects the contemporary virtuality of the Gulf War.

Like Hata, Henry Park lives a deterrent, gesturing life as he performs the role of the model minority in order to maintain his cover as an undercover agent:

> And yet you may know me. I am an amiable man. I can be most personable, if not charming, and whatever I possess in this life is more or less the result of a talent I have for making you feel good about yourself when you are with me. In this sense I am not a seducer. I am hardly seen. I won't speak untruths to you, I won't pass easy compliments or odious offerings of flattery. I make do with on-hand materials, what I can chip out of you, your natural ore. Then I fuel the fire of your most secret vanity.[116]

Henry's deterrent performance as an Asian American spy—preventing his cover from being blown—inflects the binary stereotypes of the model minority and yellow peril that typically subjectify the Asian American: He conveys the inscrutability and shiftiness of his interiority through such opaque declaration as, "And yet you *may* know me"—meaning you may not—and "I make do with on-hand materials, what I can chip out of you, your natural ore."[117] The line "Then I fuel the fire of your most secret vanity" reveals the strategy of his manipulation. He uses his "gentle-looking" face to game the objects of his espionage.[118] The shocking admission of his manipulative methods as an undercover agent continually casts a pall over his model minority gestures: "I am an amiable man. I can be most personable, if not charming, *and whatever I possess in this life is more or less the result of a talent I have for making you feel good about yourself when you are with me.*"[119] His amiability is his conniving talent that he uses to spy on his subjects. As a spy, he anticipates an apocalyptic exposure of his cover: No matter how he thinks he has ingratiated himself

---

115. Chang-rae Lee, 274.
116. Chang-rae Lee, *Native Speaker*, 7.
117. Chang-rae Lee, 7, my emphasis.
118. Chang-rae Lee, 92.
119. Chang-rae Lee, 92, my emphasis.

with his wife or in his local community, he and those associated are constantly threatened as targets of violence.

Like Hata, Henry experiences an apocalyptic moment when he witnesses the death of his seven-year-old son, Mitt, who is suffocated by a group of bullying, racist white children who had called him "mutt, mongrel, half-breed, banana, twinkie":

> I bent down and started blowing into Mitt's mouth. Lelia cried that she'd tried already. She kept screaming about it and I had to tell her to shut up. I didn't know that I was doing. I pulled open his mouth and blew anyway, a dozen times, a hundred, pumping down on his chest with all my weight, eventually pounding on him as if he were solid ground. I shudder to think that I might have injured him, hurt his delicate breastbone or ribs, or worse, that his last thought was to ask why his father was harming him.[120]

Like Hata, after K's death, Henry has an involuntary reaction ("I didn't know what I was doing. [. . .] I shudder to think that I might have injured him") as a response to the trauma of this apocalyptic moment that was driven by racism. Unlike Hata, Henry does not fuel this tragedy except for the possible neglect of his son. In addition to his dual model minority and yellow peril status, his ineffectuality during this instantaneous, apocalyptic moment hinges on what Tina Chen calls his denigrated "invisibility."[121] The successes of Henry as a corporate spy and Doc Hata as a fraudulent performer are likewise predicated on their invisibility.

As I mentioned, the race riots of the early 1990s drew attention to otherwise politically "invisible" but racially marked minorities: African Americans and Asian Americans. In other words, through media coverage and advancements in surveillance, images of police brutality against African Americans and those of African Americans and Korean Americans imperialistically waging violence against one another became visible to the American public. As in Vietnam War–period literature, minorities became visible criminals as the US policed the world, explicitly during the Vietnam War and implicitly during the Gulf War. On the other hand, the Gulf War was a significant event that marked a new era of conflict between the US and countries in the Middle East but was largely unseen and unknown by the American public, as evidenced in Lee's two novels. And yet, media coverage of the race riots proliferated during the early 1990s. As a result, surveillance during the race riots made vis-

---

120. Chang-rae Lee, 103, 105.
121. Chen, "Impersonating," 638.

ible to the American public "a mercenary Korean American shopkeeper and a thieving African American in their ostensibly natural states."[122] Conversely, surveillance was used secretly by the military during the Gulf War to play the odds, deter the enemy, and advance the American position in the war, covertly securing the capitalist monopoly on oil. The invisibility of the international Gulf War to the American public and its narrative absence is contrasted by the visible narrative of minority conflict, which reflected white American imperialism, in the contemporary media and in *Native Speaker* and *A Gesture Life*. For example, in *Native Speaker*, John Kwang ironically marvels at the hopeful relations between minority children during one of his speeches while campaigning for the mayoral position in New York City: "My friends, [. . .] I have something to tell you today. An incredible bit of news. Black and Korean children, as some in this city would have you believe, aren't yet boycotting one another's corner lemonade stands."[123] Through the recognizable humor of his comment, Kwang reveals the visibility of the era's race riots. Moreover, this tongue-in-cheek reference to the Flatbush Boycott of 1990 indicates Kwang's suburban sense of removal from the Brooklyn boycott. Even though the suburbs are the setting of deterrent lifestyles and apocalyptic moments for the novels' protagonists, both novels epitomize the postwar suburban malaise that was widely felt during the Gulf War to such an extent that American society did not acknowledge that the nation was at war.

Such suburban despondency—of being part of the coveted metropole but not quite—is described by Hata in his reflection on being perpetually remembered by the townspeople of Bedley Run, a geographical suburban sprawl, as the model minority.[124] He resigns himself to being uncomfortably anonymous when he goes on to narrate: "I must wonder then, too, whether a man like me should be happy enough with the accrued comforts of his life, accepting the minor losses."[125] For Hata, there is no alternative for his subjectivity beyond the acceptance of his lot of anonymity. Likewise, Henry Park conveys his frustration and boredom with endless sprawl of suburban life in the 1990s, which coincided with the endlessness of the virtual Gulf War, when he describes his father's compromise in confronting racism: "He came to know that the sky was never the limit, that the truer height for him was more like a handful of vegetable stores that would eventually run themselves, making him enough money that he could live in a majestic white house in Westchester and call

---

122. Chang, *Writing the Ghetto*, 167.
123. Chang-rae Lee, *Native Speaker*, 150.
124. Chang-rae Lee, *Gesture Life*, 201.
125. Chang-rae Lee, 201.

himself a rich man."[126] Park describes his father as metonymically represented through his vegetable stores and its commodities of produce. Robert Perrucci and Earl Wysong coined the term "the invisible class empire" in their book, *The New Class Society* (1999), to describe the "superclass" that controls joint political and corporate power. Dominated by the "invisible class empire" of advanced finance capital, Henry's father represents the visible small business owner who is racially condemned as an "Oriental Jew"[127] by his customers and blamed for the ills of domestic American society on account of his race.[128] By contrast, international American imperialism, which has always served as a model for small ethnic businesses in the United States, remains "virtual" and invisible in the form of the Gulf War as it ironically flies under the radar of detection in both novels.

DETERRENT GESTURES DURING THE GULF WAR

In expressing their Asian American player subjectivities, Doc Hata and Henry Park fail in performing the era's player imperialist masculinity of the world police playing family man. *A Gesture Life* reflects the apocalyptic horrors of a seemingly "fake" deterrent war as "Doc" Hata is accused by his daughter of "mak[ing] a whole life out of gestures and politeness" and by his army superior of "too much depend[ing] upon generous fate and gesture."[129] Hata and Henry nevertheless cling to their failed masculinities and play and objectify women of color. Subjectified as a model minority and effeminate man who relies on "gesture" throughout his life, Hata admits that he is a "fraud" and a "coward" and "should not have coveted and accepted as [he] had done the confidence of people, their singular regard and trust."[130] Like the players of this

---

126. Chang-rae Lee, *Native Speaker*, 333.
127. Chang-rae Lee, 53.
128. In *The Communist Manifesto*, Karl Marx and Friedrich Engels famously describe the reification, or the commodification of labor relations by stating, "The bourgeoisie cannot exist without constantly revolutionizing the instruments of production, and thereby the relations of production, and with them the whole relations of society. [. . .] Constant revolutionizing of production, uninterrupted disturbance of all social conditions, everlasting uncertainty and agitation distinguish the bourgeois epoch from all earlier ones. All fixed, fast-frozen relations, with their train of ancient and venerable prejudices and opinions, are swept away, all new formed ones become antiquated before they can ossify" (771). However, this definition of the commodity fetish, later developed as reification by Georg Lukács, referenced early forms of capitalism whereas finance capitalism involves several layers of reification and invisibility as Robert Perrucci and Earl Wysong conceptualize in their book, *The New Class Society*.
129. Baudrillard, *Gulf War*, 68; Chang-rae Lee, *Gesture Life*, 95, 266.
130. Chang-rae Lee, 274.

chapter—the constantly gesturing Hata and the ever-performing spy Henry Park—the player imperialist masculinity of the Gulf War is a violent "illusion": Baudrillard describes the Gulf War as,

> fake war, deceptive war, not even the illusion but the disillusion of war, linked not only to defensive calculation, which translates into the monstrous prophylaxis of this military machine, but also the mental disillusion of the combatants themselves, and to the global disillusion of everyone else by means of information. For deterrence is a total machine (it is the true war machine), and it not only operates at the heart of the event—where electronic coverage of the war devoured time and space, where virtuality (the decoy, programming, the anticipation of the end) devoured all the oxygen of war like a fuel-air explosive bomb—it also operates in our heads.[131]

Baudrillard compares the apocalypse of a virtual war here to a "fuel-air explosive bomb" that is simultaneously real and "operates in our heads." Asian American playerism, exemplified by Hata and Henry, reveals the apocalyptically virtual ways in which the US played Iraq and the Middle East during the Gulf War, and the other looming apocalypse of its cover being blown.

Because the Gulf War seemed to be slow and attritional, the deterrent, playing-the-odds virtual war continued despite the official end of the Gulf War in 1991.[132] Nevertheless, the apocalyptic horror of a virtual war is that it is endless, which is reflected in the geographical sprawl of, and the endless consumer spending signified by, the suburbia of Lee's novels. Lee's suburbs are culturally valuable but failed simulacra of the metropole; they are the masculinist settings of the protagonists' deterrent lifestyles and the apocalyptic moments they fail to prevent. Reflective of the protagonists' failures and victimizations, the suburbs are subordinate to the American metropole but also targeted areas for racism. As this chapter has argued, Lee's *Native Speaker* and *A Gesture Life* are Gulf War–era texts and index the illusory, masculinist

---

131. Baudrillard, *Gulf War,* 49, 68.
132. In *The Gulf War* Tucker-Jones writes, "In 1996 things came to a head when Saddam urged his air defence forces to ignore both no-fly zone and attack 'any air target of the aggressors.' These transgressions of the no-fly zones and Iraq's failure to comply with UNSCOM helped spark Operation Desert Fox two years later. American and British aircraft conducted a four-day bombardment of Iraqi targets, including air defence installations. This proved to be a failure as Iraq remained defiant and UNSCOM was expelled. The Iraqi Air Force and Air Defence Command (IADC) continued to taunt those aircrafts, patrolling the no-fly zones largely with impunity. According to the US Joint Chiefs of Staff Chairman, Air Force General Richard Myers, over a three-year period Iraqi artillery fired at coalition aircraft more than 1,000 times, launched 600 rockets and fired nearly 60 surface-to-air missiles. [. . .] Finally, in 2003 Operation Iraqi Freedom drove Saddam Hussein from power" (126–27).

political and military tactics of converting a prisoners' dilemma of capitalism and dominance in the oil market to a zero-sum game of imperial dominance or constructing adversarial difference out of similarity using the military tactic of deterring apocalypse. And yet, Baudrillard argues that the virtuality of the Gulf War was itself apocalyptic.[133] In contrast to the tautological, polarized Cold War, Baudrillard argues that the Gulf War is a large decoy that "deceive[s] itself" in failing to be a real and largely bodily-fought war.[134] In Lee's portrayals of Asian American players, masculinity is a simulacral decoy in both texts; it is an aspiration that distracts but is never attained.

Even though Asian American men have been historically feminized and African American, Latinx, and Native American men have been discursively hypermasculinized, the hyperboles of their masculinities render them racially marked—that is, inferior outsiders. Comparing Asian American and African American masculinities, Chong Chon-Smith writes, "Minority masculinities cannot surpass the universal power center of white national manhood, and black vis-à-vis Asian stereotypes articulated in certain combinations reinforce this architecture codified onto the Asian and black male body."[135] Moreover, critic Cathy J. Cohen "remind[s] us of the numerous ways that sexuality and sexual deviance from a prescribed norm have been used to demonize and to oppress various segments of the population, even some classified under the label 'heterosexual.'"[136] The Asian American characters of my study, Ichiro Yamada, Song Liling, Henry Park, and Doc Hata, oscillate between the hyperbolic, racial performances of effeminacy and hypermasculinity, that is, in playing others. Although Doc Hata and Park fail to obtain ethical manhood, they nevertheless expose the world police qua family man, imperialist masculinity of the Gulf War era through mimicry. And yet, like their Asian American simulacra, even when exposed, white hegemonic masculinity clung to its playerism during the Gulf War. The invisibility of the player imperialist, hegemonic, heterosexual white American masculinity continues to inform American foreign policy in the untraceable and seemingly endless War on Terror, which I will discuss in the next chapter.

---

133. In *The Gulf War*, Baudrillard describes the Gulf War as "war stripped of its passions, its phantasms, its finery, its veils, its violence, its images; war stripped bare by its technicians even, and then reclothed by them with all the artifices of electronics, as though with a second skin. But these too are a kind of decoy that technology sets up before itself. Saddam Hussein's decoys still aim to deceive the enemy, whereas the American technological decoy only aims to deceive itself" (64).

134. Baudrillard, 64.

135. Chon-Smith, *East Meets Black*, 4–5.

136. Cohen, "Punks, Bulldaggers, and Welfare Queens," 457.

CHAPTER 4

Playing the Endless War

The Simulacra of Illegitimacy after 9/11

The Asian American players in the texts I examined in the previous chapter declined to embrace ethical manhood during the masculine ideological conflation of family man and world police characteristic of the Gulf War; on the other hand, the American "victories" of the War on Terror, which included the execution of Saddam Hussein in 2006 for war crimes and the assassination of Osama bin Laden in 2011, and the public acknowledgment of US imperialism created an environment of optimism in which Asian American players could ethically relate to the women they had previously objectified. This new development can best be seen in Viet Thanh Nguyen's *The Sympathizer* (2015) and Frances Khirallah Noble's *The New Belly Dancer of the Galaxy* (2007). The player protagonists of each of these novels self-reflexively expose the illegitimacy, the ultimate bluff of playing, which structured the War on Terror and the Financial Crisis of 2007–8 that it caused. Like Chang-rae Lee's Henry Park, Nguyen's narrator is a self-declared spy. The sympathizer's introductory self-portrait—"I am a spy, a sleeper, a spook, a man of two faces. [. . .] I am not some misunderstood mutant from a comic book or a horror movie"—is a deliberate nod to Ellison's invisible man who memorably describes himself as "an invisible man. No, I am not a spook like those who haunted Edgar Allan Poe; nor am I one of your Hollywood-movie ectoplasms. I am a man of substance, of flesh and bone, fiber and liquids—and I might even be said to possess a mind. I am invisible, understand, simply because people refuse to see me."[1] Unlike Okada's Ichiro and Lee's Doc Hata, the sympathizer's self-comparison to a famous African American literary figure draws parallels between the racial discrimination that African Americans and Asian Americans have historically experienced. Despite this racial self-awareness, the sympathizer is a player by trade. His depiction as "a man of two faces" is a preemptive disclaimer of his honesty—as a spy, he is a self-avowed player and, in this way, his masculinity reflects the player imperialist masculinity of the War on Terror contemporary to the novel's production even though the narrative takes place during and after the Vietnam War. Living in the US during the seductive and illegitimate War on Terror, the Arab American protagonist of Noble's *The New Belly Dancer of the Galaxy*, Kahlil Gibran Hourani, nicknamed Kali, likewise plays women. When he first starts dating his wife Sophie, he cannot tell her apart from her three sisters.[2] Perpetually dishonest with his wife, he has an affair with his client Jane Plain and is thereafter disempowered by Homeland Security, which interrogates him for being a terrorist during the War on Terror. Both the unnamed sympathizer and Kali reflect preemptive US playerism during the War on Terror, but unlike the previous protagonists of this study, they disavow their playing when it is mirrored back to them by supernatural ghosts and haunting memories. Their recognition coincided with public reckoning with US imperialism after 9/11 and the War on Terror.

Although the War on Terror officially ended in 2013, the US continues to fight this endless and playing-the-odds virtual war as it did during and after the Gulf War in 1991. Freeman writes that the 9/11 attacks, which initiated the War on Terror, began a new era in American history. September 11 shocked the US: No foreign attacks had occurred on the continental US since 1814, and most Americans had understood the US to be benevolent in its foreign dealings since World War II.[3] The events of 9/11 were a sudden wake-up call from twenty years of American isolationism.[4] Historian Paul Rogers argues that the responsibility of the al-Qaida movement or Osama bin Laden for 9/11 remains questionable.[5] And yet, the US nevertheless invaded and declared war on Afghanistan following the September 11 attacks and Iraq two years later without proper evidence that either country was responsible for the attacks.[6] Officially introducing the War on Terror as a "preemptive war" in June 2002, the US government deployed preemption as a military strategy of deterrence

---

1. Nguyen, *The Sympathizer*, 1; Ellison, *Invisible Man*, 3.
2. Noble, *New Belly Dancer*, 32.
3. Freeman, *American Empire*, 466.
4. Rogers, *Why We're Losing*, 67.
5. Rogers, 68–69.
6. Hodges, *"War on Terror" Narrative*, 16; Dower, *Cultures of War*, xxiii.

through domestic surveillance and foreign incursions such as the invasion of Iraq in March 2003.[7] Historians have argued that post–Gulf War UN sanctions against Iraq and continued American military presence in Saudi Arabia motivated the terrorist attacks on 9/11.[8] Nevertheless, like Afghanistan, Iraq became part of a complete narrative in which it was the center stage of the War on Terror.[9] Other historians, such as John Davis, have argued that Bush saw September 11 as "an opportunity to revive discourse on the new world order" that moved away from "the mistakes" of US neo-isolationism that followed his father George H. Bush's 1991 Gulf War.[10] Regardless of the motivations, many historians still hold that George W. Bush's choice to start the "fictive" and illegitimate, preemptive war was founded on many falsities and misrepresentations such as the relation between Saddam Hussein and 9/11, the false intelligence information on Iraq's weapons of mass destruction, and the notion that democracy could thrive in Iraq even as US democracy was so empirically flawed.[11] The trope of illegitimacy shaped player imperialist masculinity and its compensations for it during the War on Terror. If player imperialist masculinity was figured during the Gulf War by world police masquerading as family man, it was and has been shaped by illegitimacy in the form of simulacral orphanhood during the War on Terror. Nguyen's *The Sympathizer* and Noble's *The New Belly Dancer of the Galaxy* demonstrate two Asian American—that is, Vietnamese and Arab American—players who have lost their parents and are haunted by ghosts and disturbing memories. Their womanizing compensates for this loss of parental presence, and thus familial legitimacy, and only temporarily anchors them in the stability of intimacy and proximity with others. The Asian American players index the illegitimacy, that is, the bluff of playing, which structures the War on Terror and the consequent Financial Crisis of 2007–8.

Terrorism is the ultimate example of illegitimacy, according to the US. However, there are many nations for whom terrorism is a legitimate form of warfare. For example, Osama bin Laden attempted to defend his cause for the terrorism that initiated the War on Terror: He cited "'Crusaders,' Jews, and Western involvement in the Middle East, pointed to specific historical events and political grievances, including the establishment of US military bases in Saudi Arabia prior to the first Gulf War, Western control of Middle Eastern resources, and American backing for Israel and corrupt Arab

---

7. Dower, xxiii.
8. Atwood, *War and Empire*, 223; Allen, "Fight Against Terrorism," 25.
9. Hodges, *"War on Terror" Narrative*, 50, 41.
10. Davis, "War on Terrorism," 55.
11. Stiglitz and Bilmes, *Three Trillion Dollar War*, x.

regimes."[12] September 11 made Americans question the benignity of the dual, and usually ineffective, American policy of imperialism and democratization overseas since World War II. The evolved policing image of player imperialist masculinity was finally being questioned by the American public in popular, low cultural films such as *Team America: World Police* (2004), a spoof of American war and action films and a critique of the nebulous War on Terror. Importantly, this public self-reflection on American imperialism, but also the nebulous gains of the War on Terror (that is, getting the bad guys), influenced Asian American literature, which includes Arab American literature. Many canonical texts produced since 9/11, such as *The Sympathizer* and *The New Belly Dancer of the Galaxy*, feature Asian American players who become conscious of their illegitimacy as players and orphans through their speculative hauntings and their compensatory womanizing; the sympathizer in Nguyen's novel and Noble's protagonist Kali start to recover their inclusive, ethical manhoods over the course of the texts. As we have seen throughout the last three chapters, canonical Asian American literature has explored masculinity to understand and expose American player imperialism throughout the major postmodern American wars.

Like the literary texts I discuss that were written or took place during the Korean War, the Vietnam War, and the Gulf War, the texts contemporary to the War on Terror that I study in this chapter reference or reflect the events or the political strategies of war through the subjectivities of their featured Asian American players. As I will later discuss, however, the explicitness of turning the cooperative prisoners' dilemma of fighting global terrorism into the zero-sum game of American imperialism during the War on Terror is challenged by the ethical transformations and reflections of the Asian American players in the texts that I examine.

The main portion of this chapter examines two canonical Asian American texts that feature male players who are also victims of ethnic discrimination and abuse. *The Sympathizer* and *The New Belly Dancer of the Galaxy* were both shaped by the preemptive seduction and invincibility of player imperialist masculinity that influenced US military responses to 9/11 and the Financial or Credit Crisis of 2007–8, which many economists have linked as cause and effect. According to Pema Levy, editor of *The American Prospect*, as well as economists Linda Bilmes, Joseph Stiglitz, Ryan Edwards, and Anita Dancs, war-spending in Iraq and Afghanistan after 9/11—part and parcel of the finance capitalist strategies of risk and debt—led to the economy's loss of $648 billion, the stock market's loss of $7.4 trillion, and the burst of the

---

12. Freeman, *American Empire*, 466, 467–68.

housing bubble in 2008.[13] In the spirit of finance, the US employed the costly military strategies of chance, speculation (investment), and deterrence (preemptive, counterterrorist action, rather than the brinkmanship of the Cold War) in foreign nations such as Iraq and Afghanistan, which is reflected in the individual behavior of the players when dealing with female others described in these two texts.

Like the protagonists of the two main texts I explore, the US has harnessed the seduction and invincibility of the era's white hegemonic masculinity to feign possession of the finances and egalitarian politics that it unfortunately does not have during the War on Terror. Operation Enduring Freedom in both the Afghanistan (2001–14) and Iraq (2003) wars—which stipulated that Afghanistan and Iraq were involved in the attacks of 9/11—has been ideologically contradicted by the spate of race riots since 2000 and Black Lives Matter protests since 2012 that have indicated the empirical domestic failures of democracy despite the fact that the US has been fighting in the name of democracy since World War II. A prisoners' dilemma of fighting global terrorism turned once again into a zero-sum game of American imperialism, the War on Terror has been a preemptive seduction of sorts that has led to and been fueled by a fantasy of inexhaustible funds, which led to the Financial Crisis of 2007–8. Like the US government's political approach to foreign affairs—in fighting an invisible and nebulous enemy through ephemeral means—and failing to reproduce the patriarchy of player imperialist masculinity, the players of the texts I examine express their subjectivities by turning to fantasy, even supernatural experiences, to escape and recreate reality; in turn, they exploit women even as they are being racially exploited and discriminated against as Asian American subjects. Their supernatural experiences allow them to become conscious of their orphanhoods and the playing they enact to compensate for this perceived loss. And although their womanizing ways attempt to mimic the preemptive seduction of the player imperialist masculinity of this era and compensate for their social lacks, their behavior ironically further emasculates them: Their infidelity becomes visible and they gain the reputation for being players and liars and risk ending up alone, indebted to the women they have objectified. In other words, playing inevitably creates debt—financial, material, or that of conscience, whether acknowledged or not. The self-reflection that these consequences induce further allows these characters to reclaim their ethical manhood and expose what has previously been a covert American imperialism in the form but not fact of democracy. As I have indicated, there is a homology between the discursive popularity

---

13. Levy, "Did 9/11 Cause the Financial Crisis?"

of players and US foreign policy and intervention in the Middle East since 2001. However, America's preemptive, chancing exploitation of other nations has largely remained invisible while Asian American players who have merely mimicked government actions have been visibly scapegoated as menaces to American society even in the high culture of literature.

THE WAR ON TERROR PLAYERS

The Sympathizer and *The New Belly Dancer of the Galaxy* reflect the white hegemonic masculine discourse of the counterterrorist, and thus also illegitimate, but imperialist savior that emerged from 9/11 and its attendant War on Terror. On September 11, 2001, when two airplanes crashed into the twin towers of the World Trade Center, one into the Pentagon, and one unsuccessfully headed toward Washington, DC, but exploded in Shanksville, Pennsylvania, the terrorist group al-Qaida claimed responsibility for these horrific attacks on US soil. These attacks cost the lives of nearly three thousand people and three trillion dollars in damage. In a series of speeches over the course of the days following the destructive attacks, President George W. Bush fictively transformed them from criminal acts to acts of war: On September 11, Bush addressed the nation stating, "The *victims* were in airplanes, or in their offices, secretaries, businessmen and women, military and federal workers, moms and dads, friends and neighbors. [. . .] These *acts of mass murder* were intended to frighten our nation into chaos and *retreat*."[14] The next day, on September 12, he declared, "The deliberate and deadly *attacks* which were carried out yesterday against our country were more than acts of terror. They were *acts of war*. [. . .] This *enemy attacked* not just our people, but all freedom-loving people everywhere in the world. This *battle* will take time and resolve. But make no mistake about it, *we will win*."[15] In addition to declaring a preemptive, ideological, illegitimate, and abstract war between freedom and terror, Bush began to conflate al-Qaida, Iraq, and Afghanistan as evil alliances into the "War on Terror."[16] The masculinist discourse of war that the president began to wield now assigned the role of the victim to the US and the victimizer to the Middle East but also rallied to reclaim the national "imperial" masculinity that had been compromised during the attacks.[17] Moreover, as historian Neal Allen has argued, at the forefront of the reclamation of imperial masculinity was

---

14. Hodges, *"War on Terror" Narrative*, 25, 24.
15. Hodges, 25.
16. Hodges, 69–70.
17. Scott, "Rescue in the Age of Empire," 100.

the president himself: "George W. Bush has drawn on the head of state role to recast himself as the personification of the war against terror."[18] Moreover, "that summer, a senior Bush adviser told a reporter, 'We're an empire now, and when we act, we create our own reality.'"[19] Even though it was casting itself as victim that had to save other victimized nations, player masculine American imperialism came to the fore after 9/11 in such an explicit way, as I have argued, that the public and cultural artifacts could then begin to consciously grapple with it. And yet, as we have seen in previous chapters, the consciousness of playerism does not necessarily discontinue it.

Although *The Sympathizer* is set during the Vietnam War, the player imperialist masculinity of the War on Terror contemporary to the novel's publication shapes and is reflected by the playerism of the narrator. Both protagonists find themselves locked in a player's perspective of fantasy in which the distinction between what is real and fake is unclear; insofar as both protagonists find themselves supernaturally haunted by the dead, both *The New Belly Dancer of the Galaxy* and *The Sympathizer* are speculative fiction. The protagonists' fantastic perspectives, which victimize women, are, in part, due to the trauma that Nguyen's unnamed "sympathizer" experiences from a violent civil war and torture by the Vietnamese communists for being a traitorous communist spy and the trauma that Kali experiences as an Arab American after 9/11. While Kali is haunted by his dead grandmother, the sympathizer is haunted by those he is contracted to murder: The sympathizer's trauma specifically imprisons him in redundant flashes of time and memory. Both protagonists are figuratively haunted by unpleasant memories of their parents and literally haunted by ghosts.

A spy for the Viet Cong, the sympathizer finds himself in a communist prison at the end of the novel and is criticized for his duplicity just as Song faces criticism for his homosexuality even though he is tasked by the Communist Party to have an affair with Gallimard: in *The Sympathizer*, the commandant tells him, "You are a communist only in name. In practice, you are a bourgeois intellectual."[20] Moreover, his initial self-characterizations suggest the instability of Asian American subjectivity and masculinity. And like the invisible man, the sympathizer realizes the fallacy of time and reality, particularly as he is being tortured by the same organization for which he works because they have deemed him a bourgeois and incompetent communist. While living in Los Angeles and later returning to Vietnam, the sympathizer becomes acquainted with the mistakes of universalizing ideologies—whether capitalist or communist. In Los Angeles, he is racialized and victimized by the

---

18. Allen, "Fight Against Terrorism," 21.
19. Freeman, *American Empire*, 469.
20. Nguyen, *The Sympathizer*, 306.

white department chair of Oriental Studies at the college where he works, who defines an "Oriental" as "forever homeless, a stranger, a foreigner, no matter how many generations lived on the soil of Judeo-Christian culture."[21] Likewise, not accepted by his Vietnamese comrades as he later is tortured by them, he is reduced to the nihilistic belief that all is for naught:

> What was it that I got? *The Joke.* Nothing was the punch line, and if part of me was rather hurt at being punched—by nothing, no less!—the other part of me thought it was hilarious. [. . .] Don't you get it? I cried. The answer is nothing! Nothing, nothing, *nothing!*[22]

The sympathizer emerges from the prison camp renouncing the naturalized, polarized ideologies of capitalism and communism while becoming psychically split from the trauma of his torture. Capitalism is epitomized by the racist department chair, who tells him, "You must assiduously cultivate those reflexes that Americans have learned innately, in order to counterweigh your Oriental instincts."[23] He fails at mimicry but is also encouraged to copy his white American colleagues—an impossible feat in the racist system in which he lives. The resulting schizophrenia from his racist encounters and prison torture leads him to avow a nonideological revolutionary collectivity at the conclusion of the novel as he leaves Vietnam.[24]

The sympathizer's objectifications of women are legion. Of his boss's daughter Lana, he states, "Even I was shocked by the black leather miniskirt that threatened to reveal a glimpse of that secret I had so often fantasized about."[25] A victim of racism and orphanhood, himself, the sympathizer, who introduces himself as "a man of two faces [. . .] a man of two minds," is indeed as much a sexual player as he is a political one—a spy.[26] Countering the stereotype of Asian American male effeminacy, the sympathizer's racial hypermasculinity is also consolidated by his status as a captain in the South Vietnamese army (Army of the Republic of Vietnam).

During numerous public readings, author Viet Nguyen has identified the sympathizer as "a womanizer."[27] And yet, only critic Pat C. Hoy II has offered any commentary on the sympathizer's sexist treatment of women: Hoy ana-

---

21. Nguyen, 63.
22. Nguyen, 355.
23. Nguyen, 63.
24. Nguyen, 367.
25. Nguyen, 112.
26. Nguyen, 1.
27. Nguyen, Book Reading of *The Sympathizer*, May 6, 2015; Nguyen, Book Reading of *The Sympathizer*, September 5, 2015; Nguyen, Book Reading of *The Sympathizer*, November 12, 2015.

lyzes his conversation with his childhood friends Bon and Man, in which the sympathizer tells them that his mother makes him promise to work harder than all the family members who denigrate him for being a "bastard" but sheepishly omits the part of the story when his "face [was] pressed against one comforting breast while [his] hand squeezed its plush other."[28] Man reassures the narrator that he does not need the cultural traditions from which he had been excluded since he "see[s] the lie beneath those things because [he] never got to take part."[29] In his criticism of this passage, Hoy only briefly references the narrator's objectification of his mother's body: "This double-lesson—the one gleaned from the comforting, highly charged body of a woman and the other from the mind's many-faceted splendor brought into clarity by a precocious blood brother—travels with us and with the narrator for the duration of the tale."[30] In anonymously referring to the narrator's mother as "the comforting, highly charged body of a woman," Hoy evades any mention of the narrator's incestuous feelings. In focusing my analysis of the characters' sexual exploits and taboo feelings, I argue that the sympathizer turns to the objectification of women to futilely grasp a reality that has been made abstract by his experiences with racism, orphanhood, and, in the contemporary moment of the novel's publication, by the War on Terror and its ideological companion finance capitalism.

The seduction of sexual (in addition to financial) risk, as played out in the lives of these Asian American male characters I analyze in this chapter, often results in debt—loss of property, guilt, or debt of conscience. As a form and result of risk and debt, as anthropologist David Harvey points out, finance capitalism also "relates to the future value of goods and services," which is usually not attainable or recoverable.[31] Also discussing the financialization of the US economy and culture, sociologist Giovanni Arrighi argues that the US has been an economic "player" of sorts since it succeeded Britain in dominating world trade during the Cold War: "The United States instituted a trade regime that was far less 'generous' towards the rest of the world than the British regime."[32] In particular, US globalization involved a much higher level of "multilateral" free trade than British hegemony before 1945.[33] Reflective of US economic free trade in the twentieth and twenty-first centuries, the multilateral investments that the characters examined in this chapter make

---

28. Nguyen, *The Sympathizer*, 136.
29. Nguyen, 136.
30. Hoy, "Spying with Sympathy and Love," 688.
31. Harvey, *Enigma of Capital*, 26.
32. Arrighi, *Long Twentieth Century*, 72.
33. Arrighi, 72.

in relationships, however ephemeral, incite the multiple risks of seduction, cheating, and being caught, and the debt of material loss as well as the debt of conscience or guilt they owe to their victims. The seductive and insidious player imperialist codes of preemptive and seductive risk and debt that structure finance capital have contributed to the development of the Keynesian military-industrial complex and have also directly informed US military strategy in the twenty-first century. As I discuss in the final section of this chapter, the contemporary military-industrial complex's invisible strategies of risk and debt have thus permeated the daily lives of Americans and cultural products such as speculative fiction, of which Noble's *The New Belly Dancer of the Galaxy* and Nguyen's *The Sympathizer* are examples; many scholars have argued that speculative fiction is a critical response to the financialization of American life.[34] I demonstrate the pervasiveness of this kind of risk and debt through *The Sympathizer* and *The New Belly Dancer of the Galaxy*. These works of Asian American speculative fiction depict the Asian American player or womanizer as a visible, even sensationalized, reflection of the seductive modes of American finance capital and its correlative military interventions.

Like the sympathizer, Kali objectifies most of the women in his life as part and parcel of his player imperialism. In addition to his female clients, one of whom he has an affair with, he also objectifies his only matriarch, his grandmother "Situe," who returns from the dead to meet him during his midlife crisis at age fifty-three. Kali's masculinist sexism in the novel counters Gómez-Vega's claim that he is an American "subaltern."[35] In a sexist manner, he questions Situe's intellect, "How do you know about metaphors? You can't read or write." And she responds, "You forget I'm in heaven now. I can do a lot of things I couldn't do before."[36] Able-bodied after her death, Situe proves herself to be a guide for Kali through his disempowerment and the recovery of his ethical manhood over the course of the novel, which I later discuss. Kali also objectifies his wife Sophie: He mistakes her for her sisters twice but "ma[kes] up for" it "over time with the sweetness of his nature and his way with words."[37] In this way, he reconstructs the historicized stereotype of Arab American men as threatening and sexist toward Arab American women.[38] Moreover, he admits that he failed to "sig[h] deeply whenever Sophie

---

34. Bahng, "Specters of the Pacific, 666; Carroll and McClanahan, "Fictions of Speculation: Introduction," 658; Laura Finch, "Un-real Deal," 732.
35. Gómez-Vega, "Ancestral Voices and Family History," 77.
36. Noble, *New Belly Dancer*, 3.
37. Noble, 32.
38. Bosch-Vilarrubias, *Post-9/11 Representations*, 9.

entered his thoughts."[39] He further critically objectifies Sophie's body: "From the beginning, there was a thinness about Sophie, an angularity."[40] And his thoughts drift toward "another girl, not Arab, a girl who glided over campus as though airborne, a girl so free she seemed to skim over the obstacle of daily life, [who] had said to him, 'Come with us this summer.'"[41] Kali is not a serial womanizer. Besides Jane, the client with whom he has an affair, and the free, "airborne" American girl who propositions him in college, Kali's only other romantic interest is Sophie. However, Kali's playerism exists in his occupation as an optician, which entails an insincere, physical intimacy with women that he documents. In addition to his "sweetness of [. . .] nature and his way with words," Kali charms his women clients:

> With other women, he had more success [than with his wife]. They relied on him to gauge the distance between their irises with his mother of pearl measuring stick pressing confidently, yet gently, against the bridges of their noses. They loved the way he warmed the arms of the frames so they'd fit into the indented spaces just behind their ears.
>
> "He reminds me of Omar Sharif, only a little [. . .] heavier," a customer would tell her friends. Or, "He looks like Rossano Brazzi in that old movie where he tried to steal the Englishman's wife but her children ruined everything and she went back to her husband."
>
> And to them Kali said things like, "The eyes are the windows to the soul." Rapturous words, poetic words.[42]

Even though he does not have serial affairs with his women clients he intentionally and seductively establishes physical intimacy with them by using the tools of his trade to gain otherwise illegitimate physical intimacy; he also pulls chairs out "for most of his women customers, if appropriate" based on their youth and attractiveness.[43] When Jane Plain, the client with whom later has an affair, appears at his optical store, the Oasis, Kali exercises his charm: When she asks if the store is open, Kali flatteringly states, "For you [. . .] of course," even though he had intended to close the shop early.[44]

In his seduction of his women clients, he often finds himself, in turn, seduced by them; for example, he is entranced by Jane's scent: "Pungent.

---

39. Noble, *New Belly Dancer*, 31.
40. Noble, 31.
41. Noble, 31.
42. Noble, 5.
43. Noble, 64.
44. Noble, 6.

Musky. Distracting."[45] "It's ginger and citrus," she offered. "I mix it myself."[46] Like Gallimard and Song, they begin to play fictional roles. After Kali follows her to the New Belly Dancer of the Galaxy Contest in Santa Vista, California, they start their affair when he tells her, "You are lovely, beguiling, and talented."[47] When he finally returns home after escaping from his interrogation as a suspected terrorist by what we can assume to be Homeland Security, Sophie asks him if his trip to Santa Vista—instead of Cincinnati, his supposed destination—involved another woman. He replies, "Sophie, I can tell you in all honesty, no."[48] Attempting to legitimize an illegitimate claim, he tells himself "there had been no one else."[49] He also further objectifies and dismisses Jane by telling his Homeland Security interrogators that his affair with her "was part of a larger philosophical scheme."[50] His affair and the trip to homeland security signify his fulfillment, which inevitably means failure, of Asian American playerism.

Like the other players in this study, Kali is both victimizer and victim. As critic Marta Bosch-Vilarrubias argues, he is introduced as a racially disempowered Arab American man in the wake of the 9/11 attacks and the War on Terror; she also states that 9/11 contributed to the Orientalist stereotype of Arab men as simultaneously hypermasculine and emasculated.[51] Because he is Syrian American, and despite that fact that he goes to church (but is an atheist), he is racially discriminated against as and mistaken for a Muslim "terrorist" by Jane's landlord and his Homeland Security interrogators.[52] His racial emasculation, for which he is severely beaten by the interrogators, is coupled with his physical emasculation, or the erectile dysfunction he experiences at the beginning of the novel: In addition to falling asleep while making love to his wife, "he wanted to please her. He tried. It was no use. She sent him to the doctor."[53] The Homeland Security interrogators are also aware of his erectile dysfunction when they ask him if he is "successful" in bed with Jane: "'Success in that area, confirmed,' Kali responded somewhat embarrassed."[54] His militarization of his performance of player imperialist masculinity contextualizes his experience during the War on Terror but also coincides with

---

45. Noble, 6.
46. Noble, 6.
47. Noble, 67.
48. Noble, 265.
49. Noble, 265.
50. Noble, 140.
51. Bosch-Vilarrubias, *Post-9/11 Representations*, 119, 131.
52. Noble, *New Belly Dancer,* 17, 127.
53. Noble, 1.
54. Noble, 147.

new ways Arab Americans were politically represented. Critic Samira Aghacy claims that the Gamal Abdel Nasser Era of 1967 in Egypt, also known as the June War, extended the image of a singular and peaceful pan-Arab space in armed and political defiance of joint Israeli and Western hegemony but also promoted a "compulsory heterosexuality" and "anxieties about masculinity" among men in in the Middle East in the decades following.[55] Kali's embarrassment in this moment stems from the exposure of his erectile dysfunction and his hypermasculine compensation of it through his affair with Jane Plain. Jane is an all-American girl, a green-eyed blonde woman who dons a patriotic, self-fashioned "red, white, and blue" sequined bra and harem pants for the belly dancing competition.[56] Kali's returned-from-the-dead grandmother, Situe, sardonically remarks about Jane, "Don't worry about that girl. She floats to the top. It's a gift."[57] Indeed, Jane capitalizes on her white privilege by excusing herself from Kahlil's investigation through her race, stating that he had "seduced" and "stalked" her, and starts an affair with one of the Homeland Security interrogators.[58] Kahlil is ultimately defeated by the player's logic, which was never intended for the vulnerable or racially minoritized.

In order to assert himself, Kali appeals to his identity as an American citizen and tries to play the game he thinks he knows how to play. Like Jane, the Homeland Security interrogators exercise their white privilege in sharp contrast to Kali, who protests his kidnapping and maltreatment by proclaiming his American citizenship and revealing that he doesn't "speak Arabic": "We didn't speak Arabic in the house because my father wanted us to be 'American.'"[59] Despite his "Americanness" or his mimicry of player imperialism, one of the interrogators replies, "Don't talk to us about America, buddy, [. . .] Your rights ended when you got into this car" and "You trying to get patriotic on us, Huron?"[60] The interrogators continue to demonstrate their racism by repeatedly mispronouncing Kali's last name, Hourani, and calling him a "Bedouin sonofabitch."[61] Kali's brutal Homeland Security interrogation reminds us that the War on Terror has been fought on domestic soil as well. When the interrogators whom Kali names "the fire marshal" and "the man in the brown suit" first question him, they tell him, "We don't like being cor-

---

55. Aghacy, *Masculine Identity*, 6, 9, 1–2.
56. Noble, *New Belly Dancer*, 70.
57. Noble, 90.
58. Noble, 83.
59. Noble, 119.
60. Noble, 77, 79.
61. Noble, 111.

rected, Mr. Huron. [. . .] Especially if we're wrong."[62] The duplicity of masculinist American imperialism is further articulated by Orville and Shadrack, two of the "good cop" interrogators who attempt to induce Kali to confess his terrorist crimes. Critic Ibis Gómez-Vega writes that Orville and Shadrack performatively "introduce themselves to Kahlil as a thief and a rapist."[63] As a representation of American imperialism and secretly a Homeland Security agent, Shadrack claims that Kali is being interrogated for being at the "wrong place—on top of a woman in her motel room" at the "wrong time—while she was screaming."[64] On the other hand, Orville discloses a "lifetime of deception" as he tells Kali the story of his life.[65] As I have already demonstrated, Kali performs the player imperialist masculinity that Shadrack's rape mentality espouses. Like Shadrack, he objectifies women, and like Orville, he is a serial liar. Kali's perpetual dishonesty self-reflexively exposes the player imperialist masculinity that discursively drove the War on Terror.

Kali's dishonesty shapes his playerism. Nevertheless, the third-person narrative of the novel continuously dips into free indirect discourse when it attempts to defend Kali's honesty:

> Taking risks: he was bad at that; a terrible gambler, unable to calculate odds, let alone beat them. Some people had that blind wild courage in the face of the unknown. Not him. In family poker games—assuming he could be persuaded to sit at the table with his aunts and uncles and cousins and their shot glasses of whiskey and their lopsided piles of chips—when asked how many cards he wanted, he'd say without looking at his hand, 'All' or 'None,' then fold without making a bet.[66]

And yet, though he is unable to formally gamble with deception, Kali takes informal, quotidian risks like flirting with his customers and following Jane to her contest, and he lies throughout the novel. Like the sympathizer, Kali's dishonesty is encompassed by his playerism. As he plays women, he is charming although not necessarily skilled at seduction—he calls Jane nineteen times in an eight-hour period.[67] In addition to lying to Sophie about going to an opticians' conference in Cincinnati when he actually follows Jane to her belly dancing competition, he lies to his interrogators, claiming "Sophie was

62. Noble, 94.
63. Gómez-Vega, "Ancestral Voices and Family," 75.
64. Noble, *New Belly Dancer*, 127.
65. Noble, 136.
66. Noble, 49.
67. Noble, 85.

the only person I lied to."⁶⁸ He attempts to preempt Sophie's discovery of his affair when he discourages her from following him into the airport where he had not booked a flight and raises his voice at her, which alarms the security guards.⁶⁹ When he is talking to the transgender man Benny who rescues him from the interrogators, the narrator states, "For Kali did not lie, usually, except for Cincinnati."⁷⁰ Kali mimics the deterrent, preemptive player imperialism of the contemporary War on Terror by lying to his wife about his affair with Jane. He lies to Jane when he seductively tells her what he thinks of her when he sees her dancing: "That woman, whoever she is, is far better than most of the others. [. . .] Let me rephrase. [. . .] What I meant to say was that the only dancer better than you was the teacher."⁷¹ He later admits to Jane that he lied to her—that he had not seen her dance and that he was married.⁷² He fuels his dishonesty in cheating on his wife by lying to Jane. Moreover, he also admits that "Jane [. . .] wasn't very good. An awkward, inarticulate belly dancer. He hadn't dared to think it when he was with her. He'd excused her performance in the motel room on the grounds that she had no music, the setting was wrong, she was self-conscious. But the truth was, it wasn't in her blood."⁷³ Here, he racializes Jane as an inept white person who cannot perform Middle Eastern belly dancing, even though she attempts to seduce him by performing an exoticized part of his cultural background, as an excuse for his lying. Kali also admittedly lies to Benny that his opinion of him does not change after Benny reveals that he is transgender.⁷⁴ The narrator's use of free indirect discourse in stating that "Kali lied for the second time" is, itself, a lie. Kali's deception, however, is exposed, whereas the deception of player imperialist masculinity remains under wraps. Kali suffers through an unlawful interrogation just for committing adultery, and the justice system eliminates any evidence of its wrongdoing. The mistaken, fraudulent Homeland Security interrogation by Orville, Shadrack, the fire marshal, and the man in the brown suit is covered up when some of their unidentified bodies are found in a car crash: The police's "orders were to find out what Kali knew and then put a lid on it. No further publicity, no arrests, no nothing: that was how it came down. Find out if he could be relied on to keep quiet. Determine if he would spill the

---

68. Noble, 146.
69. Noble, 37.
70. Noble, 175.
71. Noble, 62.
72. Noble, 66.
73. Noble, 149.
74. Noble, 180.

beans."[75] On the one hand, the American imperialist, preemptive interrogation is erased or made invisible; on the other hand, Kali's dishonesty, which keeps him from getting a divorce and prevents emotional debt to women, is exposed throughout the novel. In this way, American imperialism is enforced by making Kali's masculinity Other. Thus, player imperialism dismantles and reinforces itself.

It is through being Othered that Kali challenges the player imperialist masculinity of his interrogators. While he is being interrogated, he unsuccessfully lunges for the interrogator's gun and is punished for it. In reflecting upon his masculine action, he states, "Not that he had covered himself with unqualified glory, so far. But two steps forward and one step back was progress of a sort. Had the earth shifted on its axis? Was there a change of seasons? He didn't know, but whatever the explanation, he clung to its inner results."[76] His failed attempt to stand up for himself as an action hero reveals his own vulnerability and the performativity of player imperialism.

PLAYING THE LOSS OF PATRIARCHY

If player imperialist masculinity is a patriarchal ideology to which the sympathizer and Kali must but inevitably fail to adhere, the loss of patriarchy, in addition to a loss of reality, pervades both texts and drives the protagonists' fantasies of empowerment through self-discovery. Kali's father is dead at the start of the novel, but his loss of patriarchal authority is also figurative. For example, Kali confesses to his second set of interrogators, Orville and Shadrack, that when he was a child, ashamed of his unassimilated heritage in the US, he told his classmates that he was Italian, and when "the kids [at school] asked me if the colored man was my father. [. . .] I said no."[77] His father's vulnerability and his association with his father threaten to castrate him as an imperialist player and thus, his disavowal is a form of patricide. His modified castration complex, since it is his father rather than his mother who is disempowered, here mirrors the US struggle to maintain player imperialism as Great Britain's failure as the global leader loomed after World War II. In response to Kali's inherited vulnerability, Situe later scolds Kali for his disavowal of his father: "How could you be ashamed of your own father? [. . .] You should have been a better child."[78] His masculinist concern over

---

75. Noble, 255–56.
76. Noble, 117.
77. Noble, 143, 144.
78. Noble, 156.

his father's discovery of his lie, which never happens, reflects the historical Arab American cultural conflation of patriarchy and manhood.[79] His affair with Jane both betrays his bourgeois value of family but, at the same time, reinforces the larger patriarchal system that facilitates his womanizing.

In a similar vein, Nguyen's sympathizer, whose parents are both dead at the start of the novel, discovers himself through ideologically disavowing patriarchy and the bourgeois family in his playing. Early in the novel, he reveals that he is the offspring of an illicit and colonizing affair between a maid and a priest. As a result, he states,

> Having been thus produced outside of marriage, I confess to feeling very uncomfortable at the thought of being married myself. Bachelorhood is one of the unexpected benefits of being a bastard, as I was not considered much of a catch to most families. [. . .] Being a bachelor also meant I could chat without consequence with the call girls, brazenly displaying their shapely shanks among the evacuees while using yesterday's tabloid paper to fan the sweaty ravines of their cleavage, artificially enhanced by atomic age bras.[80]

The sympathizer's rejection of marriage has the potential to be a radical disavowal of bourgeois values, but it instead reinscribes them when he objectifies women as he "brazenly" stares at the "sweaty ravines of their cleavage." Even though he criticizes and disavows his father like Kali does, the sympathizer is ironically influenced by the womanizing behavior of his absent and hypocritical father. Seducing his mother and gifting her with expensive perfume before abandoning her, the sympathizer's father is a "holy m[a]n" who, according to the sympathizer, "not only had holes in his socks but also had a hole somewhere in his soul."[81] Here, he references his father's colonizing relationship with his mother as a defect in care since he not only took advantage of her but also abandoned her. Womanizing, for the sympathizer and Kali, indeed compensates for a lack of male role models or emasculation that is both gendered and racial. In addition to being symbolically castrated by his father through abandonment, the sympathizer faces many instances of racial discrimination, particularly when he arrives in the US. He is exploited by a movie producer who is directing a movie about the Vietnam War that is uncannily similar to

---

79. In *Post-9/11 Representations of Arab Men by Arab American Women Writers* Bosch-Vilarrubias writes, "Among these traditionally patriarchal traits, the issue of fatherhood is particularly important. [. . .] Amal Amireh refers to the 'ability to provide' (725) as a central trait of Arab manhood" (49).

80. Nguyen, *The Sympathizer*, 35.

81. Nguyen, 196.

Apocalypse Now and who belittles him on account of his race even as he seeks his advice on Vietnamese culture for the film.[82] Moreover, he is essentialized as a model minority, "self-effacing," "always trying to please," "usually quiet," and an effeminate "Oriental" by his department chair.[83] The sympathizer and Kali are similarly disempowered as their race and perceived effeminacy become what is most visible to the white characters in the novels.

Reflective of the US, an orphan nation that broke from Great Britain and overtook its position as a global leader in 1945, these characters compensate for these lacks in patriarchy and masculinity through their sexual exploitation of women and, in the sympathizer's case, his focus on masturbation. Masturbation, like the rejection of marriage and Cold War "momism" in the first chapter of this book, has a similar potential for revolutionizing sex and rescuing it from the bourgeois function of patriarchal procreation in service of creating an atomic family. In some ways, masturbation is a substitution for the actual objectification of women, but substitution does not necessarily comprise ethical behavior without proper analysis of the reasons for objectification in the first place. To illustrate, in *The Sympathizer*, masturbation is only a vehicle for narcissistic fantasy. "Without bidding, and utterly beyond my control, my maniacal manhood leaped to attention, luring me forward to you, inviting, bewitching, come-hither squid!"[84] In this scene from his youth, he masturbates using an uncooked squid before his mother cooks it and unknowingly forces him to eat it with a "mother's sweet love."[85] He aptly names his arousal maniacal since, according to Freud, mania is simply a form of melancholia and a psychic form of loss.[86] In short, masturbation implies loss, specifically of male role models to perpetuate patriarchy, for the narrator and Kali. Moreover, the sympathizer remorselessly defends his actions by negating the comparison of the squid to a rape victim: "Some will undoubtedly find this episode obscene. [. . .] Masturbation, even with an admittedly nonconsensual squid? Not so much. I, for one, am a person who believes that the world would be a better place if the word 'murder' made us mumble as much as the word 'masturbation.'"[87] Once again, the sympathizer's narrative has the potential of radical revision of the inhumane status quo when he indicates that murder has problematically become less shocking than masturbation. And yet, any social progress is undermined when he casually compares the scene with the

---

82. Nguyen, 172.
83. Nguyen, 62.
84. Nguyen, 76.
85. Nguyen, 77.
86. Freud, "Mourning and Melancholia," 174.
87. Nguyen, *The Sympathizer*, 77.

"admittedly nonconsensual squid" to rape. This facetious comparison is particularly violent: What haunts the sympathizer's repressed unconscious until he is tortured in the communist military camp is witnessing the gang rape of a comrade, a female agent, while he is undercover. The magnitude of pain that causes him to repress this memory launches him into ethical manhood. As he is being tortured, he hears screaming and at first states, "*Somebody was screaming and it was the agent.*"[88] The same screaming then morphs into his mother screaming and then his own screaming.[89] The confluence of screaming here suggests that as both a victimizer and victim, he identifies with the agent, for whom he cares as he does for his mother, but whom he cannot help when she is being raped. Here, he recognizes that he owes a debt of conscience to the agent for refusing to break his performance of the part of a South Vietnamese military officer to help her. The guilt, regret, and haunting of the parallel scenes of his masturbation and torture suggest that through the literal self-discovery of masturbation and inflicted pain, he recovers his ethical manhood, which is a sustainable alternative to patriarchy.[90]

PLAYING MOTHER ISSUES

Much like the relation between their racialized subject positions and the imperialist nation, the absence of or abuse by father figures precedes the symbolic castration of these protagonists. However, mourning the loss of mother figures who provide or are conventionally supposed to provide inclusive care for these protagonists likewise seems to drive the self-destructive behavior of these characters. Growing up without a father, the sympathizer looks to his mother for care: "My mother called me her love child."[91] His mother provides familial inclusion even as he is rejected by her family for being illegitimate: When his aunts and uncles give him half the sum of money as his cousins during the lunar new year and his cousin tells him that it is because he is a "bastard," his mother indignantly defends him:

> "If I could [. . .] I'd strangle him with my bare hands. [. . .] Oh they'll see!" my mother wept, squeezing me with such force I was nearly breathless, my face pressed against one comforting breast while my hand squeezed its plush other. [. . .] "You'll work harder than all of them, you'll study more than all

---

88. Nguyen, 353.
89. Nguyen, 353.
90. I thank Joan Shifflett for this excellent insight.
91. Nguyen, *The Sympathizer*, 20.

of them, you'll know more than all of them, you'll be better than all of them. Promise your mother you will!"[92]

Here, the narrator's mother, like Kali's Situe, offers him democratic inclusion and equity (and capitalist competition) in relation to her family even as they disenfranchise him as an illegitimate child. His objectification and sexualization of his inclusive, caring mother reflect the historical and paradoxical twin projects of US democratization and imperialism that drove the Vietnam War and the other major American wars after World War II. His mistreatment of his caring mother reflects the misapplication of democracy in American imperial enterprises in postmodern wars.

Reflective of the contemporary virtual and unfounded War on Terror that was ongoing during the novel's publication, the sympathizer spots the fake re-creation of the cemetery where his mother is buried and her pretend tomb on the Vietnam War movie set in the Philippines. Never having had the chance to properly mourn the death of his mother, he states:

> It was only a fake cemetery with its fake tomb for my mother, but the eradication of this creation, in its wantonness and its whimsy, hurt me with unexpected severity. I had to pay my last respects to my mother and the cemetery, but I was alone in such sentiments. [. . .] Mama, I said, my forehead on her headstone. Mama, I miss you so much."[93]

The emphasis on the "fake," unreal setting does not deter the sympathizer from expressing his genuine emotions of grief just as the illegitimate War on Terror does not prevent Asian American men from realizing their ethical manhoods; moreover, the next moment, in which the film's auteur, he later suspects, purposefully sets off an explosion that nearly kills him, reminds him of both the artifice of the scene and the real racist hatred directed toward him by the auteur. This constant mixture of artifice and reality, reflective of the invisible and nebulous War on Terror, the elusiveness of finance capital that was used to fund the Vietnam War film, and his inability to attain player imperialist masculinity, muddles the difference for the sympathizer as the memories of his mother haunt his interactions with the material world. Furthermore, the haunting loss of his mother seems to also motivate his objectification of women: He recalls, "That blissful memory of a ten-year-old's warmth and happiness was aroused by Phi Phi's fragrance, the same, nearly or so I

---

92. Nguyen, 136.
93. Nguyen, 174.

imagined, as from the one tiny vial of honey-colored perfume my mother owned, a present from my father with which she anointed herself once a year. So I fell in love with Phi Phi, a harmless enough emotion."[94] Here, the "harmless enough emotion" of "love" divulges the capriciousness of the sympathizer's pursuit of Phi Phi, a night club singer; together with his caustic critique of his absent father, he reveals his underlying Oedipal desires when he only falls in love because her perfume reminds him of his mother—his only individual representation of an inclusive, familial democracy.

His Oedipal desire for his mother and maternal figures, however, is based on power rather than selfless love. As I mentioned earlier, when he is tortured in the communist prison camp, he suddenly remembers the gang rape scene of the communist agent and his own paralysis, due to shock but also due to the need to keep his identity undercover. Even when the comrade reminds him of his own mother, he is emotionally frozen and unable to intervene, else he blow his cover:

> *Somebody was screaming and it was the agent.* I was packed tight into my mother's aquarium, knowing nothing of independence and freedom, witnessed by all my senses except the sense of sight to the uncanniest experience of all, being inside another human being I was a doll within a doll, hypnotized by a metronome ticking with perfect regularity, my mother's strong and steady heartbeat. *Somebody was screaming and it was my mother.*[95]

Imagining himself as a Russian matryoshka doll and having essentially returned to a fetus that can hear his mother's heartbeat within her uterus, the sympathizer is both within the scene and traumatically detaching himself from the scene through the slow realization that the person he imagines is screaming is his mother, who has already died. This scene is one of empathy and ethical guilt for not aiding the communist agent, who morphs into his mother and, finally, himself: "*Somebody was screaming and I knew who it was. It was me.*"[96] He, as a Vietnamese refugee, and his mother, who represents democratic inclusion and equity to the sympathizer, have been figuratively violated by the Vietnam War, and arguably all major American wars since. This simultaneous closeness and detachment from his mother, parallel to the artifice and reality that he consistently experiences, simultaneously reflects the War on Terror contemporary to the book's publication and the condition of the narrator's war-ravaged motherland after the Vietnam War in the novel.

---

94. Nguyen, 38.
95. Nguyen, 353.
96. Nguyen, 353.

Although critic Annette Kolodny has importantly pointed out the problematic conflation of women with "motherland" that is susceptible to rape and pillage, the metaphor is reproduced in *The Sympathizer* when Man tells the sympathizer of postwar Vietnam: "Now that we are the powerful, we don't need the French or the Americans to fuck us over. We can fuck ourselves just fine."[97] Here, Man, the sympathizer's childhood best friend who has ironically become the communist commissar in charge of his torture, extends the rape of the motherland metaphor to cynically describe the enduring, narcissistically masturbatory nature of imperialism; in its anxious futility, the masturbatory, self-congratulatory nature of imperialism that speaks itself without history is inevitably a loss of patriarchy, or the simulacra. Man suggests that, despite the communists' efforts to dispel foreign imperialists from Vietnam, they have nevertheless reconstructed a new imperialism that exploits its own people in the absence of democracy. Evidence of longing for empirical democracy, the Oedipal desires of the sympathizer for a mother figure ultimately become another form of exploitation for self-empowerment. The lost mother figures of democratically inclusive and equitable care in both *The Sympathizer* and *The New Belly Dancer of the Galaxy* reflect the empirical failures of democracy in the domestic US and in US imperialist military forays in the Middle East during the contemporary period of the texts.

As I have mentioned, Situe, one of the few but significant matriarchal figures in *The New Belly Dancer of the Galaxy*, represents for Kali democratic care and freedom from hegemonic, polarizing thought. Although he mentions his father, Kali declines to discuss his mother. The only other maternal figure in the novel is the woman with a mental disability at the laundromat who unknowingly hides him from the interrogators after he escapes. Without questioning him about the injuries he sustains from the interrogation, she accepts him and drinks soda with him. When she dances for him, "for the first time in a long time, Kali felt a feeling he loved: equal parts sadness and happiness. A gift from the old woman and for that he was grateful to her. He regretted having to leave her behind uncared for and hoped she wouldn't be lonely, however brief their contact."[98] Her dance represents a reciprocal care between Kali and her. For the first time in the novel, Kali admits that he cares for another woman and "hoped she wouldn't be lonely." In fact, she helps him develop an ethical manhood of care through which he returns to her at the end of the novel to give her money.[99] He also gives money to others: "He put money in other people's parking meters in front of his store, once he got the

---

97. See Annette Kolodny, *Lay of the Land*; Nguyen, *The Sympathizer*, 349.
98. Noble, *New Belly Dancer*, 154.
99. Noble, 269.

business up and running again."[100] The companionate care he develops for the woman with the disability also runs over into his relationship with Sophie when he reunites with her at the end of the novel and tells her: "I look at you, this woman I've been married to for thirty years. And you seem different. [. . .] Forgive me, Sophie. I didn't mean to be so blind."[101] Maternal figures heal Kali, a figuratively myopic optician, of his narcissism.

Situe, of course, is the main matriarch who leads him out of his narcissistic and greed-driven blindness. She does so through her stories but then disappears again at the end of the novel. However, toward the novel's conclusion, not only does she lead him back to a renewed companionate marriage, she also teaches him the historically feminine art of Middle Eastern storytelling made famous by Scheherazade in *One Thousand and One Nights*; he tells Max, the man with one arm who rescues him from a rattlesnake and gives him food and shelter, "I come from a long line of storytellers. [. . .] It's part of our tradition."[102] He starts with a story about orphans—a boy named Mansour and his siblings—which he begins with the undocumented migrants whom the truckdriver Benny transports and finishes with Max. Even though Mansour's "mother was alive," Kali states, "There's more than one way to be an orphan."[103] After Mansour's father dies and his mother remarries, his stepfather who lives in the States sends for them from Zahle, Lebanon. Espousing the ideology of American imperialism, "*Mansour was glad to be traveling to the New World. [. . .] Many from their village and the surrounding villages had heard that in America gold bricks paved the streets of the cities.*"[104] Instead, Mansour and his siblings endure abuse by their stepfather and are hired out as peddlers. After repaying their stepfather, the siblings move to Los Angeles, which "*was like the old country. Where they could grow olives and figs and anything else they wanted.*"[105] Instead of finding an imperialist America of "gold bric[k] paved [. . .] streets," Mansour and his siblings attempt to return to a place like Lebanon, never to see their mother again. Kali concludes his story, "And that's why we talk of Mansour as an orphan."[106] Like Mansour, Kali is a literal and figurative orphan after he repeatedly loses Situe, declines to mention his dead mother, and disavows his unassimilated dead father and Syrian heritage. Although he attempts to mimic player imperialist masculinity during

---

100. Noble, 270.
101. Noble, 261.
102. Noble, 229.
103. Noble, 230.
104. Noble, 231, 666.
105. Noble, 234.
106. Noble, 234.

the War on Terror, his racialization as an Arab American prevents his ability to do so as his Homeland Security interrogation demonstrates.

However, Kali meets other white characters who appear to be without an avowed lineage or history. When Benny, the truckdriver, comes out to Kali as a transgender man who used to be named Betty, he is still ashamed of his history. When he thinks Kali has told Mario, the keeper of the undocumented migrants, about his gender identity, Benny cries, "I'm going to kill myself! I'm going to blow myself up!"[107] As a transgender man who is uncomfortable with his history, Benny demonstrates the instability of white hegemonic American masculinity at the level of the individual. Even though Max is also a white man, he is also minoritized by his disability. Sincerely praising the weapons inventor John Moses Browning as "a goddam genius," whose guns were "used in Nam, in Korea, during I and II," Max continually implies that he lost his arm in the Vietnam War.[108] When Kali concludes his story about Mansour and figurative orphanhood, Max relates to the orphan Mansour and confesses that he had feigned being a decorated, masculine war hero and that he "wasn't in Nam" but had lost his arm to an inanimate windmill.[109] Whereas the Homeland Security interrogators represent player imperialist masculinity, who nevertheless disappear after the car crash and are unaccounted for, minoritized white male characters such as Benny and Max likewise demonstrate the performativity of player imperialism and its distinction from white hegemonic masculinity during the War on Terror. They suggest that player imperialism is both a political ideology and a subjective practice but is empirically unsustainable at the level of the individual and, potentially, of the nation. Of Benny and Max, Bosch-Vilarrubias writes that the flexibility of Benny's and Max's identities allows Kali to understand the complexity of his own; he thus begins to embrace the nonbinariness of his identity:

> When he got home and had time to reflect, he'd have to rethink his mixtures: how many parts Arab, how many parts husband; how many parts father; how many parts optician, church member, nonbeliever, neighbor, Chamber of Commerce member, voter (not down party lines, usually). Man?[110]

Bosch-Vilarrubias interprets this moment as Kali employing his self as metaphor, understanding that his body has many parts and he thus has many iden-

---

107. Noble, 194.
108. Noble, 221, 215, 225.
109. Noble, 237, 238.
110. Bosch-Vilarrubias, *Post-9/11 Representations*, 135; Noble, *New Belly Dancer*, 234.

tities: In this way, "gender may not be all that relevant."[111] While, like Situe, Benny and Max encourage Kali's nonbinary understanding of gender and the contemporary War on Terror, gender continues to be relevant to Kali's understanding of American imperialism. His questioning of how many parts "man" he is comes at a moment when he has been literally robbed and disempowered by the Homeland Security interrogators. Even though the Homeland Security interrogators, the representatives of white hegemonic masculine American imperialism during the War on Terror, die through a freak car accident, they are nevertheless given patriarchal legitimacy as their crimes (kidnapping and beating an innocent civilian) and deaths are covered up by the police and the government. On the other hand, Benny, Max, and Kali are exposed as failed simulacra of player imperialist masculinity.

In their seductive mimicry of and failure to attain the player imperialist masculinity, Kali and the sympathizer are figurative orphans who have lost or been abused and abandoned by patriarchy and suffered the loss of inclusive and equitable mothers and mother figures during the contemporaneous War on Terror. The questions of the prisoners' dilemma turned zero-sum game of the War on Terror remain: Who and where are the terrorists? Whom are we fighting and who is consenting to this elusive, illegitimate war? The explicit virtuality of their hauntings that remind them of their orphanhood and illegitimacy reflect the illegitimacy of American imperialist War on Terror and its lack of democracy; their hauntings also cause these countercultural characters to reflect on their playerism and make more ethical decisions toward inclusion of and equity in their treatment of gendered and racial minorities and people with disabilities in their lives. Abandoned by or emotionally detached from both their mothers and fathers, democracy and American imperialism, these protagonists seem to wander around as symbolic orphans who initially run after sex objects for self-empowerment and identity; over the course of their narratives, they are able to rehabilitate their player ways when they find themselves wholly detached from reality and alone, owing a debt of conscience to those whom they have hurt, and haunted by loss. Leann Wolley has compared positive postmodern citizenship and negative diaspora, both of which are caused by global and financial capital, to orphanhood insofar as postmodern citizens and diasporic subjects are without patriarchy and motherland, respectively.[112] These conditions of injury and privilege subjectify the masculine Asian American player. The orphaned players of these two texts are reflective of the simulacra, or copies of reality, which have structured society since the evolution of finance capital and its attendant, abstract War on Terror.

---

111. Bosch-Vilarrubias, *Post-9/11 Representations*, 135.
112. Wolley, "Orphan as Mirror."

With each passing year, the War on Terror seemed to become orphaned from 9/11, and yet there persisted the need to figure out what happened and legitimize the war. The War on Terror had and continues to have few parameters and boundaries. In the midst of the victim/victimizer and war discourses, many felt that attempting to explain the terrorist attacks of 9/11 "amount[ed] to blaming the victim."[113] And yet, what was not brought to light in the aftermath of 9/11 in Bush's speeches or the media coverage of the event was the historical US military occupation in Afghanistan and aid given to fight Soviet invasion during the Cold War from the late 1970s until 1989; thereafter, starting in 1991, the US assumed a policy of "benign neglect" in Afghanistan in which they "stopp[ed] arm shipments and military supplies" but also paradoxically supported the Rabbani regime and provided aid to the opposing Taliban regime.[114] Like the erasure of the violent Homeland Security investigators in *The New Belly Dancer of the Galaxy*, this part of the narrative leading up to 9/11 has been eradicated from popular discourse. Moreover, this problematic, gaslighting policy of avoidance after explicit involvement resulted in a series of attacks on American embassies in Nairobi, Kenya, and Dar es Salaam, Tanzania.[115] Whether this policy of avoidance was directly part of the motivation for the terrorist attacks of 9/11 is unclear, but the prehistory of US foreign relations has often been erased from narratives of the attacks to ossify the roles of victims and victimizers.

Even though the War on Terror has been fought in the name of freedom and democracy, surveillance laws such as the US Patriot Act passed after 9/11 indeed compromised and curbed the freedom of American citizens—and it is this heightened policing that Nguyen and Noble zero in on. Historian Kim Rygiel argues that surveillance was a way in which the government could reclaim its masculine dominance over its citizens.[116] Rygiel goes on to argue that surveillance undermines freedom insofar as it is a "biopolitical project" that privileges certain identities and categorizes people as "'high' and 'low risk' travelers," detaining criminalized populations.[117] Inevitably, those who have been found to be othered, discursively effeminate (that is, cowardly suicide-bombers), "high risk" terrorist suspects living in the US have been people of color who have been preemptively maligned as being in collaboration with the new, conflated Axis of Evil in the War on Terror: Iraq, Iran, and North Korea.[118]

---

113. Andrews, "Why Bush Should Explain," 33.
114. Lansford and Covarrubias, "Osama bin Laden," 13.
115. Lansford and Covarrubias, 13.
116. Rygiel, "Protecting and Proving Identity," 151.
117. Rygiel, 153, 158.
118. Rygiel, 148; Rogers, *Why We're Losing*, vii.

SPECULATIVE FICTION: PLAYING UP 9/11 AND THE FINANCIAL CRISIS

The financial speculation that has driven the elusive and, like the Gulf War, virtual War on Terror and caused the Financial Crisis of 2007–8 contributes to the blurring of reality and fiction for these two contemporarily constructed protagonists. Critic Annie McClanahan has established the conceptual overlaps between the post-9/11 doctrine of preemption and the risk of finance or speculative capital. Preemption, she argues, is a horrifying and "perverse" form of speculation that "transform[s] probability into plausibility."[119] Many critics, including McClanahan, have recently argued that speculative fiction, which often depicts alternative and futuristic realities, dialectically reflects and responds to financial speculation.[120] She and co-author Hamilton Carroll point out that the genre and supernatural conventions of "speculative fiction"—to which both of the protagonists, the sympathizer and Kali, turn in this chapter—correlate to the pretense and unrealness of speculative financial capital.[121] Critic Laura Finch has argued that financial speculation, a cycle of investment and credit, which has long been discredited as a "freewheeling" offshoot of the real economy, is actually constitutive of the current, real economy of finance capitalism.[122] Speculative fiction thus underscores the "fictionality of finance" and, at the levels of form and content, keeps the difference between the real and unreal preeminently difficult to define.[123] And it is in this place of speculation that the novels I discuss ground their critique of white, American hegemonic masculinity.

Finance capital has evolved since the early 1970s, a period that coincided with American attempts to secure its energy resources in the Middle East.[124] According to anthropologists Edward LiPuma and Benjamin Lee, finance capital was characterized by a financial group that speculated on risks related to globalization and other similar types of connections.[125] Risk and financial derivatives, or "wagers on changes in the cost of money (that is, interest rates) or the relationship among national currencies" are the underlying principles of finance or speculative capital.[126] In other words, the investments and con-

---

119. McClanahan, "Future's Shock," 52.
120. Carroll and McClanahan, "Fictions of Speculation," 658; Bahng, "Specters of the Pacific," 666.
121. Carroll and McClanahan, "Fictions of Speculation," 658.
122. Finch, "Un-real Deal," 731.
123. Finch, 732, 747.
124. Rogers, *Why We're Losing*, 61.
125. LiPuma and Lee, *Financial Derivatives*, 18.
126. LiPuma and Lee, 23.

stant movement of speculative capital are based on the educated "bets" of financial derivatives.[127] The risk and investment of speculative capital corresponds to the strategy of preemption and military deterrence during the War on Terror. The military strategy of "shock and awe" repeated from the Gulf War during the invasion of Iraq in 2003 was a correlative military form of speculative risk and deterrence.[128] Economists Joseph Stiglitz and Linda Bilmes make a strong case that links US deficit spending during the War on Terror to the Financial Crisis of 2007 and 2008.[129] Between 2003 and 2007, the Federal Reserve attempted to offset the costs of war by lowering interest rates, prompting people to borrow, sometimes against their own houses, and spend money, "enabling America to consume well beyond its means."[130] Together with the costs of a three trillion dollar war and the bursting housing bubble, the US economy entered a severe recession in 2008. The inestimable cost of the War on Terror has been the nearly sixty thousand lives of those who have fought in Iraq and Afghanistan since 9/11.[131] Carter writes that the Obama administration was "inescapably Keynesian": He writes that the Financial Crisis of 2007–8 reinvigorated Keynesianism against recommendations by neoliberal and neoclassical competitors in academia; through the recession, Americans learned very quickly about the illegitimacy and irrationality of the financial markets.[132] And thus, Obama turned to wartime Keynesian spending on the War on Terror to abate the recession. In *The New Belly Dancer of the Galaxy*, Kali likewise turns to finance capital to start his opticianry and to finance his affair with Jane. It is finally the ghost of his grandmother that calls his attention to the financial and interpersonal bluffing in his life.

Situe, whose supernatural appearance to Kali during his midlife crisis qualifies the novel as both "magical realist" and speculative fiction, questions his dishonesty in cheating on his wife and lying to those around him.[133] She tells Kali that she has been sent from heaven by the committee to transform him because they believe him to "have a good heart" and to be "eminently salvageable" even though he is dishonest, "still moderately self-absorbed and self-indulgent."[134] In her visitations to Kali, Situe tells him three stories that relate to his heritage and attempt to salvage his character. The first story is of her

---

127. LiPuma and Lee, 25, 116.
128. Stiglitz and Bilmes, *Three Trillion Dollar War*, 3.
129. Stiglitz and Bilmes, 21–22.
130. Stiglitz and Bilmes, 125–26.
131. Stiglitz and Bilmes, 60.
132. Carter, *Price of Peace*, 528–29.
133. Gómez-Vega, "Ancestral Voices and Family History," 65, 77.
134. Noble, *New Belly Dancer*, 207.

parents Tofa and Tasheeda, who fall ill and die after her brother Bashara steals their treasure and her dowry to go to the New World. Despite Kali's protests over Bashara's criminal actions, Situe concludes, "His sister would never have gotten to the New World if Bashara hadn't stolen the fortune" and "Because of Bashara, your grandfather had the means to start the store."[135] Gómez-Vega writes, "Kahlil's grandmother's very personal story teaches Kahlil the family history as it actually happened, which means that Kahlil now knows that his family history in America begins with a criminal act."[136] Influenced by the Manichean ideology of freedom fighters and terrorists of the contemporary War on Terror, Kali questions his grandmother: "Are you saying that nothing is clearly good or clearly bad? That there is no line between good and evil?"[137] She replies, "It's more complicated than you think."[138] As Gómez-Vega and Bosch-Vilarrubias point out, it is Situe who provides an avenue for multilateral or "nonbinary" thinking rather than the contemporary ideological binaries of the hegemonic War on Terror.[139] The second story she tells is of a girl named Haleema who saves one of the men who had attacked and killed her family. Incensed with self-righteous anger, Kali asks, "He helped kill her family and tribe and she helps him?"[140] Again, Situe attempts to lure him out of his binaristic thinking: "Such things do happen, Kali."[141] Gómez-Vega argues of this scene: "He also places himself in a strange position when he tells his grandmother that 'if someone had killed everyone in my caravan, I wouldn't help them. I'd happily watch them die.' [. . .] He has apparently forgotten that Haleema saves a murderer who is one of his ancestors, so Haleema is in fact doing him a favor."[142] The "strangeness" of this position more aptly reflects the binaristic thinking of the contemporary War on Terror of which Situe tries to break him.

Situe's final story takes yet another step in helping guide and save Kali from the intertwined personal and political trouble he finds himself in. The tale is about a tragic love story that takes place at a fountain, after which the townspeople build a second fountain that eventually incites war. She concludes with a moral: "*Pride and envy, they were forced to agree. They'd ignored God's plan and substituted their own. They argued and complained. They built*

---

135. Noble, 28, 29.
136. Gómez-Vega, "Ancestral Voices and Family History," 70.
137. Noble, *New Belly Dancer*, 29.
138. Noble, 29.
139. Bosch-Vilarrubias, *Post-9/11 Representations*, 135; Gómez-Vega, "Ancestral Voices and Family History," 72–73.
140. Noble, *New Belly Dancer*, 46.
141. Noble, 46.
142. Gómez-Vega, "Ancestral Voices and Family History," 72–73.

a second fountain when they had a perfectly good one already. And so on."¹⁴³ This conclusion directly convicts Kali of his womanizing when he "had a perfectly good one already," Sophie; it thus reflects the "pride and envy" of the zero-sum, endless war of white masculinist, American imperialism. Situe follows up this conclusion by giving Kali marital advice to recognize the ways in which couples balance each other in characteristics: "Every couple divides up the ten points according to their characteristics. Or, they wouldn't have gotten together in the first place."¹⁴⁴ Shortly before she gives him her advice, she supernaturally appears on billboards:

> But, oh the billboards: one of Situe selling coffee, one of Situe urging citizens to vote, another of Situe exhorting passengers to believe in the Lord Jesus Christ. Kali marveled at her apparent inability to resist playing jokes—the stoic, silent grandmother of his childhood, transformed. She had a much better sense of humor dead than she'd had when alive.¹⁴⁵

The playfulness with which Situe appears to Kali on the billboards and as a disembodied Cheshire cat like that in Lewis Carroll's *Alice in Wonderland* suggests that multiple, multilateral avenues of thinking and contentment with the self embody the true freedom and democracy that she had sought in the New World as an immigrant.¹⁴⁶

While *The Belly Dancer of the New Galaxy* and *The Sympathizer* do not appear at first to be speculative fiction, there are a multitude of speculative elements in both novels such as the sympathizer's supernatural haunting by the ghosts of the men he has murdered (the crapulent major and Sonny) and Situe's appearances to Kali.¹⁴⁷ Moreover, the sympathizer's and Kali's harrowing fantasies of apocalyptic scenarios during their interrogations and torture are meta-reflections of the indistinction between fantasy and reality in financial speculation. While the sympathizer faces the conceptual murkiness between fantasy and reality, both protagonists face realities that are dystopian and meaningless. In fact, their sexual prowess stems from the very principle of seduction, which defines player imperialist masculinity during this era, and which, according to Jean Baudrillard, "extracts meaning from discourse and

---

143. Noble, *New Belly Dancer*, 104.
144. Noble, 245.
145. Noble, 242.
146. In "Ancestral Voices and Family History" Gómez-Vega writes, "She plays tricks on him by showing her face in unusual places" (80).
147. Nguyen, *The Sympathizer*, 108–9, 291.

detracts it from its truth."¹⁴⁸ Baudrillard goes on to say, "What actually displaces [truth], 'seduces' it in the literal sense, and makes it seductive, is its very appearance: the aleatory, meaningless, or ritualistic and meticulous, circulation of signs on the surface; its inflections, and its nuances. All of this effaces the content value (*teneur*) of meaning, and this is seductive."¹⁴⁹ The tautology of seduction and its meaninglessness is what makes the players of these texts successful in their compulsive sexual conquests and also what perpetuates their debt of self-loathing and guilt when their victims discover their infidelity. And yet, the very meaninglessness and trauma of their realities alone do not incentivize these characters to break from the vicious cycles of womanizing and self-loathing. In fact, their seduction of women is the incarnation of the meaninglessness they find in their lives, since to seduce or "to simulate is to feign to have what one hasn't."¹⁵⁰ But they are all made conscious of their playing by their consequences: Kali is severely beaten during his interrogation after his affair, and the sympathizer realizes that he is and has always been haunted by the gang rape of the communist agent he had witnessed but not stopped as he is tortured in the military prison.¹⁵¹ Critics continue to deemphasize the protagonists' attainment of ethical manhood by the end of each text; while they are featured in the texts as players, they mirror, expose, and depart from the player imperialism of white hegemonic masculinity during this era.

While the War on Terror was driven by player imperialist masculinity, the unfounded reasons for the War on Terror only contributed to the unrealness of the war. This unrealness is articulated by the generic conventions of speculative fiction in *The Sympathizer* and *The New Belly Dancer of the Galaxy*. Comparing the catastrophe of 9/11 itself to an unreal "dream," Baudrillard states, this "new terrorism" that attacked the US does "not play fair" as they pretend to lie dormant until "they put their own deaths into play" and "tak[e] over all the weapons of the dominant power."¹⁵² He goes on to say that the magnitude of this violence makes it an unreal spectacle.¹⁵³ As I have mentioned, the temporal narrative of the War on Terror also became a fictive construction. Hodges argues that, in hindsight, the source from which the War on

---

148. Baudrillard, *Selected Writings*, 149.
149. Baudrillard, 149–50.
150. Baudrillard, 155, 167.
151. Nguyen, *The Sympathizer*, 353.
152. Baudrillard, *Spirit of Terrorism*, 5, 19–20.
153. Baudrillard, 27. In *The Spirit of Terrorism*, Baudrillard states, "The terrorist violence here is not, then, a blowback of reality, any more than it is a blow back of history. It is not 'real.' In a sense, it is worse: it is symbolic" (29).

Terror flows is 9/11;[154] however, the prehistory of US involvement in the Middle East has been discursively erased, and it is this very prehistory of American imperialism that, in their own way, these two novels seek to discover. The ambiguity of the term "terror" and all its derivatives has also contributed to the abstraction of the war. Describing terrorism as a "virus" that "shadows" and serves as a "double agent" to any system of domination, Baudrillard points out that "we can no longer draw a demarcation line around it."[155] Others have also indicated that terrorism, as a form of local and global violence, is illusory and ideologically difficult to define.[156] Historian Patrick Hayden also corrects the discursive antipodes of terrorism and freedom that were disseminated by the Bush administration immediately following 9/11. According to Hayden, US counterterrorism seems to be the more appropriate label for the War on Terror since it involves overt and covert deployment of the military by specialized government agencies like the CIA.[157] Instead, the rhetoric of freedom, a term that is equally as abstract as terrorism, was bandied about in Bush's speeches following 9/11: On September 20, 2001, Bush stated, "All of this was brought upon us in a single day, and night fell on a different world, a world where freedom itself is under attack."[158] The abstraction of freedom and terrorism, although empirically real, is reflected by the supernatural hauntings of Nguyen's and Noble's speculative novels.

In the midst of the reified and fictive reality that financial speculation creates, reflected by speculative fiction, social capital (social networks constructed for power and self-legitimacy) and deterrence (military and political strategies of preemption) remain and become the means of survival for these protagonists.[159] For the sympathizer and Kali, fantasies about power, citizenship, and women are mutually constitutive. Without actual capital, which financial speculation presupposes, these players seduce with the appearance of love and devotion. And yet, it is their devotion to capital—a power that does not exist for any of them—that causes them to exploit women's bodies. *The Sympathizer* and *The New Belly Dancer of the Galaxy* demonstrate that ways in which capital directly and indirectly disciplines women's bodies through the sociality of the valued and hated player.[160] These Asian American players are, in turn, disciplined and disavowed as players while the financial

---

154. Hodges, *"War on Terror" Narrative*, 52.
155. Baudrillard, *Spirit of Terrorism*, 10.
156. LiPuma and Lee, *Financial Derivatives*, 27; Hayden, "War on Terrorism," 109.
157. Hayden, 110.
158. Hodges, *"War on Terror" Narrative*, 44.
159. Bourdieu, "Forms of Capital," 241–58.
160. Szalay, "Pimps and Pied Pipers," 817–18.

and military chancing by the US government remains invisible and unquestioned. This scapegoating contributes to the framing of these protagonists as both victims and victimizers.

Though the novels I discuss play differently with time, they both deeply engage with tensions that forged the so-called War on Terror. *The Sympathizer* takes place in Vietnam and Los Angeles, California, following the Fall of Saigon in 1975; however, the novel features a protagonist who relies on the seductive and deterrent strategies of chance, risk, and preemption to carry out his sexual escapades, which ultimately hide or deter the discovery of his emasculation. *The New Belly Dancer of the Galaxy*, on the other hand, is set and published during the War on Terror. Despite the diversity in settings, the War on Terror publication era of these texts shaped the development of these characters and their masculinities, which are based on deception and preemption. Whereas *The New Belly Dancer of the Galaxy* explicitly references 9/11 and the War on Terror, *The Sympathizer* is not explicitly about 9/11 or finance capital. And yet, these protagonists are shaped by the player imperialist masculinity of seduction and fantasy, reflected by the finance capitalism that drove the War on Terror.

Like the texts I discussed in chapter three that show the invisibility of the Gulf War, the elision of any in-depth focus on US involvement in the unrest in the Middle East in *The Sympathizer* and *The New Belly Dancer of the Galaxy* reveals the abstraction of the War on Terror and the related hyperbourgeois detachment from the economy and politics in the age of finance capital. However, the explicitness of American imperialism during the War on Terror allows the characters to face the ways in which they womanize but do not quite measure up to the invincibility of player imperialist masculinity. For example, when he is first kidnapped by the Homeland Security interrogators, Kali admits that, in addition to feigning feelings for Jane, he is also playing his class qua financial speculation when he asks and states, "Are you kidnapping me? Do you want ransom? I'm not a rich man. You have nothing to gain by keeping me."[161] And yet, earlier, he told the suspicious rental car clerk that "*MONEY WAS NO OBJECT.*"[162] Without his wallet, which the interrogators have taken, he hops a train to return home at the end of the novel. Pretense also marks the sympathizer: Although an avowed communist, the sympathizer comes to believe "that true revolution also involved sexual liberation";[163] by liberation, he actually means womanizing, since he was "wont to fall in love

---

161. Noble, *New Belly Dancer*, 77.
162. Noble, 40.
163. Nguyen, *The Sympathizer*, 74.

two or three times a year and was now well past due."¹⁶⁴ Here, he recognizes the whimsy of his love and his objectification of women. His behavior consciously reflects the hyper-bourgeois, imperialist strategies of the US during the War on Terror in its narcissistic disregard of financial and political realities. He is eventually tortured by Vietnamese communists for his bourgeois tendencies that are evident in his sexist attitudes toward women, particularly communist comrades, and his heavily stylized writing and narration, like Ichiro's in *No-No Boy*.

The sexual exploits, involving investment, risk, and debt, of Nguyen's sympathizer and Noble's protagonist Khalil exemplify the player imperialist masculine discourse that the sociologist Randy Martin has famously called "the financialization of daily life," which has been a preemptive seduction of sorts to and a bluff of the American people;[165] that is to say, they are seduced by and feign possession of capital: again, as Deleuze and Guattari call it, the "crisis of desire." Over the course of the latter half of the twentieth century, the American government's Keynesian spending trickled down to the American people so that by the late twentieth and early twenty-first centuries, most Americans were financing their everyday lives. Speculative capitalism is so pervasive that it seems that everyone plays the bluffing game of finance in this postwar era, and it seems impossible to cheat this postmodern condition. The question then remains, who are the victims that playing leaves in its wake?

Martin argues that, since the 1980s, but particularly since the turn of the twenty-first century, the American counterculture of play has morphed into financialization: It has become "both subjectivity and moral code"; even though financialization presumes that capitalism is profane, it still suggests that all people, regardless of their circumstances, embrace risk that should be in the hands of professionals.[166] He indicates that the serious game of financial risk, driven by the mutually constitutive risks of historical American military deterrence and large-scale Keynesian economics—that is, deficit spending that has been historically used to deter communism, Middle Eastern capitalism, and terrorism—has become "routine" in American culture and a seductive enterprise that is "a means of price setting on the promise that a future is attainable."[167] Sociologist Greta Krippner similarly argues that the US economy and US culture have "undergone a process of financialization" in which preemptive risk is substituted for profit.[168] Martin's and Krippner's analyses

---

164. Nguyen, 74, 38.
165. Martin, *Financialization of Daily Life*, 9.
166. Martin, 9, 12.
167. Martin, 107, 105.
168. Krippner, *Capitalizing on Crisis*, 23, 4.

of the hegemony of financialization of American culture focus mainly on the economy. Since the Bretton Woods conference in 1944, which solidified US Keynesian economics and deficit spending in the military-industrial complex, the ideology of financialization also permeates the sexual activities and attitudes of Asian Americans as portrayed in these texts—that is, preemptively feigning what you do not have whether it is money or love only to hide your deceit and growing financial or emotional deficit. Asian American players are all considered inferior outsiders but attempt to overcompensate for their racializations and orphanhoods through womanizing; in this way, they are all the abusers and the abused—a cycle they begin to realize and ethically abandon through the loss that haunts them.

REALIZATIONS AND ETHICAL MANHOOD

The sympathizer becomes the "bourgeois" artifice he uses to seduce women for empowerment;[169] however, this realization and loneliness spur him onto attaining an ethical manhood of authentic relationships with other human beings:

> No, we cannot be alone! Thousands more must be staring into darkness like us, gripped by scandalous thoughts, extravagant hopes, and forbidden plots. We lie in wait for the right moment and the just cause, which, at this moment, is simply wanting to live. [. . .]
> *We will live!*[170]

Here, the sympathizer's schizophrenia, resulting from his torture, morphs into a revolutionary collective that will proclaim a new, democratic life that includes women. The sympathizer's and Kali's initial objectifying and womanizing behaviors both enhance and disrupt social capital or social obligations through pretense and betrayal.[171] At first, these characters often find themselves in love or obsessed with sexual fantasy and briefly invest in relationships. Reflecting the contemporary strategy of speculative or finance capital and imperialism, the romantic investments of these protagonists are brief and quickly aborted for the new, seemingly better opportunity to imperialistically be the best. The Asian American players discussed in this chapter epitomize the antinomies of this subject position through their victimizations as racial

---

169. Nguyen, *The Sympathizer*, 306.
170. Nguyen, 366–67.
171. Bourdieu, "Forms of Capital," 3.

others and their masculine victimizations of women. Their own victimizations ultimately allow them to empathize with their victims. Faced with the ghosts of those they victimized, unlike the other players of this study, Kali and the sympathizer come to grips with their own playerism.

Just as the American public faced the ghosts of 9/11 and what caused it during and after the War on Terror in spoofs like *World Police*, Kali and the sympathizer grapple with the domestic and international scars of this war. Recognizing the ways in which the War on Terror has often needlessly victimized other nations, President Obama declared that the focus of the US would no longer be on an abstract global War on Terror but would be redirected toward specific extremists that threaten the nation in 2013.[172] The adjusted focus on extreme terror organizations nevertheless remains vague for all the reasons cited before. Moreover, the legacies of Bush's War on Terror have endured: From the American perspective, the post-9/11 Manichean "axis of evil" emerged as Iraq, Iran, and North Korea. The zero-sum, binary (democratic freedom fighters / lawless terrorists) Manicheanism of the War on Terror was reinforced in gendered discourses recasting the terrorist as a feminine or at least "subordinate masculine identity," which, in turn, "reinforce[ed] and rescu[ed] Anglo-American hegemonic masculinity."[173] The imperialism of American democracy (as a theory rather than practice) in the failed projects of nation-building and democratizing Middle Eastern nations nevertheless fortified the ideology of American exceptionalism.[174] Beyond the calcification of Manichean ideologies, the War on Terror aimed to secure American energy sources in the Middle East, which ultimately exploited poorer Middle Eastern countries "in favor of the [American] metropole."[175] Moreover, as LiPuma and Lee argue, financial derivatives, which are the cornerstones of the speculative capital that aided in driving the War on Terror, remain invisible to regular economistic views even as they are "financial weapons of mass destruction" whose risk threatens to destroy the global economy.[176] The Manichean discourse of good American democracy and finance capital versus the bad, lawless, effeminate terrorist was propagated by Bush and his administration.[177] Once again, white hegemonic masculinity became synonymous with American imperialism. Such discourses have since become reiterated "sound bites" in the media and performances by American citizens, particularly

---

172. Shinkman, "Obama."
173. Rygiel, "Protecting and Proving Identity," 148.
174. Dower, *Cultures of War*.
175. LiPuma and Lee, *Financial Derivatives*, 49.
176. LiPuma and Lee, 64, 104.
177. Scott, "Rescue in the Age of Empire," 111; Rygiel, "Protecting and Proving Identity," 148.

Asian American men who are constantly challenged with impossibly proving their player imperialist, *white* American masculinity in the age of terror. This dynamic is explicitly reflected in the behaviors of the Asian American players of the texts that this chapter examines.

The player society that each of these works depicts is reflective of contemporary finance capital and US imperialism in which the dominant powers briefly invest in either business or political relationships and then quickly withdraw when most convenient for them. At the center of these societies is psychic, personal, or democratic loss, particularly for women and women of color, who represent democratic inclusion and equity in each of these texts: Nguyen's sympathizer mourns the death of his inclusive mother and the gang rape of the communist agent. Kali mourns the loss of his grandmother Situe, who eventually leaves him again after teaching him about freedom of thought and companionate marriage; he also disavows his father and fails to mention his mother. All of these painful losses of care signify the loss of inclusive democracy in the contemporary American imperialist War on Terror and historical military enterprises in the East and are the origins of these characters' misogynistic addictions, which later become their remedies. At the end of *The New Belly Dancer of the Galaxy*, when Kali is rehabilitated by Situe and reunited with his wife, he feels his new soul "coating his skin. His mind. His heart": "He thought of it as an invisible cloak. And he hoped that, as time passed, he would absorb it into himself. He wished he'd weighed himself the first day he felt it to see if he was heavier, like people are weighed before and after death to see if there's a difference. To see if there's a soul."[178] Uncertain yet if he has attained a new soul, Kali is nevertheless on his way to healing himself of his anxious and narcissistic playing, which had taken the hegemonic forms of coping with illegitimacy through deception and preemption, at the end of the novel. To heal, or at least take a long respite from playing, the sympathizer and Kali realize and come to accept that—in this nation, now world, of imperialism, artifice, and simulacra—real, inclusive, and equitable democracy can be realized in interpersonal relationships of authentic care; moreover, they recognize that one does not have to be the best—an illusion in itself—to have value. This illusion is one of the many ways in which American imperialism has seduced, deluded, and betrayed them.

---

178. Noble, 263.

CONCLUSION

The Anxieties of Postmodern Wars

POSTMODERN ANXIETY AND MASCULINITY

The Asian American players I examine in this book index and challenge but do not necessarily undo the hegemony of player imperialist, white masculinity. Their performances, however, demonstrate the performativity of player imperialism and its possible distinction from white hegemonic masculinity. By demonstrating these points through Asian American players after World War II, this book postmodernizes[1] or politicizes these players and contributes to the study of the difficult, elusive concept of postmodernism. The Asian American player is a figure and phenomenon that performs himself as if he were without history: That is, he loses or disavows his influences and parental figures like the sympathizer and Kali or he refuses to start a new history by influencing others through childrearing or mentorship; nevertheless, he reflects his historical moment of postmodern war that is driven by player imperialist masculinity. Like the simulacra of player imperialism that he imitates, the Asian American player is a symbol of postmodernism. The Asian American player is a figure who performs multiply and delineates subjectification as he is both empowered and disempowered, victimizer and victimized. He mimics the player imperialist masculinities that have been shaped

---

1. Appiah, "Is the Post- in Postmodernism," 343.

by and informed each major US war since World War II. The counterculture of play that emerged after 1945 was incorporated into American imperialism and reared its head in the political player ideologies of domestic containment during the Korean War, polarizing "remasculinization" during the Vietnam War, world police qua family man during the Gulf War, and the illegitimate orphanhood of the War on Terror. I chose to focus on canonized and well-known Asian American texts as established case studies to exemplify the enduring and evolving political phenomenon of player imperialist masculinity and the Asian American players that subjectively mimic and expose it.

As demonstrated by the characters Benny and Max in *The New Belly Dancer of the Galaxy*, the player imperialism of white hegemonic masculinity is untenable at the level of the individual precisely because it is a political ideology that is premised on the inherently unstable temporality of anxiety. Player imperialism is a true simulacrum that continually seduces others to follow suit. It supposes that one ethnic group, white Americans, is superior to others, particularly feminized Asian Americans, based on a temporary and gendered performance of seemingly permanent strength, might, and invincibility. In other words, player imperialism is, even as a subjectivity, and symptom, counterposed to humanity. Thus, player imperialism inevitably distinguishes itself from white hegemonic masculinity. Nevertheless, Breitenberg asserts that "the phrase 'anxious masculinity' is redundant."[2] He goes on to clarify that masculinity is fostered and sustained by patriarchy and its assumptions about the naturalness of male superiority in "power, privilege, sexual desire, the body;" thus masculine anxiety is ineluctable and imperative in perpetuating patriarchy even as it discloses its "fissures and contradictions."[3] The "fissures" of patriarchy lie in its exclusions; while patriarchy is meant to protect its subordinates, those whom it keeps intact in the postwar United States are a select homogenous group of white, cisgender heterosexual men and sometimes the minorities who deconstruct and perpetuate this ideology: Asian American players. As Breitenberg points out, anxiety paradoxically exposes the unstable foundations of patriarchy and continues it, propelling it forward. Thus, war—particularly post–World War II American wars, which were propelled by player imperialist masculinity—as the quintessential expression of masculine might and dominance is inherently anxious and anxiety-inducing.

As reflected in the novels I have studied in this book, the United States emerged from World War II in a notably masculine and anxious position as victor and unstable world superpower. Historian Jessica Wang indicates

---

2. Breitenberg, *Anxious Masculinity*, 1.
3. Breitenberg, 1–2.

America's precarious and anxious status as the world superpower after the release of the atomic bombs on Hiroshima and Nagasaki that ended World War II: She states that the war allowed the US to emerge as world victor and power, but there was no guarantee for the endurance of this prosperity, which was threatened by further atomic war.[4] American masculinity was fueled by anxiety. Wang likens American anxiety about its world power to the instability of the atomic bomb.[5] After the atomic bombs were dropped, the US leveled its anxiety about its newly acquired superpower status at communist countries such as Russia and China. Communism became the enemy and scapegoat for these anxieties over nuclear holocaust.[6] While the US maintained its masculine and hard demeanor in the Cold War, the communists, like Asian Americans, were discursively cast as feminine and soft.[7] The gendered polarization between capitalists and communists during the Cold War appears in Ichiro's reactionary hypermasculinity and his criticism of his mother as improperly butch in *No-No Boy* (1957) and in the polarization between the disempowering, stereotyping metaphor of the effeminate Asian butterfly in *M. Butterfly* (1988) and the discourse of player imperialist masculinity.[8] Likewise, during the wars in the Middle East following the Cold War, Middle Easterners and terrorists have been problematically figured as feminine and unpredictable: During the Gulf War, the US believed that Iraq's impulsive invasion of Kuwait and neighboring countries needed to be deterred. Likewise, if counterterrorism was a form of masculine reclamation of power, terrorism is framed as feminine, illegitimate, and excessive.[9] Excess, or anything else that masculinity cannot accept about itself, is always projected onto femininity.[10] Terrorist suicide bombings, for example, during the War on Terror, have been portrayed as excessive and cowardly, and thus offensively feminine, since they indiscriminately kill civilians and military, alike. On the other hand, the precise and invisible virtuality of the Gulf War and the War on Terror exemplifies the masculinity of American war strategies. Although some of the Asian American characters I examine, such as Ichiro and Henry Park, suffer from social invisibility because of racism—while the texts and media castigate other Asian American players and the 1990s race riots by visibility—a privileged invisibility has been used by player imperialism to distract from America's perpetual

---

4. Wang, *American Science*, 1.
5. Wang, 1.
6. Wang, 2.
7. See Cuordileone, "'Politics in an Age of Anxiety,'" 515–45.
8. Okada, *No-No Boy*, 12.
9. Rygiel, "Protecting and Proving Identity," 151.
10. Thomas, *Male Matters*, 2.

state of war since World War II. All different incarnations of deterrence, the American war strategies in major wars after World War II have been heavily influenced by the same game theory of poker that involves bluffing, reduction to bipolarities, playing the odds, preemption, and risk with the aim of securing patriarchal masculinity. Fighting totalitarianism and terrorism is a democratic prisoners' dilemma of many nations that the US has historically and continually turned into a zero-sum game of American imperialism under the guise of democracy. This repeated bait-and-switch strategy, used by the US throughout the Cold War and the wars in the Middle East, exemplifies Nash's game theory of equilibrium in which players reiteratively use the same strategies to arrive at an equilibrium against the anxiety of loss. To win the zero-sum game of American player imperialism, the US has used Keynesian economics—a game of bluffing about wealth and playing the odds of public and private spending to boost private economy—in the military-industrial complex throughout all of the postmodern wars. Keynesian economics ultimately paved the way for finance capitalism, which contributed to the financialization of the everyday lives of Americans in the twenty-first century. American imperialism has always been racially gendered as white hegemonic masculinity but has come to the fore through the mimicry of ethnic, specifically Asian American men after World War II.

In the previous chapters, I have also briefly placed popular postmodern thinkers such as Michel Foucault, Jacques Lacan, and Jean Baudrillard in the polarizing contexts of the Cold War, the Gulf War, and the War on Terror to historicize the ahistoricism of postmodern theories. Moreover, Foucault's theory of the carceral, Lacan's theory of the *imago* and fragmentation of the "mirror stage," and Baudrillard's theory of the simulacra all share the common themes of empowerment and disempowerment. The form of power that I discuss consistently throughout this book—one that is both enduring and unsustainable—is player imperialist American masculinity or what is now commonly known as "bro-hood."

US incursions into the discursively feminized Far and Middle East since World War II have been a specifically masculine endeavor and have consolidated stereotypes of Asian American male effeminacy. Art historian Amy Lyford argues that, specifically in France, but also universally, the scaffolding of post–World War II society and politics relied on the familiar notions of sexual difference; thus, after the war, women's return to domesticity and masculine anxiety stalled feminist progress.[11] After World War II, the US attempted to stabilize its anxious masculinity as a world superpower by returning to

---

11. Lyford, *Surrealist Masculinities*, 11.

structures of sexual difference domestically and internationally by invading feminized Far and Middle Eastern countries. Fueling a seemingly permanent state of war, different presidential administrations and the US military have abided by Nash's game theory of equilibrium of turning prisoners' dilemmas of fighting totalitarianism and terrorism into the zero-sum game of American imperialism since World War II; specifically, the US has used variations of the player's logic of deterrence—that is, polarizing brinkmanship (objectifying minoritized others while subjectifying the self) and deterrent, preemptive strikes (masking the deceptive bluff of empowerment) in the Cold War and the wars in the Middle East, respectively. As my study demonstrates, war—particularly, a permanent state of war—is not fought in isolation from civilians and war veterans: The anxious masculinity of the US imperialist interventions in the Far and Middle East, as I have argued, has been reflected by Asian American (hyper)masculinity and hypersexuality in cultural productions ever since World War II. In this way, civilian Asian American male characters deploy hybridity in mimicking their military and governmental superiors, but, in addition to deconstructing and deauthorizing white hegemonic masculinity as hybridity does to authority, their mimicry exposes even as it legitimizes the political white playerism of the US military and its government. In other words, contributing to American imperialism and a perpetual state of war since 1945, Asian American masculinity traces—that is, is symptomatic, constitutive, and deconstructive of—player imperialist masculinity. Despite their mimicry, the Asian American players are racialized as victimizing inferior outsiders.

By the same token, white hegemonic masculinity is not synonymous with player imperialism. In fact, the Asian American mimicry of player imperialist, white hegemonic masculinity, as this book demonstrates, suggests that ethical manhood is possible for any recovered player when he can begin to identify and empathize with his victims. On the other hand, the Asian American player plays to survive within a player imperialist society but never wins. He is always "other": By mimicking the imperialism that oppresses him, he betrays himself.

The player imperialist, hegemonic white American masculinity that was championed by the Cold War and the wars in the Middle East has been mimicked by Asian American male players who are emasculated and victimized by the very ideology they seek, but fail, to imitate. By reflecting American imperialism, the Asian American player, or the ethnic player more broadly, offers ethnic studies a historicized unit of comparison and a mode of discussing the "elephant in the room" of American imperialism in the multidisciplinary field that attempts to claim and complexify America. As the texts of this study have sociologically demonstrated, Asian American male players, in turn, victimize women of color and, at times, white women, to compensate for their emasculation and to anxiously continue their imitation of American foreign policy after World War II. The same could be said of African American players, such as Ralph Ellison's invisible man, Latinx players, such as Junot Díaz's Yunior, and Native American players, such as Sherman Alexie's Victor and Junior from *The Lone Ranger and Tonto Fistfight in Heaven*. Ethnic American men, with the very general exception of Asian American men, are associated with violence and delinquency.[12] As receptacles of violence and abuse, ethnic American men sometimes, themselves, become abusers of others and often play or objectify women of color. *The Moynihan Report*, a 1965 sociological study of African American families, cites the social abuse given and endured by African American men.[13] Moreover, critic Hazel V. Carby and theorist Cornel West state that the African American bodies are often stylized as macho and thus invite sexual encounters with women but also violent encounters with others, including the police; this quest for power often ends up perpetuating the status quo of the criminal justice system.[14] On the other hand, critic Marlon Moore writes that male femininity has historically been rejected by Black leadership and patriarchal African American interpersonal relationships.[15] There have been exceptions: As critic Jonathan Fenderson points out, the famous African American editor Hoyt Fuller's homosexuality and experiences deny the assumed dichotomy between Black nationalism and queer sexualities within the Black Arts movement.[16] However, African American heteronormative hypermasculinity remains hegemonic and has created dysfunctions within the African American community: bell hooks observes that psychically wounded African American men often find problems in romantic relationships: "As the saying goes, 'hurt people hurt people.'"[17]

The same hypermasculine dynamic that plagues Asian American players appears in other communities. In the Latinx community, as critic Jacqueline

---

12. There are, of course, exceptions to this general assumption. As Eric Tang points out in *Unsettled: Cambodian Refugees in the New York City Hyperghetto*, Cambodian refugees are often criminalized and, thus, hypermasculinized and contradict the model minority stereotype (13).

13. In *The Moynihan Report: The Negro Family—The Case for National Action*, Daniel Moynihan writes, "As a direct result of this high rate of divorce, separation, and desertion, a very large percent of Negro families are headed by females. [. . . In] 1963, a prosperous year, 29.2 percent of all Negro men in the labor force were unemployed at some time during the year. Almost half of these men were out of work 15 weeks or more" (9, 21).

14. Carby, *Race Men*, 32.

15. Moore, *In the Life*, 29.

16. Fenderson, *Building the Black Arts Movement*, 13–14.

17. bell hooks, *We Real Cool*, 126.

Reich argues, the hypermasculine "Latin lover" becomes a product that is consumed by the masses and thus becomes a feminized object.[18] And thus, many Latinx men continue to set out to prove their masculinity in a society that denies them dignity. Likewise, masculinity is complicated in the Native American community. Critics Robert Alexander Innes and Kim Anderson argue of Indigenous men that hegemonic masculinity has encouraged Indigenous men to dominate Indigenous women and women of color, white women, and other Indigenous men who do not espouse a cisgender, heteronormative identity.[19] Alexie's *The Lone Ranger and Tonto Fistfight in Heaven* and Díaz's *The Is How You Lose Her* contain prime examples of ethnic American players whose hypermasculinities are recognizable despite their womanizing exploits. African American, Latinx, and Native American countercultures appear to be the primary avenue of rebellion for young Asian American men against dominant white culture and the attendant binary stereotypes of them as model minorities and the yellow peril in recent literature and popular culture. Thus, Asian American players often attempt to cast off their model minority/yellow peril racial stereotypes and perform African American, Latinx, and Native American countercultural identities. However, it is nonhyperbolic ("just right"), legitimate white hegemonic masculinity that ethnic American players ultimately seek to perform for the purposes of empowerment.

The ethnic American player, which this study has only begun to examine, is an effective unit of comparison among the different fields of ethnic studies and relates the discipline to studies of American imperialism. In examining the Asian American player during the postmodern era, this study reveals that they are subjectified by the binary, racializing stereotypes of the abuser and the abused. This subjectification contributes to Claire Jean Kim's formulation of US racializing paradigms of superior/inferior and insider/outsider.[20] For these portrayed Asian American players—Ichiro Yamada, Song Liling, Franklin Hata, Henry Park, the sympathizer, and Kali—machismo and anxiety are coupled motivations for players' deceptions. Because of their binary racializations, Asian American players seduce others by performing either a docile hyperfemininity (Song—who speaks in American English—Hata and Park) or a criminalized hypermasculinity (Ichiro and the sympathizer) that is more akin to other ethnic players. All the Asian American players' anxious performances of hegemonic white American masculinity deceive their victims and themselves.

18. Reich, *Beyond the Latin Lover*, xiv.
19. Innes and Anderson, *Indigenous Men and Masculinities*, 11.
20. C. Kim, *Bitter Fruit*, 16.

Nevertheless, the backdrop of war in all these texts, in content and publication, influences the masculinities of all of these Asian American players. For example, when Ichiro is discriminated against by the returning veteran Eto at the beginning of *No-No Boy,* Okada reinforces the notion that the soldier is the quintessential embodiment of masculinity. In addition to the military, sport and superhero popular culture are other representations of indefatigable masculinity in the US. As my final chapter demonstrates, after the public questioning of American player imperialism since 9/11, Asian American players have themselves become an outdated trope—the binary counterpart to the ideology of legitimate white American masculinity, which enjoys the privilege of being either visible or invisible whenever convenient; the Asian American players I examine in my fourth chapter choose to embrace ethical manhood as a result of their contemporary moment of challenging American imperialism. Their temporal moves in choosing ethical manhood after playing offer an alternative to the toxic masculinity of the player imperialism that white hegemonic masculinity often espouses. Asian American players, throughout this study, mimic the US government's incorporation of American counterculture of spontaneity and whimsical play that began after World War II but was corporately used to dominate Eastern nations. At times, Asian American "playing" performs the democratic work of exposing American imperialism as inequitable. Whereas player imperialist, white American masculinity can enforce its invisible patriarchy, Asian American male players have been visibly painted or racialized as sexual deviants and outlaws during each major war. Whether the Asian American players embrace ethical manhood seems dependent on the ethos of the era: That is, during the Korean War, in which the US victoriously established the 38th parallel, the Asian American players could adopt ethical manhoods; however, during the explicitly and implicitly remasculinizing eras of the Vietnam War and the Gulf War, the Asian American players I examine decline to do so; it is not until the national self-questioning of American imperialism during the War on Terror that the Asian American players attain their ethical manhoods. As the texts of this study have shown, Asian American men fail to live up to the imperialist, hegemonic ideal of masculinity, which invisibly victimizes others, and visibly default to playerism. Without many options for ways of identifying in the US, as Asian American players, they exemplify and challenge, by collapsing, the polarizing metaphors of racial stereotypes—variations of the stereotypes of superior/inferior, insider/outsider, *and* the abuser / the abused. In comparing the privilege of whiteness to masculinity, Lyford writes that whiteness is often an invisible foundation of the discourse about race and identity and is therefore also wedded to anxiety.[21] In maintaining its dominance in the American racial landscape, whiteness must continually attempt to legitimize its social construction as superior, insider, and recovering from abuse or altogether exempt from the binary of the abuser and the abused. The bipolarities that subjectify and racialize the Asian American player are perpetuated by the contexts of post–World War II binary ideologies of communism/capitalism and terrorists/freedom fighters. As this book has demonstrated, civilian Asian American players who have not participated in warfighting, no matter how diversely they identify themselves, remain unconsciously locked in the war prisons of binary racial and gendered stereotypes. Since World War II, American wars have become increasingly abstract and virtual and thus contribute to a postmodern lack of reality and identity for these constantly performing players in their attempts to subjectify themselves.

Given that the polarization that structures the Cold War and the wars in the Middle East pervades the racialization of ethnic others in the United States after World War II, it seems particularly apt to suggest that multi-ethnic literature, which emerged as an academic field during the Civil Rights era of the 1960s and 1970s, culminates in representing groups who are depicted as inferior outsiders during this period. The figure of the ethnic American player merges Claire Jean Kim's paradigm of ethnic American others as either superior or inferior and insiders or outsiders with Lynn Mie Itagaki's analysis of white civility and nonwhite uncivility by also subjectifying ethnic others as either the abuser or the abused. The structure of abuse—in which the abused perpetuate the paradigm of the abuser and the abused by enabling or, in turn, enacting abuse—offers multi-ethnic literature what Spivak terms "responsible comparativism" and situates ethnic studies in relation to American imperialism.[22] In her critical discussion of the field of comparative literature, she calls for a "discipline to come," through a vocabulary that allows "access to textuality" in order to "responsibly" understand cultural diversity diachronically through a multicultural history without preconceived ideas.[23] The perpetuated paradigm of the abuser and the abused that is dialectically confronted by political protest through social movements and literature offers a common unit of comparison for African American, Asian American, Latinx, and Native American studies that are otherwise informed very differently by histories of slavery, segregation, racial exclusion, deportation, and genocide. Indeed, the

---

21. Lyford, *Surrealist Masculinities*, 8.
22. Spivak, *Death of a Discipline*, 12–13.
23. Spivak, 14–15.

cycle of violence of the abused and its confrontation by social protest define Asian American literature and multi-ethnic literature, broadly. Diachronically tracing the development of multi-ethnic literature through the Cold War and the wars in the Middle East would usefully divulge the hegemony of player imperialist, white, heterosexual, cisgender American masculinity after World War II and the consequent struggles of ethnic American men who never quite attain this ideal and the ethnic women who are often victimized as a result. Player imperialist, white, cisgender, heterosexual masculinity enacts its hegemony in American foreign policy and domestic politics through its intoxicating normativity, even unmarked invisibility, after World War II. As this study has shown, masculine strategies of war become more and more abstract through the Cold War, the Gulf War, and the War on Terror. Polarizing Cold War ideologies such as domestic containment and brinkmanship are premised on and perpetuate patriarchal anxiety whereas the deterrent, virtual preemption of the Gulf War and the War on Terror converts patriarchal anxiety into more abstract addictions for Asian American men as we see in *The Sympathizer*. Defined by these historically evolving structures of anxiety and masculinity, the cycle of violence and abuse that informs ethnic studies renders all ethnic American subjects part of an underclass. The Asian American player that enacts social, sometimes physical, violence on its minoritized victims finds its analogue in other ethnic literatures.

It would be remiss and irresponsible of me to fail to acknowledge that a few of the successful authors in this conclusion have been publicly charged with sexual harassment as part of the Me Too movement—a democratic call for gender equity which came about in October 2017 after the sexual harassment allegations against Harvey Weinstein emerged. That this study features Asian American male protagonists who recover their ethical manhood suggests that rehabilitation is possible for all; however, as Gallimard, Song, Henry Park, and Doc Hata show, exposing the playerism does not always put an end to it. On the other hand, as Ichiro, the sympathizer, and Kali demonstrate, empathizing with their disempowered victims and recognizing their own inherent disempowerment allows them to recover an ethical manhood of inclusive care and an empirical, interpersonal form of democracy. I would also venture to argue that, in addition to the hard work of fourth-wave feminists, the public questioning of player imperialist masculinity after 9/11 and during the War on Terror helped to spur the Me Too movement, just as some historical eras incited the players in my study to recognize the harmfulness of their actions and embrace ethical manhoods through care, inclusion, and promoting equity. Moreover, this book is not meant to perpetuate the condemning shame that asymmetrically punishes the victim (usually more so) and the victimizer in playerism and the allegations of sexual harassment to which they often lead. Instead, it examines the mutual but asymmetrical structures of imperialism and its corollaries of emasculation, unworthiness, and gendered, sometimes racial, insecurities in which harassment occurs. Sexual harassment, molestation, and assault occur in abusive, player patriarchies to which most cisgender men and women have historically consented. And victims and allies who protest or make complaints about such behavior are often persecuted for disrupting the status quo—even when it is traditionally comprised of unethical violence—or, worse, blamed for seeking negative attention.

Shame is the primary executioner in playing and other forms of sexual abuse. It unfortunately does not discriminate. It incriminates the victim as well as the victimizer and, by association and complicity, the communities of these figures. Since abusers unfortunately tend to victimize more than once, shame sometimes deters the offender from enacting further offenses. Repeat offenses of victimization, as in the case of Harvey Weinstein, reveal that the sexual abuse of playerism is based on a masculinity that is inherently anxious. That is to say, the seriality of his offenses demonstrates his compulsion to assert an unstable masculinity. As this study argues, anxious masculinity is a historical phenomenon that pervades American foreign policy after World War II. Consequently, the discursive paradigm of the abuser and the abused subjectifies Asian American men as players in this postmodern period. Race can unfortunately constitute an identity associated with violence through victimization and abuse.

Asian American Players explores the intersections of Asian American masculinity, American player imperialism, and the ever-elusive concept of postmodernity through the lens of war and wartime in fiction and drama during different periods following World War II. This book points out that, in addition to celebrating culture and difference, Asian American studies specifically takes the toxic (that is, abusive, selfish, imperialist, homogenous, and genocidal), hegemonic masculinity of American imperialism as its common point of reference even as it is implicated in it. Asian American studies thus divulges the ways in which the abused themselves become anxious abusers or enablers of hegemonic, player ideologies of heterosexual, cisgender, white American masculinity. Since the end of World War II, the postmodern Asian American player who finally attains his ethical manhood reveals that democracy, unlike imperialism, is not a game to play. Instead, it is a principle used to repair nation states and their apparatuses, which have had deficiencies in diversity, equity, inclusion, and social justice. For all of us, democracy is the ultimate romance—one that we eagerly desire to usher into empirical reality.

BIBLIOGRAPHY

Abe, Frank, Greg Robinson, and Floyd Cheung, eds. *John Okada: The Life & Rediscovered Work of the Author of* No-No Boy. Seattle: University of Washington Press, 2018.

Aghacy, Samira. *Masculine Identity in the Fiction of the Arab East since 1967.* Syracuse, NY: Syracuse University Press, 2009.

Allen, Neal. "The Fight Against Terrorism in Historical Context: George W. Bush and the Development of Presidential Foreign Policy Regimes." In *America's War on Terror,* edited by Patrick Hayden, Tom Lansford, and Robert P. Watson, 37–48. Burlington, VT: Ashgate, 2003.

Allinson, Gary D. *Japan's Postwar History.* Ithaca, NY: Cornell University Press, 1997.

Amoko, Apollo O. "Resilient ImagiNations: *No-No Boy, Obasan* and the Limits of Minority Discourse." *Mosaic: A Journal for the Interdisciplinary Study of Literature* 33, no. 3 (September 2000): 35–56.

Andrews, Kristin. "Why Bush Should Explain 11 September." In *America's War on Terror,* edited by Patrick Hayden, Tom Lansford, and Robert P. Watson. Burlington, VT: Ashgate, 2003.

Appiah, Kwame Anthony. "Is the Post- in Postmodernism the Post- in Postcolonial?" *Critical Inquiry* 17, no. 2 (Winter 1991): 336–57.

Arendt, Hannah. *Between Past and Future: Eight Exercises in Political Thought.* New York: Penguin Classics, 1954.

Arrighi, Giovanni. *The Long Twentieth Century: Money, Power, and the Origins of Our Times.* New York: Verso, 1994.

Atwood, Paul L. *War and Empire: The American Way of Life.* New York: Pluto Press, 2010.

Bahng, Aimee. "Specters of the Pacific: Salt Fish Drag and Atomic Hauntologies in the Era of Genetic Modifications." *Journal of American Studies* 49, Special Issue 04 (November 2015): 663–83.

Bak, John S. "'Vestis Virum Reddit': The Gender Politics of Drag in Williams's 'A Streetcar Named Desire' and Hwang's 'M. Butterfly.'" *South Atlantic Review* 70, no. 4. "Tennessee Williams in/and the Canons of American Drama" (Fall 2005): 94–118.

Ball, W. Macmahon. *Japan: Enemy or Ally?* New York: The John Day Company, 1949.

Bascara, Victor. *Model-Minority Imperialism*. Minneapolis: University of Minnesota Press, 2006.

Baudrillard, Jean. *America*. New York: Verso, 1988.

———. *The Gulf War Did Not Take Place*. Bloomington: Indiana University Press, 1991.

———. *Selected Writings*. Edited by Mark Poster. Stanford, CA: Stanford University Press, 1988.

———. *Simulacra and Simulation*. Translated by Sheila Glaser. Ann Arbor: University of Michigan Press, 1994.

———. *The Spirit of Terrorism*. 2001. New York: Verso, 2002.

Belgrad, Daniel. *The Culture of Spontaneity: Improvisation and the Arts in Postwar America*. Chicago: The University of Chicago Press, 1998.

Bhabha, Homi. "Of Mimicry and Man: The Ambivalence of Colonial Discourse." In *The Location of Culture*. New York: Routledge, 1994.

Blair, Clay. *The Forgotten War: America in Korea 1950 to 1953*. New York: Anchor Books, 1989.

Blang, Eugenie M. *Allies at Odds: America, Europe, and Vietnam, 1961–1968*. Lanham, MD: Rowman and Littlefield, 2011.

Bloom, Gina. *Gaming the Stage: Playable Media and the Rise of English Commercial Theater*. Ann Arbor: University of Michigan Press, 2018.

Bodnar, John. *The "Good War" in American Memory*. Baltimore, MD: The Johns Hopkins University Press, 2010.

———. *Remaking America: Public Memory, Commemoration, and Patriotism in the Twentieth Century*. Princeton, NJ: Princeton University Press, 1992.

Bosch-Vilarrubias, Marta. *Post-9/11 Representations of Arab Men by Arab American Women Writers: Affirmation and Resistance*. New York: Peter Lang, 2016.

Bourdieu, Pierre. "The Forms of Capital." *Handbook of Theory and Research for the Sociology of Education* (New York, Greenwood): 241–58. https://www.marxists.org/reference/subject/philosophy/works/fr/bourdieu-forms-capital.htm.

Bradford, Richard. *Roman Jakobson: Life, Language, Art*. London: Routledge, 1994.

Breitenberg, Mark. *Anxious Masculinity in Early Modern England*. Cambridge, UK: Cambridge University Press, 1996.

Brown, Wendy. *States of Injury: Power and Freedom in Late Modernity*. Princeton, NJ: Princeton University Press, 1995.

———. *Undoing the Demos: Neoliberalism's Stealth Revolution*. New York: Zone Books, 2015.

Brune, Lester H., ed. *The Korean War: Handbook of the Literature and Research*. Westport, CT: Greenwood Press, 1996.

Brune, Lester H., and Mark Leach. "Congress during the Korean War." In *The Korean War: Handbook of the Literature and Research*, edited by Lester H. Brune, 342–400. Westport, CT: Greenwood Press, 1996.

Butler, Judith. *Gender Trouble: Feminism and the Subversion of Identity*. New York: Routledge, 1990.

Cándida Smith, Richard. *Utopia and Dissent: Art, Poetry, and Politics in California*. Berkeley: University of California Press, 1995.

Carby, Hazel V. *Race Men: The W. E. B. Du Bois Lectures*. Cambridge, MA: Harvard University Press, 1998.

Carroll, Hamilton. "Traumatic Patriarchy: Reading Gendered Nationalisms in Chang-rae Lee's *A Gesture Life.*" *Modern Fiction Studies* 51, no. 3 (Fall 2005): 592–616.

Carroll, Hamilton, and Annie McClanahan. "Fictions of Speculation: Introduction." *Journal of American Studies* 49, Special Issue 04 (November 2015): 655–61.

Carter, Zachary D. *The Price of Peace: Money, Democracy, and the Life of John Maynard Keyes*. New York: Random House, 2020.

Chan, Jachinson. *Chinese American Masculinities: From Fu Manchu to Bruce Lee*. New York: Routledge, 2001.

Chan, Sucheng. *Asian Americans: An Interpretive History*. Detroit, MI: Gale Cengage Learning, 1991.

Chang, Yoonmee. *Writing the Ghetto: Class, Authorship, and the Asian American Ethnic Enclave*. New Brunswick, NJ: Rutgers University Press, 2010.

Chapman, William. *Inventing Japan: The Making of a Postwar Civilization*. New York: Prentice Hall Press, 1991.

Chen, Tina. *Double Agency: Acts of Impersonation in Asian American Literature and Culture*. Stanford, CA: Stanford University Press, 2005.

———. "Impersonating and Other Disappearing Acts in *Native Speaker* by Chang-rae Lee." *Modern Fiction Studies* 48, no. 2 (Fall 2002): 637–67.

Cheng, Anne Anlin. *The Melancholy of Race: Psychoanalysis, Assimilation, and Hidden Grief*. Oxford: Oxford University Press, 2001.

———. *Ornamentalism*. Oxford: Oxford University Press, 2019.

———. "Race and Fantasy in Modern America: Subjective Dissimulation/ Racial Assimilation." *Multiculturalism and Representation, Literary Studies: East and West*. Honolulu: University of Hawai'i, College of Languages, Linguistics, and Literature.

Cheung, Floyd. "Early Chinese American Autobiography: Reconsidering the Works of Yan Phou Lee and Yung Wing." In *Recovered Legacies: Authority and Identity in Early Asian American Literature*, edited by Keith Lawrence and Floyd Cheung, 24–40. Philadelphia, PA: Temple University Press, 2005.

Childers, Joseph, and Gary Hentzi, eds. "Postmodernism." In *The Columbia Dictionary of Modern Literary and Cultural Criticism*. New York: Columbia University Press, 1995.

Chin, Frank. Afterword to *No-No Boy*, by John Okada, 253–60. Seattle: University of Washington Press, 1976.

Chin, Frank, Jeffery Paul Chan, Lawson Fusao Inada, and Shawn Wong, eds. *Aiiieeeee!: An Anthology of Asian American Writers*. New York: Mentor, 1991.

Chiu, Monica. *Scrutinized!: Surveillance in Asian North American Literature*. Honolulu: University of Hawai'i Press, 2014.

Chon-Smith, Chong. *East Meets Black: Asian and Black Masculinities in the Post-Civil Rights Era*. Jackson: University Press of Mississippi, 2015.

Cohen, Cathy J. "Punks, Bulldaggers, and Welfare Queens: The Radical Potential of Queer Politics?," *GLQ* 3: 437–65.

Cuordileone, K. A. "'Politics in an Age of Anxiety': Cold War Political Culture and the Crisis in American Masculinity, 1949–1960." *The Journal of American History* 87, no. 2 (September 2000): 515–45.

Davis, John. "The War on Terrorism on President Bush: Completing His Father's Legacy and Defining His Own Place in History." In *America's War on Terror*, edited by Patrick Hayden, Tom Lansford, and Robert P. Watson, 105–18. Burlington, VT: Ashgate, 2003.

Deleuze, Gilles, and Félix Guattari. *Anti-Oedipus: Capitalism and Schizophrenia*. New York: Penguin Books, 1972.

Denning, Michael. *The Cultural Front: The Laboring of American Culture in the Twentieth Century*. London and New York: Verso, 1997.

Derrida, Jacques. *Of Grammatology*. Translated by Gayatri Chakravorty Spivak. Baltimore, MD: The Johns Hopkins University Press, 1997.

———. *Specters of Marx*. Translated by Peggy Kamuf. New York: Routledge, 1994.

Dixit, Avinash K., and Barry J. Nalebuff. *Thinking Strategically: The Competitive Edge in Business, Politics, and Everyday Life*. New York: W. W. Norton, 1991.

Doherty, Thomas. *Cold War, Cool Medium: Television, McCarthyism, and American Culture*. New York: Columbia University Press, 2003.

Dower, John W. *Cultures of War: Pearl Harbor / Hiroshima / 9-11 / Iraq*. New York: W. W. Norton, 2010.

———. *Embracing Defeat: Japan in the Wake of World War II*. New York: W. W. Norton, 1999.

Dudziak, Mary. *Cold War Civil Rights: Race and the Image of American Democracy*. Princeton, NJ: Princeton University Press, 2000.

Ehrhart, William D. "Ch. 3: Above All, the Waste: American Soldier-Post and the Korean War." In *Remembering the 'Forgotten War': The Korean War through Literature and Art*, edited by Philip West and Suh Ji-moon, 40–54. Armonk, NY: East Gate, 2001.

Ellison, Ralph. *Invisible Man*. 1952. New York: Vintage International, 1995.

Enloe, Cynthia. *Bananas, Beaches and Bases: Making Feminist Sense of International Politics*. Berkeley: University of California Press, 1990.

Eng, David L. *Racial Castration: Managing Masculinity in Asian America*. Durham, NC: Duke University Press, 2001.

Entin, Joseph. "'A Terribly Incomplete Thing': *No-No Boy* and the Ugly Feelings of Noir." *MELUS* 35, no. 3, Crime, Punishment, and Redemption (Fall 2010): 85–104.

Fenderson, Jonathan. *Building the Black Arts Movement: Hoyt Fuller and the Cultural Politics of the 1960s*. Urbana: University of Illinois Press, 2019.

Fickle, Tara. *The Race Card: From Gaming Technologies to Model Minorities*. New York: New York University Press, 2019.

Finch, Laura. "The Un-real Deal: Financial Fiction, Fictional Finance, and the Financial Crisis." *Journal of American Studies* 49, Special Issue 04 (November 2015): 731–53.

Finlan, Alastair. *The Gulf War, 1991, Essential Histories*. Oxford: Osprey Publishing, 2003.

Foot, Rosemary. *The Wrong War: American Policy and the Dimensions of the Korean Conflict, 1950–1953*. Ithaca, NY: Cornell University Press, 1985.

Foucault, Michel. *Discipline and Punish: The Birth of the Prison*. Translated by Alan Sheridan. New York: Vintage Books, 1995.

Freeman, Joshua B. *American Empire: The Rise of a Global Power, the Democratic Revolution at Home, 1945–2000*. New York: Penguin Books, 2012.

Freud, Sigmund. "Mourning and Melancholia." In *General Psychological Theory*, 164–79. New York: Touchstone, 1997.

Galbraith, P. W. "Refugees from the War in Iraq: What Happened in 1991 and What May Happen in 2003." *Migration Policy Institute* 2 (8 September 2003): 1–11.

Garber, Marjorie. *Vested Interests: Cross-Dressing & Cultural Anxiety*. New York: Routledge, 2011.

Gates, Scott, and Brian D. Humes. *Games, Information, and Politics: Applying Game Theoretic Models to Political Science*. Ann Arbor: The University of Michigan Press, 1997.

Glickman, Lawrence B. *Free Enterprise: An American History*. New Haven, CT: Yale University Press, 2019.

Gómez-Vega, Ibis. "Ancestral Voices and Family History in Frances Khirallah Noble's *The New Belly Dancer of the Galaxy*." *Athens Journal of Philology* 6, no. 2 (June 2019): 65–82.

Gray, Chris Hables. *Postmodern War: The New Politics of Conflict*. New York: The Guilford Press, 1997.

Hanson, Victor Davis. "Why Did We Invade Iraq?" *National Review*, March 26, 2013. http://www.nationalreview.com/article/343870/why-did-we-invade-iraq-victor-davis-hanson.

Harper, Phillip Brian. *Are We Not Men?: Masculine Anxiety and the Problem of African-American Identity*. Oxford: Oxford University Press, 1996.

———. *Framing the Margins*. New York: Oxford University Press, 1994.

Harvey, David. *The Enigma of Capital and the Crises of Capitalism*. Oxford: Oxford University Press, 2010.

Hastings, Max. *The Korean War*. New York: Simon and Schuster, 1987.

Hawthorne, Melanie C. "'Du Du That Voodoo': M. Venus and M. Butterfly." *L'Esprit Créateur* 3, no. 4 (Winter 1997): 58–66.

Hayden, Patrick. "The War on Terrorism and the Just Use of Military Force." In *America's War on Terror*, edited by Patrick Hayden, Tom Lansford, and Robert P. Watson, 49–72. Burlington, VT: Ashgate, 2003.

Herring, George C. *America's Longest War: The United States and Vietnam, 1950–1975*. Philadelphia, PA: Temple University Press, 1986.

Hill, Samantha Rose. *Hannah Arendt*. London: Reaktion Books, 2021.

Hoang, Nguyen Tan. *A View from the Bottom: Asian American Masculinity and Sexual Representation*. Durham, NC: Duke University Press, 2014.

Hodges, Adam. *The "War on Terror" Narrative: Discourse and Intertextuality in the Construction and Contestation of Sociopolitical Reality*. Oxford: Oxford University Press, 2011.

hooks, bell. *We Real Cool: Black Men and Masculinity*. New York: Routledge, 2004.

Hong, Christine. *A Violent Peace: Race, U.S. Militarism, and Cultures of Democratization in Cold War Asia and the Pacific*. Stanford, CA: Stanford University Press, 2020.

Hoy, Pat C., II. "Spying with Sympathy and Love." *Sewanee Review* 123, no. 4 (Fall 2015): 685–90.

Huang, Betsy. "Citizen Kwang: Chang-rae Lee's *Native Speaker* and the Politics of Consent." *Journal of Asian American Studies* 9, no. 3 (October 2006): 243–69.

Huey, Gary L. "Public Opinion and the Korean War." In *The Korean War: Handbook of the Literature and Research*, edited by Lester H. Brune, 409–17. Westport, CT: Greenwood Press, 1996.

Hwang, David Henry. *M. Butterfly*. New York: Plume, 1986.

Innes, Robert Alexander, and Kim Anderson. *Indigenous Men and Masculinities: Legacies, Identities, Regeneration*. Winnipeg: University of Manitoba Press, 2015.

Itagaki, Lynn Mie. *Civil Racism: The 1992 Los Angeles Rebellion and the Crisis of Racial Burnout*. Minneapolis: University of Minnesota Press, 2016.

Jackson, Lawrence. *Ralph Ellison: Emergence of Genius*. New York: John Wiley & Sons, 2002.

Jakobson, Roman. "Two Aspects of Language and Two Types of Aphasic Disturbances." In *On Language*, edited by Linda R. Waugh and Monique Monville-Burston, 115–33. Cambridge, MA: Harvard University Press, 1990.

Jameson, Fredric. *The Political Unconscious: Narrative as a Socially Symbolic Act.* Ithaca, NY: Cornell University Press, 1981.

———. *Postmodernism, or, The Cultural Logic of Late Capitalism.* Durham, NC: Duke University Press, 1991.

Jeffords, Susan. *Hard Bodies: Hollywood Masculinity in the Reagan Era.* New Brunswick, NJ: Rutgers University Press, 1994.

———. *The Remasculinization of America: Gender and the Vietnam War.* Bloomington: Indiana University Press, 1989.

Jehlen, Myra. *Class and Character in Faulkner's South.* New York: Columbia University Press, 1976.

Jie, Li. "Changes in China's Domestic Situation in the 1960s and Sino-U.S. Relations." In *Reexamining the Cold War: U.S.-China Diplomacy, 1954–1973*, edited by Robert S. Ross and Jiang Changbin, 288–320. Cambridge, MA: Harvard University Press, 2001.

Jun, Helen Heran. *Race for Citizenship: Black Orientalism and Asian Uplift from Pre-Emancipation to Neoliberal America.* New York: New York University Press, 2011.

Kahn, Suzanne. *Divorce, American Style: Fighting for Women's Economic Citizenship in the Neoliberal Era.* Philadelphia: University of Pennsylvania Press, 2021.

Kaplan, Amy. *The Anarchy of Empire in the Making of U.S. Culture.* Cambridge, MA: Harvard University Press, 2002.

———. "Black and Blue on San Juan Hill." In *The Anarchy of Empire in the Making of U.S. Culture*, 121–45. Cambridge, MA: Harvard University Press, 2002.

Kaplan, Amy, and Donald E. Pease, eds. *Cultures of United States Imperialism.* Durham, NC: Duke University Press, 1993.

Kerpen, Beate. "Negotiations of Race and Gender in Ralph Ellison's Invisible Man." Master's thesis, Universität Trier, 2011.

Kim, Claire Jean. *Bitter Fruit.* New Haven, CT: Yale University Press, 2000.

Kim, Daniel Y. *The Intimacies of Conflict: Cultural Memory and the Korean War.* New York: New York University Press, 2020.

———. "Once More, with Feeling: Cold War Masculinity and the Sentiment of Patriotism in John Okada's *No-No Boy*." *Criticism* 47, no. 1 (Winter 2005): 65–83.

———. *Writing Manhood in Black and Yellow: Ralph Ellison, Frank Chin, and the Literary Politics of Identity.* Stanford, CA: Stanford University Press, 2005.

Kim, Jodi. "From Mee-Gook to Gook: The Cold War and Racialized Undocumented Capital in Chang-rae Lee's *Native Speaker*." *MELUS* 34, no. 1. "Witnessing, Testifying, and History" (Spring 2009): 117–37.

Kolodny, Annette. *The Lay of the Land.* Chapel Hill: University of North Carolina Press, 1975.

Kondo, Dorinne. *About Face: Performing Race in Fashion and Theater.* New York: Routledge, 1997.

Kramer, Michael J. *The Republic of Rock: Music and Citizenship in the Sixties Counterculture.* Oxford: Oxford University Press, 2013.

Krippner, Greta R. *Capitalizing on Crisis: The Political Origins of the Rise of Finance.* Cambridge, MA: Harvard University Press, 2011.

Kuznick, Peter J., and James Gilbert, eds. *Rethinking Cold War Culture.* Washington, DC: Smithsonian Institute Press, 2001.

Lacan, Jacques. *Écrits.* Translated by Bruce Fink. New York: W. W. Norton, 2006.

———. *The Four Fundamental Concepts of Psychoanalysis: The Seminar of Jacques Lacan, Book XI.* Edited by Jacques-Alain Miller. Translated by Alan Sheridan. New York: W. W. Norton, 1998.

Lake, David. *Power, Protection, and Free Trade: International Sources of U.S. Commercial Strategy, 1887–1939*. Ithaca, NY: Cornell University Press, 2018.

Lansford, Tom, and Jack Covarrubias. "Osama bin Laden, Radical Islam and the United States." In *America's War on Terror*, edited by Patrick Hayden, Tom Lansford, and Robert P. Watson, 17–36. Burlington, VT: Ashgate, 2003.

Lee, Chang-rae. *A Gesture Life*. New York: Riverhead Books, 1999.

———. *Native Speaker*. New York: Riverhead Books, 1995.

Lee, Christopher. "Form-Giving and the Remains of Identity in *A Gesture Life*." *Journal of Asian American Studies* 14, no. 1 (February 2011): 95–116.

Lee, Robert G. *Orientals: Asian Americans in Popular Culture*. Philadelphia: Temple University Press, 1999.

Lee, Young-Oak. "Gender, Race, and the Nation in *A Gesture Life*." *Critique* 46, no. 2 (Winter 2005): 146–59.

———. "Transcending Ethnicity: Diasporacity in *A Gesture Life*." *Journal of Asian American Studies* 12, no. 1 (February 2009): 65–81.

Lew-Williams, Beth. *The Chinese Must Go: Violence, Exclusion, and the Making of the Alien in America*. Cambridge, MA: Harvard University Press, 2018.

Levering, Ralph B. *The Cold War: A Post-Cold War History*. Arlington Heights, IL: Harlan Davidson, 1994.

Levy, Pema. "Did 9/11 Cause the Financial Crisis?" *The American Prospect*, September 10, 2011. http://prospect.org/article/did-911-cause-financial-crisis.

Lim, Shirley. "Not Waving but Drowning: Creativity and Identity in Diaspora Writing." *Diaspora, Identity, and Language Communities: Studies in the Linguistic Sciences* 31, no. 1 (Spring 2001): 31–49.

Ling, Jinqi. *Narrating Nationalisms: Ideology and Form in Asian American Literature*. New York and Oxford: Oxford University Press, 1998.

———. "*No-No Boy*." *A Resource Guide to Asian American Literature*. New York: The Modern Language Association of America, 2001.

———. "Race, Power, and Cultural Politics in John Okada's *No-No Boy*." *American Literature* 67, no. 2 (June 1995): 359–81.

LiPuma, Edward, and Benjamin Lee. *Financial Derivatives and the Globalization of Risk*. Durham, NC: Duke University Press, 2004.

Lye, Colleen. *America's Asia: Racial Form and American Literature, 1893–1945*. Princeton, NJ: Princeton University Press, 2005.

———. "*M. Butterfly* and the Rhetoric of Anti-Essentialism: Minority Discourse in an International Frame." In *The Ethnic Canon: Histories, Institutions, and Interventions*, edited by David Palumbo-Liu, 260–90. Minneapolis: University of Minnesota Press, 1995.

Lyford, Amy. *Surrealist Masculinities: Gender Anxieties and the Aesthetics of Post–World War I Reconstruction in France*. Berkeley: University of California Press, 2007.

Lyotard, Jean-Francois. *The Postmodern Condition: A Report on Knowledge*. Translated by Geoff Bennington and Brian Massumi. Minneapolis: University of Minnesota Press, 1988.

Ma, Sheng-mei. "Orientalism in Chinese American Discourse: Body and Pidgin." *Modern Language Studies* 23, no. 4 (Autumn 1993): 104–17.

Macey, David. *The Lives of Michel Foucault: A Biography*. New York: Vintage Books, 1993.

Martin, Randy. *The Financialization of Daily Life*. Philadelphia: Temple University Press, 2002.

Marx, Karl, and Friedrich Engels. *The Communist Manifesto, The Norton Anthology of Theory and Criticism*. Edited by Vincent B. Leitch. New York: W. W. Norton, 2001.

May, Elaine Tyler. *Homeward Bound: American Families in the Cold War Era*. New York: Basic Books, 1988.

May, Lary. "Ch. 7: Reluctant Crusaders: Korean War Films and the Lost Audience." In *Remembering the "Forgotten War": The Korean War through Literature and Art*, edited by Philip West and Suh Ji-moon, 110–36. Armonk, NY: East Gate, 2001.

McMahon, Robert J. Introduction to *The Cold War in the Third World*, edited by Robert J. McMahon. Oxford: Oxford University Press, 2013.

Menand, Louis. *The Free World: Art and Thought in the Cold War*. New York: Farrar, Straus and Giroux, 2021.

Miller, James. *The Passion of Michel Foucault*. Cambridge, MA: Harvard University Press, 1993.

Moy, James S. "David Henry Hwang's 'M. Butterfly' and Philip Kan Gotanda's 'Yankee Dawg You Die': Repositioning Chinese American Marginality on the American Stage." *Theatre Journal* 42, no. 1 (March 1990): 48–56.

McAlister, Melani. *Epic Encounters: Culture, Media, and U.S. Interests in the Middle East, 1945–2000*. Berkeley: University of California Press, 2001.

McClanahan, Annie. "Future's Shock: Plausibility, Preemption, and the Fiction of 9/11." *symploke* 17, no. 1 (2009): 41–62.

McKinley, Maggie. *Masculinity and the Paradox of Violence in American Fiction, 1950–74*. New York: Bloomsbury, 2015.

Moore, Marlon R. *In the Life and in the Spirit: Homoerotic Spirituality in African American Literature*. Albany, NY: SUNY Press, 2014.

Moser, Keith. "A Baudrillardian Exploration of Two Victims of Hyper-Real, Erotic Simulations in Joseph Gordon-Levitt's Film *Don Jon*." *Studies in Popular Culture* 37, no. 1 (September 2014): 75–92.

Moynihan, Daniel. *The Moynihan Report: The Negro Family—The Case for National Action*. New York: Cosimo Classics, 2018.

Mulvey, Laura. "Visual Pleasure and Narrative Cinema." *Screen*. Oxford Journals 16, no. 3 (Autumn 1975): 6–18.

Narkunas, J. Paul. "Surfing the Long Waves of Global Capital with Chang-rae Lee's *Native Speaker*: Ethnic Branding and the Humanization of Capital." *Modern Fiction Studies* 54, no. 2 (Summer 2008): 327–52.

Ngai, Sianne. *Our Aesthetic Categories: Zany, Cute, Interesting*. Cambridge, MA: Harvard University Press, 2012.

Nguyen, Viet Thanh. Book Reading of *The Sympathizer*, May 6, 2015, Politics and Prose Bookstore, Washington, DC.

———. Book Reading of *The Sympathizer*, September 5, 2015, National Book Festival, Washington, DC.

———. Book Reading of *The Sympathizer*, November 12, 2015, Library of Congress, Washington, DC.

———. *Race and Resistance: Literature and Politics in Asian America*. Oxford and New York: Oxford University Press, 2002.

———. *The Sympathizer*. New York: Grove Press, 2015.

———. "We Still Live in Ralph Ellison's Moment." Library of America, June 15, 2015. https://www.loa.org/news-and-views/658-viet-thanh-nguyen-we-still-live-in-ralph-ellisons-moment.

———. "Wounded Bodies and the Cold War: Freedom, Materialism, and Revolution in Asian American Literature, 1946–1957." In *Recovered Legacies*, edited by Keith Lawrence and Floyd Cheung, 158–82. Philadelphia: Temple University Press, 2005.

Noble, Frances Khirallah. *The New Belly Dancer of the Galaxy*. Syracuse, NY: Syracuse University Press, 2007.

Okada, John. *No-No Boy*. Seattle, WA: Combined Asian American Resources Project, 1976.

Okihiro, Gary Y. *Common Ground: Reimagining American History*. Princeton, NJ: Princeton University Press, 2001.

Omi, Michael, and Howard Winant. *Racial Formation in the United States, From the 1960s to the 1990s*. 2nd ed. New York: Routledge, 1994.

Park, Michael. "Asian American Masculinity Eclipsed: A Legal and Historical Perspective of Emasculation through U.S. Immigration Practices." *The Modern American* 8, no. 1 (2013): 5–17.

Palumbo-Liu, David. "Discourse and Dislocation: Rhetorical Strategies of Asian-American Exclusion and Confinement." *Literature Interpretation Theory* 2, no. 1 (1990): 1–7.

Pease, Donald E. "New Perspectives on U.S. Culture." In *Cultures of United States Imperialism*, edited by Amy Kaplan and Donald E. Pease, 22–40. Durham, NC: Duke University Press, 1993.

Perrucci, Robert, and Earl Wysong. *The New Class Society: Goodbye American Dream?* Lanham, MD: Rowman and Littlefield, 2013.

Phillips, Kimberly L. *War! What Is It Good For?: Black Freedom Struggles and the U.S. Military from World War II to Iraq*. Chapel Hill: University of North Carolina Press, 2012.

Puar, Jasbir K. *Terrorist Assemblages: Homonationalism in Queer Times*. Durham, NC: Duke University Press, 2007.

Qiang Zhai. *China and the Vietnam Wars, 1950–1975*. Chapel Hill: University of North Carolina Press, 2000.

Reich, Jacqueline. *Beyond the Latin Lover: Marcello, Mastroianni, Masculinity, and Italian Cinema*. Bloomington: Indiana University Press, 2004.

Remen, Kathryn. "The Theatre of Punishment: David Henry Hwang's *M. Butterfly* and Michel Foucault's *Discipline and Punish*." *Modern Drama* 37, no. 3 (Fall 1994): 391–400.

Roberts, John W. *From Trickster to Badman: The Black Folk Hero in Slavery and Freedom*. Philadelphia: University of Pennsylvania Press, 1989.

Rogers, Paul. *Why We're Losing the War on Terror*. Malden, MA: Polity Press, 2008.

Rossini, Jon D. "From *M. Butterfly* to Bondage: David Henry Hwang's Fantasies of Sexuality, Ethnicity and Gender." *Journal of American Drama and Theatre* 18, no. 3 (Fall 2006): 55–76.

Rygiel, Kim. "Protecting and Proving Identity: The Biopolitics of Waging War through Citizenship in the Post-9/11 Era." In *(En)Gendering the War on Terror: War Stories and Camouflaged Politics*, edited by Krista Hunt and Kim Rygiel, 145–68. Burlington, VT: Ashgate, 2006.

Sato, Gayle K. Fujita. "Momotaro's Exile: John Okada's *No-No Boy*." In *Reading the Literatures of Asian America*, edited by Shirley Geok-lin Lim and Amy Ling, 239–58. Philadelphia: Temple University Press, 1992.

Scott, Catherine V. "Rescue in the Age of Empire: Children, Masculinity, and the War on Terror." In *(En)Gendering the War on Terror: War Stories and Camouflaged Politics*, edited by Krista Hunt and Kim Rygiel, 97–120. Burlington, VT: Ashgate, 2006.

Sedgwick, Eve Kosofsky. "Gosh, Boy George, You Must Be Awfully Secure in Your Masculinity!" In *Constructing Masculinity*, edited by Maurice Berger, 11–20. New York: Routledge, 1995.

Seshadri-Crooks, Kalpana. *Desiring Whiteness: A Lacanian Analysis of Race*. London: Routledge, 2000.

Šesnić, Jelena. *From Shadow to Presence: Representations of Ethnicity in Contemporary American Literature*. Amsterdam, Netherlands: Rodopi, 2007.

Shimakawa, Karen. *National Abjection: The Asian American Body Onstage*. Durham, NC: Duke University Press, 2002.

———. "'Who's to Say?' or, Making Space for Gender and Ethnicity in 'M. Butterfly.'" *Theatre Journal* 45, no. 3 (October 1993): 349–62.

Shimizu, Celine Parreñas. *Straitjacket Sexualities: Unbinding Asian American Manhoods in the Movies*. Stanford, CA: Stanford University Press, 2012.

Shin, Andrew. "Projected Bodies in David Henry Hwang's 'M. Butterfly' and 'Golden Gate.'" *MELUS* 27, no. 1. "Contested Boundaries" (Spring, 2002): 177–97.

Shinkman, Paul D. "Obama: 'Global War on Terror' Is Over." *U.S. News & World Report*, May 23, 2013, https://www.usnews.com/news/articles/2013/05/23/obama-global-war-on-terror-is-over.

Skloot, Robert. "Breaking the Butterfly: The Politics of David Henry Hwang." *Modern Drama* 33, no. 1 (Spring 1990): 59–66.

Smith, Richard G., and David B. Clarke, eds. *Jean Baudrillard: From Hyperreality to Disappearance: Uncollected Interviews*. Edinburgh, UK: Edinburgh University Press, 2015.

Sokolowski, Jeanne. "Internment and Post-War Japanese American Literature: Toward a Theory of Divine Citizenship." *MELUS* 34, no. 1, "Witnessing, Testifying, and History" (Spring 2009): 69–93.

Sollors, Werner. *Beyond Ethnicity: Consent and Descent in American Culture*. Oxford: Oxford University Press, 1986.

Spivak, Gayatri Chakravorty. "Can the Subaltern Speak?" In *Colonial Discourse and Postcolonial Theory*, edited by Patrick Williams and Laura Chrisman, 66–111. New York: Columbia University Press, 1993.

———. *Death of a Discipline*. New York: Columbia University Press, 2003.

Stiglitz, Joseph E., and Linda J. Bilmes. *The Three Trillion Dollar War: The True Cost of the Iraq Conflict*. New York: W. W. Norton, 2008.

Stueck, William. "Ch. 10: In Search of Essences: Labeling the Korean War." In *Remembering the 'Forgotten War': The Korean War through Literature and Art*, edited by Philip West and Suh Ji-moon, 187–202. Armonk, NY: East Gate, 2001.

Sugg, Katherine. "*The Walking Dead*: Late Liberalism and Masculine Subjection in Apocalypse Fiction." *Journal of American Studies* 49, Special Issue 04 (November 2015): 793–811.

Suh, Ji-moon. "Ch. 6: The Korean War in the Lives and Thoughts of Several Major Korean Writers." In *Remembering the 'Forgotten War': The Korean War through Literature and Art*, edited by Philip West and Suh Ji-moon, 92–109. Armonk, NY: East Gate, 2001.

Sullivan, Marianna P. *France's Vietnam Policy: A Study in French-American Relations*. Westport, CT: Greenwood Press, 1978.

Summers, Martin. *Manliness and Its Discontents: The Black Middle Class & The Transformation of Masculinity, 1900–1930*. Chapel Hill: University of North Carolina Press, 2004.

Szalay, Michael. "Pimps and Pied Pipers: Quality Television in the Age of Its Direct Delivery." *Journal of American Studies* 49, Special Issue 04 (November 2015): 813–44.

Szmańko, Klara. "The Conflict between African Americans and Korean Americans in Chang-rae Lee's *Native Speaker*." *Transitions: Race, Culture, and the Dynamics of Change* (January 1, 2006): 67–90.

Takaki, Ronald. *Strangers from a Different Shore: A History of Asian Americans*. New York: Penguin Books, 1989.

Tamaki, Julie. "Japanese Americans Recall Role in Korean War." *Los Angeles Times*, February 16, 1997.

Tang, Eric. *Unsettled: Cambodian Refugees in the New York City Hyperghetto*. Philadelphia: Temple University Press, 2015.

Thangaraj, Stanley I. *Desi Hoop Dreams: Pickup Basketball and the Making of Asian American Masculinity*. New York: New York University Press, 2015.

Thomas, Calvin. *Male Matters: Masculinity, Anxiety, and the Male Body on the Line*. Urbana: University of Illinois Press, 1996.

Tindall, George Brown, and David E. Shi. *America: A Narrative History*. 4th ed. Vol. 2. New York: W. W. Norton, 1996.

Tomine, Adrian. *Shortcomings*. Montreal: Drawn & Quarterly, 2007.

Trachtenberg, Alan. *The Incorporation of America: Culture and Society in the Gilded Age*. New York: Hill and Wang, 2007.

Tso, Tiffany Diane. "The Bamboo Glass Ceiling." *Slate,* August 8, 2018. https://slate.com/human-interest/2018/08/asian-american-women-face-a-glass-ceiling-and-a-bamboo-ceiling-at-work.html.

Tucker-Jones, Anthony. *The Gulf War: Operation Desert Storm, 1990–1991*. New York: Pen & Sword Military, 2014.

Wang, Jessica. *American Science in an Age of Anxiety: Scientists, Anticommunism, and the Cold War*. Chapel Hill: University of North Carolina Press, 1999.

Westad, Odd Arne. *The Global Cold War*. Cambridge, UK: Cambridge University Press, 2007.

Williams, Raymond. *The Country and the City*. New York: Oxford University Press, 1973.

Wolley, Leann. "The Orphan as Mirror: Postmodern Alienation and Societal Crisis in Japanese Film." *Global Tides* 3, Article 2 (2009): http://digitalcommons.pepperdine.edu/globaltides/vol3/iss1/2.

Yang, Gene Luen. *American Born Chinese*. New York: Square Fish, 2006.

Yaqub, Salim. "The Cold War and the Middle East." In *The Cold War in the Third World,* edited by Robert J. McMahon, 11–26. Oxford: Oxford University Press, 2013.

Yoon, Seongho. "'Being in a Place and Not Being There'—Asian American Space, the American Suburb, and Transnational Imageries in Chang-rae Lee's *A Gesture Life*." *The American Village in a Global Setting: Selected Papers from an Interdisciplinary Conference in Honour of Sinclair Lewis and Ida K. Compton* (January 1, 2007): 272–85.

Zhang, Baijia. "The Changing International Scene and Chinese Policy toward the United States, 1954–1970." In *Re-examining the Cold War: U.S.-China Diplomacy, 1954–1973,* edited by Robert S. Ross and Jiang Changbin, 46–76. Cambridge, MA: Harvard University Press, 2001.

Zunz, Oliver. *Why the American Century?* Chicago: University of Chicago Press, 1998.

INDEX

abuser and abused paradigm, 169, 170, 171, 173

Afghanistan: American policy after Soviet invasion of, 151; brinkmanship in, 130; and containing communism, 23; finance capital strategies in, 35, 129; September 11, 2001, attacks and, 127, 130; in War on Terror, 128, 131, 153

African American studies, 27, 171

African Americans: Asian American men influenced by, 169; Asian Americans and, 99, 104, 110, 115, 121, 122, 125, 127; capital ownership by, 116; and Double Victory campaign, 18; as hypermasculinized, 16, 19, 30, 44, 45, 46, 47, 125, 168; in Korean War, 38; in Lee's *A Gesture Life*, 110; masculinist identity politics among, 9; masculinity of, 26, 45, 46, 47; Okada's *No-No Boy* and, 32, 44–45, 46–47, 55; patriarchy among, 168; "player" as slang term among, 3; postcolonial criticism among, 28; and race riots, 97, 99, 121; racial exclusion of, 9; trickster hero of, 30. *See also* African American studies

Aiiieeeee! (anthology), 8–9

Alexie, Sherman, 168, 169

American (US) imperialism: Asian American literature and, 12; Asian American masculinity and, 31, 166, 167; Asian American players and, 167–68, 170; Asian Americans' attempt to delegitimate, 16; binary limits of, 19; containment in, 38, 49; counterculture in, 164, 170; democracy and, 166; deterrence in, 15, 23, 28, 165, 167; domesticity conflated with nation in, 10; economic, 19–25; ethical manhood conflated with, 70–71, 80, 92, 96, 97, 109; game theory in, 15, 22–23, 166, 167; gender and, 150; Gulf War and, 95, 96, 100, 108, 123; in Hwang's *M. Butterfly*, 69, 76; during Korean War, 40; in Lee's *A Gesture Life*, 106; minority conflict and, 122; in Nguyen's *The Sympathizer*, 130, 150, 157, 159, 162; in Noble's *The New Belly Dancer of the Galaxy*, 130, 139, 141, 148, 150, 157, 162; in Okada's *No-No Boy*, 58, 64; origins of, 5, 12, 40; paternalism of, 39, 62, 99–100, 108; patriarchy of, 39, 47, 48, 51, 62, 64; performativity and instability of, 18, 31; player imperialist masculinity and, 5–9, 13, 29, 36, 113, 141, 165–66; as playerism, 2–3, 3–4, 16–17, 20, 25, 35, 39; racism of, 34, 100; September 11, 2001, attacks and, 129, 170, 172; waning of, 94; in War on Terror,

158; white hegemonic masculinity in, 26, 90, 92, 125, 150, 161, 166; as world police, 71, 80, 93, 97, 109; as zero-sum, 22, 23, 77, 95, 129, 130, 155, 166, 167

American exceptionalism, 7, 161

anxiety: of Asian American masculinity, 8; of Asian American players, 12, 27, 169; in Hwang's *M. Butterfly*, 85, 86–87; in Lee's *A Gesture Life*, 119–20; of loss, 22, 166; masculinity and, 6, 16, 17, 26, 91, 138, 164, 165, 166–67, 172, 173; in Okada's *No-No Boy*, 43; patriarchal, 172; of player imperialism, 36, 164; in postwar America, 164–65; of white hegemonic masculinity, 7; whiteness and, 171

Arab Americans: emasculation of men, 24, 137; literature of, 34, 129; in Noble's *The New Belly Dancer of the Galaxy*, 35, 127, 128, 132, 135, 137, 142, 149; patriarchy among, 142n79; political representation of, 138

Asia (the East): as feminized, 10, 32, 40, 51, 73, 85, 87, 89, 93; in Hwang's *M. Butterfly*, 67; rape mentality toward, 82; and submissive Asian woman, 67, 68, 69, 70, 71, 72, 78, 79; US intervention in, 48, 65. *See also* Far East; Middle East; Vietnam War

Asian American literature: American imperialism and emergence of, 12; Asian American player in, 4, 129; cycle of violence and confrontation by protest and, 172; Lee's place in, 98; Okada's *No-No Boy* in canon of, 38; postcolonial criticism in, 28; reinforced masculinities in, 9; War on Terror influencing, 129

Asian American masculinity, 1–5; African American masculinity contrasted with, 45; American imperialism and, 31, 166, 167; anxiety of, 8, 169; complexity of, 8; as discursively hyperbolic, 31; domestic containment and, 23; as emasculated, 66; ethical manhood and, 145; as feminized, 7, 9, 12, 20, 92, 97, 106, 125, 133, 166; hybridity of, 167; instability of, 9, 132; in Lee's *A Gesture Life*, 103; in Lee's *Native Speaker*, 103, 107–8; in literature, 9–11, 27; in Okada's *No-No Boy*, 43, 46; rebellion against white American culture and, 22; white hegemonic masculinity and, 9, 19–20, 26, 162, 167. *See also* Asian American players

Asian American players: American imperialism and, 167–68, 170; anxiety of, 12, 27; in Asian American literature, 4, 129; binaristic thinking in, 14; bluffing by, 12, 19, 128; capitalist-communist polarity and, 66; during Civil Rights era, 8–9, 26; as criminalized, 29; as delinquent, 32; domestic containment and, 28, 64, 66; dominance sought by, 28; as emasculated, 4, 38, 68, 167, 168; ethical manhood and, 30–31, 33, 35, 36, 167, 170, 172, 173; as feminized, 10, 27, 30; in Hwang's *M. Butterfly*, 10–11, 29, 33, 66, 69, 73, 78, 81–87, 89, 93; hypermasculinity of, 30, 38, 76, 167; impersonation and, 26; inclusion and, 3; Keynesian economics and, 21; in Lee's *A Gesture Life*, 11, 29, 34, 96–97, 101, 106–7, 117, 123–24; in Lee's *Native Speaker*, 11, 29, 34, 96–97, 101, 106, 123–24; as limit of capitalist seduction, 17–18; logic of preemption and, 25; model minority myth and, 27, 104, 169; in Nguyen's *The Sympathizer*, 10–11, 29, 35, 126, 127, 128, 135, 150, 160–61; in Noble's *The New Belly Dancer of the Galaxy*, 35, 126, 127, 128, 132, 135, 136, 137, 138, 139, 150, 160–61; in Okada's *No-No Boy*, 10–11, 29, 37, 38, 45, 49, 50–51, 53, 55, 56, 59, 63, 65; as orphans, 150; as outdated trope, 170; patriarchy and, 164; as performers, 11, 27, 28, 163; pervasiveness of trope of, 29; player imperialism and, 3, 10, 14, 17, 18, 25, 26, 28, 31, 36, 94, 114, 163–64, 167; as postmodern, 8, 10, 13, 18, 25, 163; as racialized, 38, 45, 167, 170; racism experienced by, 4, 19, 35; scapegoating of, 131, 157–58; and survival, 17; victim and victimizer cycle in, 17, 35–36, 64, 158, 160–61, 163, 167; white hegemonic masculinity and, 2, 7, 12, 13, 18, 25, 26, 29, 30, 31, 163, 169; as womanizers, 11, 18, 129, 160; as working class, 19; yellow peril myth and, 27, 104, 169

Asian American studies, 27, 98, 171, 173

Asian Americans: as abject, 18; African Americans and, 99, 104, 110, 115, 121, 122, 125, 127; assimilation of, 16, 41; binaries associated with, 26; criminalization of women, 79; as feminized, 16, 18, 44, 46, 89, 164; fictionalized representations of, 2; financialization and, 160; as "gaming," 4; hyperfemininity attributed to, 66, 69, 71, 73, 76, 78, 80, 81, 90; hypersexuality attributed to, 27, 31, 76, 167; ideology shaping, 48; immigration laws against, 1–2; modernism and, 25; as nerds, 8, 27,

45, 47; in Okada's *No-No Boy*, 38, 46, 47; as perpetual outsiders, 27, 30, 47; sexual stereotypes of, 30. *See also* Asian American masculinity; Asian American studies; Chinese Americans; Japanese Americans; Korean Americans; model minority; yellow peril

assimilation: of Asian Americans, 16, 41; cultural hybridity versus, 28; cultural nationalism versus, 8–9; of Japanese Americans, 38, 49; in Lee's *A Gesture Life*, 97, 117; in Lee's *Native Speaker*, 97; in Noble's *The New Belly Dancer of the Galaxy*, 141; player imperialist masculinity as, 31; of "white" immigrants, 16

atomic bombs, 8, 12, 40, 48, 165

Baudrillard, Jean, 98, 102, 118, 124, 125, 125n133, 155–57, 166

Belgrad, Daniel, 15, 71

Bhabha, Homi, 25–26, 28

Bilmes, Linda, 129, 153

Bin Laden, Osama, 24, 126, 127, 128–29

binaristic thinking, 14, 154

bluffing: in American imperialism, 167; by Asian American players, 12, 19, 128; economic, 19, 21; financialization and, 159; in game theory, 166; as gendered and racial privilege, 11; in Nguyen's *The Sympathizer*, 126; in Noble's *The New Belly Dancer of the Galaxy*, 126; in Okada's *No-No Boy*, 39, 55, 57, 58, 59, 64; preemption and, 25

Bodnar, John, 6, 7

Bosch-Vilarrubias, Marta, 137, 142n79, 149–50, 154

breadwinner liberalism, 3

Breitenberg, Mark, 6, 164

Bretton Woods agreement, 20–21, 160

brinkmanship: in Cold War, 66, 67, 68, 69, 72, 82, 130, 172; deterrence and, 25, 167; Hwang's *M. Butterfly* and, 67, 68, 69, 77, 82

Bush, George H. W., 24, 100, 114

Bush, George W., 24, 128, 131, 132, 151, 157, 161

Butler, Judith, 25, 26, 28

Cándida Smith, Richard, 15, 16

capitalism: in American imperialism, 100; Asian American players and, 18; as binary and linear, 17, 20, 33, 68; bipolarity with communism, 27, 33, 62, 66, 70, 79, 80, 114, 165, 171; bluffing in, 19; commodity fetish in, 123n128; competing capitalisms, 28, 34, 114; finance, 35, 115, 116, 123n128, 129, 134, 152–53; free-market, 2; game and performance theories in, 4; global, 25, 91; Gulf War and, 115, 122; heteropatriarchy and, 17; in Hwang's *M. Butterfly*, 69, 70, 90, 91; Japanese, 41; late, 13; Middle East and, 101; in Nguyen's *The Sympathizer*, 35, 133, 134, 135, 145; schizophrenia and, 17, 68, 68n5. *See also* finance capital

Carroll, Hamilton, 111, 152

Carter, Zachary D., 21, 21n74, 68, 113, 153

castration, 59, 64, 86, 141, 142, 144

Chen, Tina, 26, 109, 109n62, 121

Cheng, Anne Anlin, 57, 87

Chin, Frank, 8–9, 98

China: becoming communist, 42; Chinese man in Hwang's *M. Butterfly*, 66, 69, 74, 75, 78; on Cold War, 69, 73–75, 77, 89; homosexuality and, 83, 87; US relations with, 40, 63

Chinese Americans, 1, 2, 4

Chon-Smith, Chong, 45, 125

citizenship: for Asian American players, 3; in Noble's *The New Belly Dancer of the Galaxy*, 138, 157; nonwhite American, 27; nuclear family and, 55; in Okada's *No-No Boy*, 46, 55, 57, 58; postmodern, 150; white male hegemonic, 18

Civil Rights era, 8–9, 26, 98, 171

Cold War: bipolarity of, 24, 78, 79, 90, 92, 93; Bretton Woods agreement and, 21; brinkmanship in, 66, 67, 68, 69, 72, 82, 130, 172; China on, 69, 73–75, 77, 89; containment in, 25, 66; counterculture during, 15; deterrence in, 23, 28, 38, 72; economic motives of, 20; end of, 23; France on, 77; Hwang's *M. Butterfly* and, 33; ideologies of, 33, 39, 50, 53, 55–56, 63, 64, 172; Lee's *Native Speaker* and, 98; momism in, 143; Okada's *No-No Boy* and, 38, 65; in permanent state of war, 6; propaganda in, 32, 39; as proxy war, 101; remasculinization and, 101; US as masculinist player in, 32; as victimizing gameplaying, 24; as zero-sum, 70, 79, 82

colonialism, 6, 28, 90, 100, 106

communism: anticommunism, 40, 50, 56, 77; bipolarity with capitalism, 27, 33, 62, 66, 70, 79, 80, 114, 165, 171; in China, 42; Cold War propaganda against, 32; containment of, 23, 39, 48, 55, 62, 63, 102; deterrence of, 23, 39, 41, 159; as feminized, 165; in Hwang's *M. Butterfly*, 70, 90, 91; in Japan, 41; Middle East and, 101; in Nguyen's *The Sympathizer*, 132, 133, 144, 146, 147, 158, 159, 162; in Vietnam War, 69, 74

containment: in Cold War, 25, 66; of communism, 23, 39, 48, 55, 62, 63, 102; as deterrence, 38, 102; foreign, 28, 66; during Korean War, 38, 41, 49, 50, 57, 64, 164; in Middle East, 115; momism and, 53n89. *See also* domestic containment

corporatization, 15–16

counterculture, 15–16, 71, 150, 159, 164, 169, 170

counterterrorism, 131, 157, 165

crisis of desire, 68, 69, 70, 81, 159

de Gaulle, Charles, 74, 77

debt: debt ceiling crises, 21; of military-industrial complex, 135; in Nguyen's *The Sympathizer*, 130, 134, 135, 150, 156; in Noble's *The New Belly Dancer of the Galaxy*, 130, 134, 135, 150, 156

deconstruction, 8, 10, 13, 14, 27, 28–29

deficit spending: as bluff, 19, 21; as deterrent, 159; in Financial Crisis of 2007–8, 153; Keynesian, 18, 20, 21, 68, 73, 75, 116, 159, 160; by military-industrial complex, 58, 160; in player imperialism, 73; suburbs and, 116; in Vietnam War, 68, 75

Deleuze, Gilles, 17, 20, 33, 68, 79, 159

democracy: American imperialism and, 166; Asian American players and, 30, 31; democratic inclusion, 3, 28, 145, 146, 147, 160, 162; democratization in US foreign policy, 16; democratization of Japan, 40, 41; ethical manhood and, 35, 65, 70, 172; failures of, 14, 18, 100, 128, 130, 147; Gulf War and, 115; Iraq War and, 128; legitimacy conferred by, 50; for Middle East, 95, 96, 161; in Okada's *No-No Boy*, 61, 64, 65; promise of, 55; September 11, 2001, attacks and, 129; unfulfilled, 19; in US incursion into the East, 66; Vietnam War and, 68, 69, 71, 145; War on Terror and, 150, 151

deterrence: in American imperialism, 15, 23, 28, 165, 167; of China, 40; in Cold War, 23, 28, 38, 72; of communism, 23, 39, 41, 159; containment as, 32, 38, 39, 41, 57, 65, 102; as gendered and racial privilege, 11; in Gulf War, 23, 100, 102, 124, 165; in Lee's *A Gesture Life*, 103, 115, 116–17, 118, 123; in Lee's *Native Speaker*, 103, 105, 115, 120; in Nguyen's *The Sympathizer*, 34, 35, 157; in Noble's *The New Belly Dancer of the Galaxy*, 34, 35, 140, 157; nuclear, 23, 66, 72, 100; in Okada's *No-No Boy*, 37–38, 57, 64, 65; preemption and, 23, 25, 34, 35, 102, 127–28, 140, 153, 157, 167, 172; suburbs and, 122; virtual, 96, 100; in War on Terror, 23, 25, 34, 130, 153

Díaz, Junot, 168, 169

Dixit, Avanish K., 22, 68, 82, 114, 115n93

domestic containment: Asian American masculinities and, 23; Asian American players and, 28, 64, 66; binaristic thinking in, 14; as deterrence, 32, 38, 39, 41, 57, 65; Gulf War and, 96; Korean War and, 50; nuclear family for, 32, 38, 39, 55; in Okada's *No-No Boy*, 32, 38, 39, 41, 55, 56, 57, 63, 64, 65, 66; patriarchal anxiety and, 172; player imperialism and, 49, 56, 164

dominance: American desire for, 7; Asian American players and, 18, 28; brinkmanship and, 68; capitalistic, 100; East seen as desiring to be dominated, 73; in Gulf War, 95; in Hwang's *M. Butterfly*, 69, 91; imperial, 16, 95, 125; in Lee's *A Gesture Life*, 105–6, 109, 111; in Lee's *Native Speaker*, 105, 106, 108, 109; masculinity and, 2; in Okada's *No-No Boy*, 52; player's illusion of, 5; surveillance and, 151; in Vietnam War, 71; wars for maintaining, 6

Dragon Lady, 79, 89

East, the. *See* Asia (the East)

Eisenhower, Dwight D., 21, 57–58

emasculation: of Arab men, 24, 137; of Asian American men, 66; of Asian American players, 4, 38, 68, 168; castration, 59, 64, 86, 141, 142, 144; in Hwang's *M. Butterfly*, 72, 76, 83, 84, 85; in Lee's *Native Speaker*, 108; in Nguyen's *The Sympathizer*, 130,

142, 158; in Noble's *The New Belly Dancer of the Galaxy*, 130, 137, 142; in Okada's *No-No Boy*, 44, 45, 49, 50

Eng, David L., 1, 26, 72

Entin, Joseph, 51, 55

ethical manhood, 30; American imperialism as, 70–71, 80, 92, 96, 97, 109; for Asian American men, 145; Asian American players and, 30–31, 33, 35, 36, 167, 170, 172, 173; democracy and, 35, 65, 70; in Hwang's *M. Butterfly*, 67, 92, 93, 172; imperialism conflated with, 70–71, 80, 92; as inclusive, 35, 63, 65, 70, 71, 129; in Lee's *A Gesture Life*, 109, 125, 172; in Lee's *Native Speaker*, 109, 125, 172; in Nguyen's *The Sympathizer*, 35, 129, 130, 144, 156, 160, 172; in Noble's *The New Belly Dancer of the Galaxy*, 35, 129, 130, 147, 156, 172; in Okada's *No-No Boy*, 53, 62, 63, 64, 65, 70, 172

family man: American imperialism as, 108, 109; in Lee's *A Gesture Life*, 114, 115, 123, 125; in Lee's *Native Speaker*, 103, 108, 113, 114, 115, 123, 125; player imperialist masculinity as, 34; white hegemonic masculinity as, 96; world police in guise of, 106, 125, 128, 164

Far East: as feminized, 10, 11, 16, 23, 166, 167; Western domination of, 10. *See also* China; Japan; South Korea

father figures, 106, 144, 150

femininity: in African American men, 168; Asian American men as feminized, 7, 9, 12, 20, 92, 97, 106, 166; Asian American players as feminized, 10, 4, 30; Asian Americans as feminized, 16, 18, 44, 46, 89, 125, 133, 164; communism as feminized, 165; East as feminized, 10, 32, 40, 51, 73, 85, 87, 89, 93, 166, 167; in Hwang's *M. Butterfly*, 85, 165; Middle East as feminized, 10, 11, 16, 23, 165, 166, 167; terrorism as feminized, 161; white hegemonic, 106. *See also* hyperfemininity

feminism, 70, 166, 172

Fickle, Tara, 4, 37, 51

finance capital: deterrence ideology and, 34; Gulf War and, 113; invisible class empire of, 123; Keynesian economics and, 166; in Nguyen's *The Sympathizer*, 35, 134, 135, 145, 150, 157, 158, 160, 162; in Noble's *The New Belly Dancer of the Galaxy*, 35,

135, 150, 153, 157, 158, 160, 162; risk and debt in, 134, 135; speculative, 152–53, 155, 159, 161

Financial Crisis of 2007-8, 126, 128, 129, 152, 153

financialization, 134, 135, 159–60, 166

Finlan, Alastair, 95, 101, 102, 113n85

Foucault, Michel, 8, 93, 166

free trade, 134

Freeman, Joshua B., 21, 58, 80, 91, 100, 116n98, 127

game theory: in American imperialist strategy, 15, 22–23, 166, 167; brinkmanship and, 72; in capitalism, 4; deficit spending and, 21; Nash on, 22, 166, 167; in nuclear deterrence, 66; in Okada's *No-No Boy*, 37–38, 51. *See also* prisoners' dilemma; zero-sum games

Garber, Marjorie, 88, 89

gender: American imperialism and, 150; in Asian American stereotypes, 2, 29; as construct, 61; conventions, 46; equity, 172; essentialism, 51; in Hwang's *M. Butterfly*, 73, 75, 76, 85, 86, 88, 89, 92; identity, 43, 149; Japanese Americans as gendered, 51; nonbinary, 150; in Okada's *No-No Boy*, 43, 52, 57, 61; perceptions of, 31; performance of, 3, 25, 26, 28, 29, 30, 52, 57, 61, 72, 93, 164; polarities, 67–68, 69, 70, 75, 76, 87; postmodern military strategies as gendered, 31; privilege by, 11; stereotypes based on, 29, 75, 76, 79, 85, 88, 171; Western imperialism as gendered, 6. *See also* femininity; masculinity

Gesture Life, A (Lee): African Americans in, 110; American imperialism in, 106; anxiety in, 119–20; Asian American masculinity in, 103; Asian American player in, 11, 29, 34, 96–97, 106–7, 117, 123–24; assimilation in, 97, 117; deterrence in, 103, 115, 116–17, 118, 123; dominance in, 105–6, 109, 111; ethical manhood in, 109, 125, 172; family man in, 114, 115, 123, 125; Gulf War and, 34, 97, 98, 109, 114, 115, 123, 124–25; Japanese Americans in, 109, 117; Korean Americans in, 109–10; model minority in, 104, 106, 109, 117, 122, 123; objectification of women in, 110, 111, 123; paternalism in, 99–100, 110, 119; patriarchy in, 100, 107, 109, 111; player imperialist masculinity in, 100, 106, 114, 115,

119, 123; race in, 106; race riots in, 34, 98, 100, 109, 115; racism in, 105, 108, 110, 117; rape in, 111–12, 118–19; on segregation, 99; suburban malaise in, 115–16, 122, 124; victim and victimizer cycle in, 96, 104; white hegemonic masculinity in, 103, 117, 125; yellow peril in, 34, 109; zero-sum game in, 34, 125

Gómez-Vega, Ibis, 135, 139, 154

Guattari, Félix, 17, 20, 33, 68, 79, 159

Gulf War: American imperialism of, 95, 96, 100, 108, 123; casualties in, 102–3; continuation of, 124, 124n132; as decoy, 125, 125n133; deterrence in, 23, 100, 102, 124, 165; economic motives of, 23–24; in Lee's *A Gesture Life*, 34, 97, 98, 114, 115, 123, 124–25; in Lee's *Native Speaker*, 34, 97, 98, 114, 115, 123, 124–25; neo-isolation after, 128; as new era of conflict, 121; in permanent state of war, 6; player imperialist masculinity in, 113, 114, 115, 119, 124, 128; preemption in, 28, 35, 102, 172; race riots and, 98, 100, 109; shock-and-awe tactics in, 24, 25, 114, 153; South Asian Americans, representations of, during, 8; surveillance in, 98, 115, 122; as victimizing gameplaying, 24; as virtual, 34, 95, 97, 100, 101, 102, 118, 120, 122, 123, 124, 127, 152, 158, 165; as zero-sum, 114–15

Harper, Phillip Brian, 13, 26

Hastings, Max, 23, 42, 70

Hawthorne, Melanie C., 89, 90

homophobia, 78, 81

homosexuality: African American male, 168; of Asian American gay men, 2; Hussein and Bin Laden associated with, 24; in Hwang's *M. Butterfly*, 78, 81, 82, 83, 87, 90, 132; in liberalization of sexuality, 16; in stereotype of Asian Americans, 9, 30

Hussein, Saddam, 24, 102, 113, 114, 125n133, 126, 128

Hwang, David Henry. See *M. Butterfly* (Hwang)

hybridity, 27, 28–29, 167

hyperfemininity: of Asian American women, 66, 69, 71, 73, 76, 78, 79, 80, 81, 90; in Hwang's *M. Butterfly*, 67, 72, 79, 169

hypermasculinity: of African Americans, 16, 19, 30, 44, 45, 46, 47, 125, 168; of Arab men, 137; of Asian American players, 30, 38, 76, 167; attributed to nonwhite immigrants, 16; ethnic, 26, 27; in Hwang's *M. Butterfly*, 91; of Latinxs, 19; in Nguyen's *The Sympathizer*, 133, 169; in Noble's *The New Belly Dancer of the Galaxy*, 138; in Okada's *No-No Boy*, 45, 47, 165, 169

hypersexuality: Asia as hypersexualized, 10; attributed to Asian Americans, 27, 31, 76, 167; Fu Manchu character as hypersexual, 2; in Hwang's *M. Butterfly*, 76, 80, 92

Iran-Iraq War, 113

Iraq: in "axis of evil," 161; Kuwait invaded by, 24, 100, 113–14, 165; weapons of mass destruction of, 128. *See also* Gulf War; Iraq War

Iraq War, 24, 127, 128, 129

Jakobson, Roman, 33, 80

Jameson, Fredric, 13, 14

Japan: colonization of China, 75; as feminized, 32, 51, 62, 64; imperialism in Korea, 41, 110; in Korean War, 47, 49; in Okada's *No-No Boy*, 47–48, 60, 61, 62; US occupation of, 40, 47, 48; US relation with, 38, 40–41, 49–50, 63–64

Japanese Americans: assimilation of, 38, 49; figured as feminine, 51; image projected after World War II, 41; internment camps for, 43; in Korean War, 50; in Lee's *A Gesture Life*, 109, 117; masculinization after World War II, 9; no-no boys, 43; in Okada's *No-No Boy*, 32, 37, 38, 40, 44, 46–47, 48, 53, 56, 57, 58, 59–60; as racialized, 43–44; war veterans, 44, 47, 48, 56, 58

Jeffords, Susan, 70, 71, 78, 95–96

Jun, Helen Heran, 9, 43, 44, 46, 47

Kaplan, Amy, 5, 10, 12, 14–15

Kennedy, John F., 75, 77

Keynesianism, 20; as bipartisan, 21, 21n74; Bretton Woods agreement, 20–21, 160; deficit spending in, 18, 19, 20, 21, 58, 68, 73, 75, 116, 159; deterrence and, 25; Gulf War and, 23–24; of military-industrial complex, 14, 57, 135, 160, 166; neoliberalism and, 2; of Obama, 153; in Vietnam War, 91

Kim, Claire Jean, 99, 104, 169, 171

Kim, Daniel Y., 9, 38, 47, 51, 52–53, 53n89

Kondo, Dorinne, 88, 89

Korean Americans: capital ownership by, 116; in Lee's *A Gesture Life*, 109–10; in Lee's *Native Speaker*, 108; in race riots, 99, 121, 122

Korean War: containment in, 38, 41, 49, 50, 57, 64, 164; as cover-up war, 50, 74; Eisenhower's trip to Korea, 57–58; as Forgotten War, 32, 42, 43, 62; as measured victory for US, 23, 32, 63, 65, 101; Okada's *No-No Boy* as novel of, 32, 37–41, 47, 61, 64; Vietnam War and, 23, 42, 69, 70, 74

Kramer, Michael, 15, 71

Lacan, Jacques, 8, 64, 84, 84n88, 85, 166

Latinx studies, 27, 171

Latinxs: Asian American men influenced by, 169; Asian Americans compared with, 104; feminization and hypermasculinization of, 16, 125, 168–69; masculinist identity politics among, 9. *See also* Latinx studies

Lee, Benjamin, 152, 161

Lee, Chang-rae: *On Such a Full Sea*, 98. *See also Gesture Life, A* (Lee); *Native Speaker* (Lee)

Lee, Young-Oak, 106, 110

Levering, Ralph B., 50, 79, 101n25

Ling, Jinqi, 11, 38, 41, 48, 51, 54, 61

LiPuma, Edward, 152, 161

Lotus Blossom: in Hwang's *M. Butterfly*, 67, 72, 73, 77, 78, 80, 83, 85, 92; as stereotype, 66, 67, 73, 79

Lowe, Lisa, 28, 98

Lye, Colleen, 10, 88, 89

Lyford, Amy, 166, 170–71

M. Butterfly (Hwang): American imperialism in, 69, 76; anxiety in, 85, 86–87; aphasic speech in, 33, 80–81, 87, 93; Asian Americans in, 67; Asian player in, 10–11, 29, 33, 66, 69, 73, 78, 81–87, 89, 93; binary reception of, 88–94; breaking fourth wall in, 81–82; brinkmanship in, 67, 68, 69, 77, 82; capitalism in, 69, 70, 90, 91; Chinese man in, 66, 69, 74, 75, 78; Cold War and, 33; communism in, 70, 90, 91; dominance in, 69, 91; duality of good/evil in, 80; emasculation in, 72, 76, 83, 84, 85; ethical manhood in, 67, 92, 93, 172; femininity in, 85, 165; as frame narrative, 85; gender in, 73, 75, 76, 85, 86, 88, 89, 92; homosexuality in, 78, 81, 82, 83, 87, 90, 132; hyperfemininity in, 67, 72, 79, 169; hypermasculinity in, 91; hypersexuality in, 76, 80, 92; Lotus Blossom in, 67, 72, 73, 77, 78, 80, 83, 85, 92; masculinity in, 67, 72, 78, 83, 84, 86, 87, 89, 90, 91–92; model minority in, 33, 79; objectification of women in, 67, 73, 83–84, 93; patriarchy and, 89; player imperialist masculinity in, 33, 67, 69–70, 71, 73, 75–76, 77, 78, 79, 80, 81, 85, 86, 89, 90, 92, 93; prison in, 33, 76, 79–80, 81, 82, 83, 84, 86, 90, 92, 93; race in, 85, 87, 88, 89, 92; remasculinization in, 32–33; as specifically American play, 67, 69, 75; surveillance in, 77; transvestism in, 67, 72, 83, 87, 88; true story as basis of, 73; underclass in, 93; as Vietnam War play, 67, 69, 71, 72, 83, 86, 89, 90; white hegemonic masculinity in, 33, 67, 68, 70, 71, 72, 76, 77, 78, 79, 84, 92, 93; womanizing in, 33, 71, 76, 81, 83, 92, 93; yellow peril in, 33, 79, 80, 92

Ma, Sheng-mei, 89, 90

Madame Butterfly (Puccini), 69, 73, 75, 76, 81, 87, 92

Mao Zedong, 73–74

markets, 2, 3, 113n85, 125

masculinity: African American, 26, 45, 46, 47; as anxious, 6, 16, 17, 26, 91, 138, 164, 165, 166–67, 172, 173; Chinese American men seen as less masculine, 1, 2; in Hwang's *M. Butterfly*, 67, 72, 78, 83, 84, 86, 87, 89, 90, 91–92; identity politics of, 8, 9; imperialist, 26, 28, 131–32; military associated with, 10, 11, 43, 44, 46, 49, 170; as multiple, 29; in Okada's *No-No Boy*, 32, 39, 45–46, 47, 51, 52–53, 54, 56, 57, 61, 63, 170; patriarchal, 18, 19, 22, 23, 164, 166; as performance, 9, 25, 26, 29, 31, 62, 72; postmodern dismantling of, 11; power and strength associated with, 17; as tied to male bodies, 31; toxic, 52, 170, 173; unstable, 6, 19, 27, 91, 173; wars and perception of, 28. *See also* Asian American masculinity; emasculation; ethical manhood; hypermasculinity; player imperialist masculinity; remasculinization; white hegemonic masculinity

masturbation, 143–44

May, Lary, 42, 50

McAlister, Melani, 24, 31, 40

McClanahan, Annie, 24, 34, 152

Me Too movement, 172

melancholia, 56; mania and, 143; in Okada's *No-No Boy*, 56–57, 58, 64; racial, 26, 57

metaphors, 33, 79–81, 87

Middle East: as American interest, 24, 34, 35; Cold War and, 101; containment in, 115; democracy for, 95, 96, 161; as feminized, 10, 11, 16, 23, 165, 166, 167; oil from, 113; storytelling in, 148; wars of competing capitalisms in, 28, 34, 114; Western domination of, 10, 128–29, 131, 157, 159. *See also* Afghanistan; Arab Americans; Gulf War; Iraq

military-industrial complex: Asian American players mimicking, 35–36; Bretton Woods conference and, 160; Cold War and, 20; corporatized masculinity and playing in, 15, 58; deficit spending and, 19; Eisenhower on, 21; Keynesianism and, 14, 57, 135, 160, 166; racialized masculinities undergirding, 14

mimetic abjection, 18

model minority: Asian American player and, 27, 104, 169; as Asian American stereotype, 1, 30, 103–4, 117; capital ownership and, 116; debunking myth of, 104–5; in Hwang's *M. Butterfly*, 33, 79; in Lee's *A Gesture Life*, 104, 106, 109, 117, 120, 122, 123; in Lee's *Native Speaker*, 104, 105, 109, 120, 121; in Nguyen's *The Sympathizer*, 143; in Okada's *No-No Boy*, 45

momism, 53, 53n89, 56, 63, 64, 143

mother figures, 144–48, 150

multipolarity, 74, 77, 87

Nalebuff, Barry J., 22, 68, 82, 114, 115n93

Native American studies, 27, 171

Native Americans: Asian American men influenced by, 169; feminization and hypermasculinization of, 16, 125; masculinity in, 9, 169; players among, 168. *See also* Native American studies

Native Speaker (Lee): Asian American masculinity in, 103, 107–8; Asian American player in, 11, 29, 34, 96–97, 106, 123–24; capital in, 116; Cold War and, 98; deterrence in, 103, 105, 115, 120; dominance in, 105, 106, 108, 109; emasculation in, 108; ethical manhood in, 109, 125, 172; family man in, 103, 108, 113, 114, 115, 123, 125; Gulf War and, 34, 97, 98, 114, 115, 123, 124–25; Korean Americans in, 108; model minority in, 104, 105, 109, 120, 121; objectification of women in, 112, 123; paternalism in, 99–100, 108, 112, 113; patriarchy in, 100, 107, 108, 109; player imperialist masculinity in, 100, 105, 106, 112, 113, 114, 115, 123; race riots and, 34, 97, 98–99, 100, 108, 109, 115, 122; racism in, 105, 108, 121, 122, 165; suburban malaise in, 115–16, 122–23, 124; surveillance in, 98, 117, 120–21; transnational scope of, 98; victim and victimizer cycle in, 96, 109, 109n62; white hegemonic masculinity in, 103, 108, 112, 125; yellow peril in, 34, 103, 109, 120, 121; zero-sum game in, 34, 125

neoliberalism, 2–3, 21, 153

nerds, 8, 27, 45, 47

New Belly Dancer of the Galaxy, The (Noble): American imperialism in, 130, 139, 141, 148, 150, 157, 162; Arab American in, 35, 127, 128, 132, 135, 137, 142, 149; Asian American player in, 35, 126, 127, 128, 135, 136, 137, 138, 139, 150, 160–61; bluffing in, 126, 153; castration in, 141, 144; citizenship in, 138, 157; debt in, 130, 134, 135, 150, 156; deterrence in, 34, 35, 140, 157; emasculation in, 130, 137, 142; ethical manhood in, 35, 129, 130, 147, 156, 172; father figure in, 141–42, 147, 148, 150, 162; finance capital in, 35, 135, 150, 153, 157, 158, 160, 162; hypermasculinity in, 138; mother figure in, 147–48, 150, 162; objectification of women in, 130, 135–36, 137, 139, 150, 160; patriarchy in, 141, 142, 143, 150; player imperialist masculinity and, 129, 130, 135, 137–38, 139, 141, 148–49, 150, 158–59, 164; preemption in, 34, 35, 127, 129, 130, 140, 141, 157, 162; racism in, 138; rape in, 139; as speculative fiction, 132, 135, 153, 155–56, 157; storytelling in, 148, 153–55; terrorism in, 127, 135, 139; transgenderism in, 140, 149; victim and victimizer cycle in, 137, 158; Vietnam War in, 149; War on Terror in, 35, 127, 137, 138, 150, 158, 161; white hegemonic masculinity in, 35, 131, 149, 150, 152, 156; womanizing in, 35, 128, 130, 135, 136–37, 139–40, 142, 155, 156, 158 new world order, 96, 128

Ngai, Sianne, 12, 13

Nguyen, Viet Thanh: *Asian American Players* and work of, 9; on Okada's *No-No Boy*, 38, 45. See also *Sympathizer, The* (Nguyen)

Nixon, Richard, 91, 94

Noble, Frances Khirallah. See *New Belly Dancer of the Galaxy, The* (Noble)

No-No Boy (Okada): African Americans and, 32, 44–45, 46–47, 55; American imperialism in, 58, 64; anxiety in, 43; Asian American player in, 10–11, 29, 37, 38, 45, 49, 50–51, 53, 55, 56, 59, 63–65; Asian Americans in, 38, 46, 47; bluffing in, 39, 55, 57, 58, 59, 64; citizenship in, 46, 55, 57, 58; democracy in, 61, 64, 65; deterrence in, 37–38, 57, 64, 65; domestic containment in, 32, 39, 41, 55, 56, 57, 63, 64, 65, 66; dominance in, 52; emasculation in, 44, 45, 49, 50; ethical manhood in, 53, 62, 63, 64, 65, 70, 172; Faulknerian writing in, 59–60, 61, 62, 64; game theory in, 37–38, 51; hypermasculinity in, 45, 47, 165, 169; Japan in, 47–48, 60, 61, 62; Japanese Americans in, 32, 37, 38, 40, 44, 46–47, 48, 53, 56, 57, 58, 59–60; as Korean War novel, 32, 37–41, 47, 61, 64; masculinity in, 32, 39, 45–46, 47, 51, 52–53, 54, 56, 57, 61, 63, 170; melancholia in, 56–57, 58, 64; model minority in, 45; nuclear family in, 55–56, 63, 64, 65; objectification of women in, 48–49, 50–51, 54, 57, 58, 59, 63, 64; player imperialist masculinity in, 32, 38, 46, 51, 52, 53, 57, 61, 62, 64, 65; prison in, 44, 48; racism in, 37, 41, 44–45, 46, 51, 165; reception of, 41; remasculinization in, 53; split nationality in, 47–48, 58–59; title's meaning, 43; victim and victimizer cycle in, 41–56, 63; white hegemonic masculinity in, 43, 44, 45–46, 53, 57, 62; womanizing in, 32, 37, 39, 45, 51, 54, 55, 56, 59, 62, 63, 64; yellow peril in, 45, 46

nuclear family: in Cold War propaganda, 32, 39, 55; domestic containment and, 32, 38, 39, 55; momism and, 53n89; in Okada's *No-No Boy*, 55–56, 63, 64, 65; as patriarchal, 3, 143; in suburbs, 116n98. See also family man

Obama, Barack, 21, 24, 153, 161

objectification of women: by Asian American players, 4, 14; in Hwang's *M. Butterfly*, 67, 73, 83–84, 93; in Lee's *A Gesture Life*, 110, 111, 123; in Lee's *Native Speaker*, 112, 123; in Nguyen's *The Sympathizer*, 130, 133–34, 142, 143, 145–46, 150, 159, 160; in Noble's *The New Belly Dancer of the Galaxy*, 130, 135–36, 137, 139, 150, 160; in Okada's *No-No Boy*, 48–49, 50–51, 54, 57, 58, 59, 63, 64

oil, 6, 100, 113–14, 122, 125

Okada, John: Cold War impacts, 47. See also *No-No Boy* (Okada)

Orientalism, 9, 10, 88–89, 137

ornamentalism, 57

Page Act (1875), 79

Palumbo-Liu, David, 43, 48

paternalism: of American policy, 39, 62, 99–100, 108; in Gulf War, 109; toward Japan, 40; in Lee's *A Gesture Life*, 99–100, 110, 119; in Lee's *Native Speaker*, 99–100, 108, 112, 113; in player imperialist masculinity, 106

patriarchy: among African Americans, 168; of American policy, 39, 47, 48, 51, 62, 64; American society as patriarchal, 17; as anxious, 172; among Arab Americans, 142n79; Asian American players and, 164; Cold War, 32, 55–56; distress associated with, 6; Hwang's *M. Butterfly* and, 89; in Lee's *A Gesture Life*, 34, 100, 107, 109, 111; in Lee's *Native Speaker*, 34, 100, 107, 108, 109, 112; in Nguyen's *The Sympathizer*, 141, 142, 143, 144, 147, 150; in Noble's *The New Belly Dancer of the Galaxy*, 141, 142, 143, 150; nuclear family and, 3, 143; patriarchal masculinity, 18, 19, 22, 23, 164, 166; philandering as form of, 63; of player imperialist masculinity, 130, 141; women's rights movement challenging, 70

performance: of gender, 3, 25, 26, 28, 29, 30, 52, 57, 61, 72, 93, 164; of masculinity, 3, 25, 26, 28, 29, 30, 52, 57, 61, 72, 93, 164; of player imperialist masculinity, 29, 31, 141, 149, 163; of stereotypes, 29; theory, 4, 25–27, 28, 29

persuasion, 7, 31

play, 15–16, 71, 159, 164

player imperialist masculinity: American imperialism and, 5–9, 13, 29, 35, 36, 113, 141, 165–66; in American wars, 14; anxiety in, 36, 164; Asian American players and, 3, 10, 14, 17, 18, 25, 26, 28, 31, 36, 94, 114, 163–64, 167; as assimilation, 31; brinkmanship in, 68; capitalist-communist polarity and, 66; domestic containment and, 49, 56, 164; domination as characteristic of, 2; as exclusionary, 6; in Gulf War, 113, 114, 115, 119, 124, 128; in Hwang's *M. Butterfly*, 33, 67, 69–70, 71, 73, 75–76, 77, 78, 79, 80, 81, 85, 86, 89, 90, 92, 93; as invisible, 29, 43, 114, 172; Korean War and, 39–40; in Lee's *A Gesture Life*, 100, 106, 114, 115, 119, 123; in Lee's *Native Speaker*, 100, 105, 106, 112, 113, 115, 123; in Nguyen's *The Sympathizer*, 127, 129, 130, 132, 141, 145, 150, 158–59; in Noble's *The New Belly Dancer of the Galaxy*, 129, 130, 135, 137–38, 139, 141, 148–49, 150, 158–59, 164; in Okada's *No-No Boy*, 32, 38, 46, 51, 52, 53, 57, 61, 62, 64, 65; patriarchy of, 130, 141; as performance, 29, 31, 141, 149, 163; "playing house" in, 63–64; preemption in, 135; as racially specific, 17; seduction in, 155–56; tracking, in literature, 9–11; as undetected, 43; victim and victimizer cycle in, 3; on Vietnam War, 69; War on Terror and, 127, 128, 132, 139, 149, 156; war required by, 26; white hegemonic masculinity and, 41, 52, 53, 62, 63, 67, 96, 149, 163, 164, 167, 170; as world police, 34, 96, 106, 115, 123, 128, 129. *See also* Asian American players

players: American imperialism as playerism, 2–3, 3–4, 16–17, 20, 25, 35, 39; debt incurred by, 130; ethnic American, 168–69, 171; as imperialist figures, 5; love-hate obsession with, 5, 13; military-industrial complex as form of, 58; performance of stereotypes and playerism, 29; postwar, 93; as psychically fragmented, 4; as spending what they don't have, 20; as stock character, 5; woman, 73, 80; womanizers and, 3, 5, 7, 37. *See also* Asian American players; player imperialist masculinity

polarization: binary reception of Hwang's *M. Butterfly*, 88–94; brinkmanship as, 167; between capitalism and communism, 27, 33, 62, 66, 70, 79, 80, 114, 165, 171; in Cold War, 24, 78, 79, 90, 92, 93; gender polarities, 67–68, 69, 70, 75, 76, 87; geopolitical, 87–88, 90; in Hwang's *M. Butterfly*, 77, 79, 83, 86, 88–89; multipolarity, 74, 77, 87; racial binarisms, 75

postcolonial theory, 28

postmodernism, 11–19; Asian American players as postmodern, 8, 10, 13, 18, 25, 163; confluence of high and low culture in, 4; as conservative, 13; and deconstruction, 8, 10, 13, 14, 27, 28–29; historicizing, 166; postmodern wars, 7, 18, 22, 27, 31, 145, 163, 171; unresolved fragmentation in, 4, 8, 13

preemption: Asian American players and, 25; deterrence and, 23, 25, 34, 35, 102, 127–28, 140, 153, 157, 167; financialization and, 159; as gendered and racial privilege, 11; in Gulf War and War on Terror, 28, 35, 102, 172; in Iraq War, 128; in Nguyen's *The Sympathizer*, 34, 35, 127, 129, 130, 157, 158; in Noble's *The New Belly Dancer of the Galaxy*, 34, 35, 127, 129, 130, 140, 141, 157, 158, 162; in player imperialist masculinity, 135; September 11, 2001, attacks and, 24; as speculation, 152, 153; virtual, 172; in War on Terror, 25, 127, 130, 131

prison: Foucault on, 93; in Hwang's *M. Butterfly*, 33, 76, 79–80, 81, 82, 83, 84, 86, 90, 92, 93; in Nguyen's *The Sympathizer*, 132, 133, 146, 156; in Okada's *No-No Boy*, 44, 48

prisoners' dilemma: in foreign affairs, 22; Gulf War and, 114–15, 125; Iran-Iraq War as, 115n93; in Lee's *A Gesture Life*, 34, 125; in Lee's *Native Speaker*, 34, 125; in US wars, 23; Vietnam War and, 77, 82, 89; War on Terror and, 129, 130, 150, 166; zero-sum games and, 23, 34, 77, 82, 89, 129, 130, 150, 167

al-Qaida, 24, 127, 131

Qiang Zhai, 74, 74n22, 78

race: American racializing paradigms, 169; Asian American players as racialized, 38, 45, 167, 170; binarisms of, 75; citizenship and, 27, 58; Cold War and, 38; deconstruction of, 28–29; discrimination based on, 9, 55, 104, 127, 129, 130, 137, 142; divisions in America, 53–54; as external identification of ethnicity, 26–27; in Hwang's *M. Butterfly*, 85, 87, 88, 89, 92;

in Lee's *A Gesture Life,* 106; racial hierarchy of women, 51; racial melancholia, 26, 57; racialization of American politics, 19; racialized hypermasculinity, 26; stereotypes based on, 29, 30, 73, 78, 87, 88, 93, 170, 171; subject determined by, 86–87; violence associated with, 173. *See also* race riots; racial minorities; racism; white hegemonic masculinity

race riots: Asian American and African American conflict in, 121; as domestic failure of democracy, 130; in Lee's *A Gesture Life,* 34, 98, 100, 109, 115; in Lee's *Native Speaker,* 34, 97, 98–99, 100, 108, 109, 115; surveillance during, 121–22; visibility of, 165

racial minorities: capital ownership by, 116; control of, 116; players' treatment of, 150; US wars against, 18; violence and delinquency associated with, 168; violent tension between, 109, 115, 122. *See also* African Americans; Asian Americans; Latinxs; Native Americans

racism: of American imperialism, 34, 100; Asian American players experiencing, 4, 19, 35; in Asian American stereotypes, 104; in Lee's *A Gesture Life,* 105, 108, 110, 117; in Lee's *Native Speaker,* 105, 108, 121, 122, 165; in Nguyen's *The Sympathizer,* 133, 134, 145; in Noble's *The New Belly Dancer of the Galaxy,* 138; in Okada's *No-No Boy,* 37, 41, 44–45, 46, 51, 165; in suburbs, 124

rape: in Lee's *A Gesture Life,* 111–12, 118–19; mentality, 73, 82, 139; of motherland, 147; in Nguyen's *The Sympathizer,* 143, 144, 146, 156, 162; in Noble's *The New Belly Dancer of the Galaxy,* 139

Reagan, Ronald, 21, 72

remasculinization: binaristic thinking in, 14; Cold War and, 101; Gulf War and, 97; in Hwang's *M. Butterfly,* 32–33; in Okada's *No-No Boy,* 53; in Vietnam War, 70, 71, 72, 94, 96, 101, 164, 170

Remen, Kathryn, 85, 89

Rogers, Paul, 24, 127

Said, Edward, 10, 40

schizophrenia, 17, 68, 68n5, 133, 160

seduction, 155–56, 159

September 11, 2001, attacks: Afghanistan and Iraq blamed for, 10, 128; American imperialism and, 129, 170, 172; Hussein and, 128; policy of avoidance and, 151; War on Terror and, 24, 127, 131, 151, 156–57

sexual harassment, 172–73

sexuality: increasing liberalization of, 16. *See also* homosexuality; hypersexuality

Shimakawa, Karen, 18, 89

Shimizu, Celine Parreñas, 30, 64–65

social capital, 157, 160

South Asian Americans, 8

South Korea: as feminized, 32, 51, 62, 64; split between North and, 47; US relations with, 38, 39, 49, 64. *See also* Korean War

speculative fiction, 132, 135, 153, 155–56, 157

Stiglitz, Joseph, 129, 153

suburban malaise, 115–16, 122–23, 124

surveillance: Asian American masculinity and, 23; in Gulf War, 98, 115, 122; in Hwang's *M. Butterfly,* 77; international, 25; in Lee's *Native Speaker,* 98, 117, 120–21; privileging certain identities and categories, 151; of race riots, 121–22; in War on Terror, 128, 151

Sympathizer, The (Nguyen): American imperialism in, 130, 150, 157, 159; Asian American player in, 10–11, 29, 35, 126, 127, 128, 132, 135, 150, 160–61, 162; bluffing in, 126; castration in, 142, 144; communism in, 132, 133, 144, 146, 147, 158, 159, 162; debt in, 130, 134, 135, 150, 156; democratic inclusion in, 145, 146, 147, 160, 162; deterrence in, 34, 35, 157; Ellison's *The Invisible Man* and, 126–27, 132; emasculation in, 130, 142, 158; ethical manhood in, 35, 129, 130, 144, 156, 160, 172; father figure in, 144, 146, 150; finance capital in, 35, 133, 134, 145, 150, 157, 158, 160, 162; hypermasculinity in, 133, 169; masturbation in, 143–44; model minority in, 143; mother figure in, 134, 144–46, 147, 150, 162; objectification of women in, 130, 133–34, 142, 143, 145–46, 150, 159, 160; patriarchy in, 141, 142, 143, 144, 147, 150; player imperialist masculinity and, 127, 129, 130, 132, 141, 145, 150, 158–59; preemption in, 34, 35, 127, 129, 130, 157, 158; prison in, 132, 133, 146, 156; racism in, 133, 134, 145; rape in, 143, 144, 146, 156, 162; schizophrenia in, 133, 160; as speculative fiction, 132,

135, 155–56, 157; victim and victimizer cycle in, 144, 158; Vietnam War and, 127, 132, 142–43, 145, 146; Vietnamese American in, 35, 128, 146; War on Terror in, 35, 127, 134, 145, 146, 150, 158, 159, 161; white hegemonic masculinity in, 35, 131, 152, 156; womanizing in, 35, 128, 130, 133, 135, 142, 156, 158–59

Taiwan, 40

Takaki, Ronald, 10, 104

terrorism: ambiguity of term, 157; deterrence of, 159; as feminized, 161; freedom fighters versus, 23, 154, 161, 171; legitimacy of, 128; "new," 157; in Noble's *The New Belly Dancer of the Galaxy*, 127, 135, 139; South Asian Americans and, 8; who are the terrorists?, 150, 151. *See also* September 11, 2001, attacks; War on Terror

Thangaraj, Stanley I., 8, 29

totalitarianism, 6–7, 15, 31, 39, 77

transgenderism, 30, 31, 140

transvestism, 67, 72, 83, 87, 88

Truman, Harry S, 38, 40, 42

Tucker-Jones, Anthony, 102–3, 124n132

underclass, 80, 92, 93, 104, 109n61, 172

universalism, 25, 26, 40, 61, 132

victim and victimizer cycle: in Asian American players, 17, 35–36, 64, 158, 160–61, 163, 167; in Lee's *A Gesture Life*, 96, 104, 109; in Lee's *Native Speaker*, 96, 109, 109n62; in Nguyen's *The Sympathizer*, 144, 158; in Noble's *The New Belly Dancer of the Galaxy*, 137, 158; in Okada's *No-No Boy*, 41–56, 63; in player imperialist masculinity, 3; in players, 4, 68; in War on Terror, 131–32

Vietnam War: asymmetrical bipolarity of US and Russia in, 33; communism and, 69, 74; counterculture during, 15; as defeat for US, 23, 67, 70, 72, 92, 101; democracy and, 68, 69, 71, 145; films of, 10, 71, 78, 79; France on, 77; gender polarities in, 70; Gulf War and, 95; Hwang's *M. Butterfly* and, 67, 69, 71, 72, 77, 83, 86, 89, 90; Korean War and, 23, 42, 69, 70, 74; Nguyen's *The Sympathizer* and, 127, 132, 142–43, 145, 146; in Noble's *The New Belly Dancer of the Galaxy*, 149; remasculinization in, 70, 71, 72, 94, 96, 101, 164, 170; US motives in, 68–69; as zero-sum, 74

War on Terror: American imperialism in, 158; binaries in, 154; as counterterrorism, 157; deficit spending for, 153; deterrence in, 23, 25, 34, 130, 153; end of, 24, 127, 161; gains of, 126, 129; as illegitimate, 150, 151, 164; in Nguyen's *The Sympathizer*, 35, 127, 134, 145, 146, 150, 158, 159, 161; in Noble's *The New Belly Dancer of the Galaxy*, 35, 127, 137, 138, 149, 150, 158, 161; in permanent state of war, 6; player imperialist masculinity and, 127, 128, 132, 139, 156; preemption in, 25, 28, 127, 130, 131, 172; September 11, 2001, attacks and, 24, 127, 131, 151, 156–57; South Asian Americans, representations of, during, 8; victim and victimizer cycle in, 131–32; as victimizing gameplaying, 24; as virtual, 127, 152, 158, 165; white hegemonic masculinity and, 130; as zero-sum, 129, 150, 161

Weathersby, Kathryn, 42, 62n131

Western imperialism: communism versus, 77; as gendered, 6; in Middle and Far East, 10. *See also* American (US) imperialism

white hegemonic masculinity: in American imperialism, 26, 90, 92, 125, 150, 161, 166; anxieties of, 7; Asian American masculinity and, 9, 19–20, 26, 162, 167; Asian American players and, 2, 7, 12, 13, 18, 25, 26, 29, 30, 31, 163, 169; Asian and African Americans seen as inferior to, 99; ethnic American players and, 169; family man and, 96; in Hwang's *M. Butterfly*, 33, 67, 68, 70, 71, 72, 76, 77, 78, 79, 84, 92, 93; Korean War and, 39–40; in Lee's *A Gesture Life*, 103, 117, 125; in Lee's *Native Speaker*, 103, 108, 112, 125; in Nguyen's *The Sympathizer*, 35, 131, 152, 156; in Noble's *The New Belly Dancer of the Galaxy*, 35, 131, 149, 150, 152, 156; nuclear family threatened by, 39; in Okada's *No-No Boy*, 43, 44, 45–46, 53, 57, 62; player imperialism and, 41, 52, 53, 62, 63, 67, 96, 149, 163, 164, 167, 170; in popular culture, 71; in postmodern wars, 7, 9; in Vietnam War, 70; War on Terror and, 130; as world police, 96, 97

white privilege, 105, 138

white supremacy, 43, 105

womanizers: Asian American players as, 11, 18, 129, 160; ethnic American players as, 169; in Hwang's *M. Butterfly*, 33, 71, 76, 81, 83, 92, 93; in Nguyen's *The Sympathizer*, 35, 128, 130, 133, 135, 142, 156, 157, 158–59; in Noble's *The New Belly Dancer of the Galaxy*, 35, 128, 130, 135, 136–37, 139–40, 142, 155, 156, 157, 158; in Okada's *No-No Boy*, 32, 37, 39, 45, 51, 54, 55, 56, 59, 62, 63, 64; players and, 3, 5, 7, 37; US military intervention and, 10

women: capital and bodies of, 157; democratic inclusion and, 162; feminism, 70, 166, 172; motherland and, 147; perfect woman, 66, 69, 84; as players, 73, 80; racial hierarchy of, 51; return to domesticity, 166; submissive Asian, 67, 68, 69, 70, 71, 72, 78, 79; women's rights movement, 70. *See also* femininity; objectification of women; womanizers

world police: American imperialism as, 71, 80, 93, 97, 109; as family man, 106, 128, 164; player imperialist masculinity as, 34, 96, 106, 115, 123, 128, 129; surveillance and, 98; white hegemonic masculinity as, 96, 97

yellow peril: Asian American player and, 27, 104, 169; as Asian American stereotype, 1, 117, 118; capital ownership and, 116; in Hwang's *M. Butterfly*, 33, 79, 80, 92; in Lee's *A Gesture Life*, 34, 109, 118; in Lee's *Native Speaker*, 34, 103, 109, 120, 121; in Okada's *No-No Boy*, 45, 46

zero-sum games: Asian American players and, 18, 29; Cold War polarization as, 70, 79, 82; containment as, 39; Gulf War as, 114–15; imperialism as, 22, 23, 77, 95, 129, 130, 155, 166, 167; Korean War as, 62; in Lee's *A Gesture Life*, 34, 125; in Lee's *Native Speaker*, 34, 125; prisoners' dilemma and, 23, 34, 77, 82, 89, 129, 130, 150; Vietnam War as, 89; War on Terror as, 129, 150, 161

Zhang, Baijia, 74, 74n23

www.ingramcontent.com/pod-product-compliance
Lightning Source LLC
Chambersburg PA
CBHW020732240426
43665CB00052B/458